T0260470

Learning the iOS 4 SDK for
JavaScript Programmers

Learning the iOS 4 SDK for JavaScript Programmers

Danny Goodman

O'REILLY®

Beijing · Cambridge · Farnham · Köln · Sebastopol · Tokyo

Learning the iOS 4 SDK for JavaScript Programmers
by Danny Goodman

Copyright © 2011 Danny Goodman. All rights reserved.
Printed in the United States of America.

Published by O'Reilly Media, Inc., 1005 Gravenstein Highway North, Sebastopol, CA 95472.

O'Reilly books may be purchased for educational, business, or sales promotional use. Online editions are also available for most titles (*http://my.safaribooksonline.com*). For more information, contact our corporate/institutional sales department: (800) 998-9938 or *corporate@oreilly.com*.

Editors: Andy Oram and Brian Jepson	**Indexer:** Ellen Troutman Zaig
Production Editor: Holly Bauer	**Cover Designer:** Karen Montgomery
Copyeditor: Amy Thomson	**Interior Designer:** David Futato
Proofreader: Kiel Van Horn	**Illustrator:** Robert Romano

Printing History:
December 2010:   First Edition.

Nutshell Handbook, the Nutshell Handbook logo, and the O'Reilly logo are registered trademarks of O'Reilly Media, Inc. *Learning the iOS 4 SDK for JavaScript Programmers*, the image of a King Charles Spaniel, and related trade dress are trademarks of O'Reilly Media, Inc.

Many of the designations used by manufacturers and sellers to distinguish their products are claimed as trademarks. Where those designations appear in this book, and O'Reilly Media, Inc. was aware of a trademark claim, the designations have been printed in caps or initial caps.

While every precaution has been taken in the preparation of this book, the publisher and author assume no responsibility for errors or omissions, or for damages resulting from the use of the information contained herein.

ISBN: 978-1-449-38845-4

[LSI]

1291231709

Table of Contents

Preface

You don't have to be an Apple fanboy or fangirl to give Apple Inc. credit for redefining mobile gadgetry and its surrounding industries. First the company used the iPod to reshape the music industry and strongly influence how we acquire and consume tunes. Just count the number of people wearing iPod-connected earbuds in a subway car. Then the iPhone rewrote the cellular telephone industry manual, while opening the world's eyes to the potential of being connected to the Internet nearly everywhere, all the time. It's happening again with the iPad, where electronic publishing is evolving right before our eyes.

Although the iPhone was an early success with just the workable but limited set of Apple-supplied applications that came with the phone, programmers couldn't wait to get their hands on the platform. The first word that Apple let drop about third-party developers, however, landed with a bit of a thud: they were graciously allowed to create web apps. Sure, the iPhone's WebKit-based browser let creative HTML, CSS, and JavaScript programmers create far more than dull web pages, but the apps still faced frustrating limits compared to Apple's native apps.

It took some additional months, but Apple eventually released a genuine software development kit (SDK) to allow third-party programmers to create native applications for what was then called the iPhone OS. Part of Apple's task was also creating the App Store to distribute apps—yet another industry-transforming effort. Many existing Mac OS X developers rejoiced because the iPhone OS was derived from Mac OS X. The iPhone SDK was based on the same Xcode tools that Mac developers had been using for some time. The language of choice was Objective-C.

As a happy iPhone early adopter, I eagerly awaited the iPhone SDK. Unfortunately, despite my years of being a dedicated Mac user since 1984 and a scripter since 1987 and the HyperCard days, I had never done any Mac OS X programming. I didn't know much about C and next to nothing about Objective-C. Still, I thought perhaps my years of experience in JavaScript would be of some help. After all, at one time I even learned enough Java to write a small browser applet to demonstrate how JavaScript code in a web page can communicate with the applet. At least I knew what a compiler did.

When the iPhone SDK landed on my Mac, I was simply overwhelmed. The old meta-phor of trying to sip from a firehose definitely applied. The more I read Apple's early developer documentation, the more I felt as though I had to know a lot more than I knew just to understand the "getting started" texts. With JavaScript having been the most recent language acquisition for me (albeit back in late 1995), I looked for anything I could borrow from that experience to apply to iPhone app development. I'd see occasional glimmers, but I was basically flying blind, not knowing what I had to discard and what I could keep.

The SDK was evolving during that time as well. I'd read a tutorial here and there, but I wasn't making much headway at first. Some tools, especially Interface Builder, felt incomplete to me. Frankly, I had a couple of false starts where I walked away until a future SDK version appeared. Finally, I reached a point that was "put up or shut up." After sticking with it and reading many of the documents many times, I was, indeed, getting tastes from the firehose. Working on iPhone development as a part-time effort over a three-month period, I managed to go from the starting line to submitting my first app to the App Store in January 2009.

Since then I've been monitoring the developer communities on both the native app and web app sides. I've even sat in online courses for web app developers to see what they're saying in the chat room. A lot of web app developers seem to look enviously to native iPhone and iPad development. I suspect many have gone through the same false starts that I did. And yet I know from my own experience that it is possible to make the transition from web app to native app developer if you know how to channel your JavaScript knowledge into what is now known as the iOS SDK environment.

What You Need to Start

I have written this book specifically for the web developer who is comfortable in the JavaScript language. Even if you use a bit of JavaScript to glue together apps from third-party JavaScript libraries and frameworks, you should be ready for this book. Unlike most entry-level iOS programming books, this one assumes that you have not necessarily worked in a compiled language before. You probably have little or no experience with C or Objective-C. But you do know what a string and an array are because you use them in your JavaScript work. I will be introducing you to the way Objective-C works by comparing and contrasting what you use in JavaScript. It's the kind of hand-holding that I wish I had when I started learning iPhone app development.

You will get more from this book if you are the adventurous type. By adventurous, I mean that you will follow the instructions throughout to try things for yourself. Along the way I will help you build an app called Workbench, where you will be able to play and learn by experimenting with little pieces of code here and there. Creating projects, editing files, and building apps is the only way to really get to know the SDK.

Of course, you'll need a Macintosh running Mac OS X version 10.6 (Snow Leopard) or later. I'll have more details about getting set up with hardware and SDK software in Chapter 2.

What's in This Book

Perhaps because my programming knowledge has been completely self-taught over the decades, this book does not follow what some might term traditional programming language training. First of all, you already come to the book with specialized knowledge. The goal of the book is to pick up where that knowledge leaves off and fill in the gaps with the new material. There's no doubt about it: there is a lot of new material for you. But I have tried to establish a learning progression that will make sense and keep you interested while you learn the decidedly unglamorous—but essential—parts of iOS programming.

Chapter 1 goes into detail about the differences between web app and native app programming for devices running iOS. It's not all roses for native app development, as you'll see, but I believe the positives outweigh the negatives. In Chapter 2, you will install the iOS SDK, inspect one of the sample apps, and run it on the iOS Simulator. Then in Chapter 3, I put you to work to create your first iPhone app—the Workbench app that you'll use throughout the rest of the book. The steps are intended to help you get more comfortable with Xcode and learn what it's like to work on an app in the environment.

In Chapter 4, you will use the Workbench app to build your first Objective-C object and compare the process against building the same object in JavaScript. You will spend a lot of time in Xcode. And if you've used JavaScript frameworks for your web app development, wait until you get a peek at the frameworks you'll be using in iOS app development.

The focus of Chapter 5 is understanding how the code you write commands an iOS device to launch your app and get it ready for a user to work with. In the process, you'll learn a great deal about how an app works. In fact, by the end of this chapter, you will add a second screen to Workbench and animatedly switch between the two.

Sometimes while learning new material, you have to take your medicine. That happens in Chapter 6, where you meet three programming concepts that are foreign to what you know from JavaScript: pointers, data typing, and memory management. There will be plenty of sample code for you to try in the Workbench app to learn these new concepts.

Objective-C is built atop the C language. There is still a bit of C that you should know to be more comfortable in the newer language. Chapter 7 shows you what you need to know from C. The good news is that a fair amount of it is identical to JavaScript. Hooray! And most of the esoterica isn't needed because it's all covered in more robust and friendly ways in Objective-C, as covered in Chapter 8. There you'll learn how Objective-C handles strings, arrays, and other data collections.

The final chapter, Chapter 9, is also the longest. It provides a catalog of programming tasks you're accustomed to, but implemented in the iOS SDK. Most of the jobs will be familiar to you—formatting numbers, performing date calculations, sorting arrays, working with user-entered text, having Ajax-like communications with a server, and even dragging an item around a screen. I don't expect you to learn and remember everything described in Chapter 9, but know what's there and how to find it when the need arises in your own iOS development.

Two appendixes round out the offering. One provides tips on using the iOS SDK's documentation to its fullest extent. The other presents a list of common Xcode compiler errors that beginners encounter and what the errors really mean. Unintelligible error messages in the early going of learning a new environment can be very frustrating and discouraging. Appendix B makes it possible to learn more quickly from newbie mistakes.

Conventions Used in This Book

The following typographical conventions are used in this book:

Plain text
: Indicates menu titles, menu options, menu buttons, and keys.

Italic
: Indicates new terms, URLs, email addresses, filenames, file extensions, and directories.

`Constant width`
: Indicates variables, methods, types, classes, properties, parameters, values, objects, XML tags, the contents of files, and logging output.

`Constant width bold`
: Highlights new code or code of special importance in examples.

`Constant width italic`
: Shows text that should be replaced with user-supplied values.

 This icon signifies a tip, suggestion, or general note.

 This icon indicates a warning or caution.

Using Code Examples

This book is here to help you get your job done. In general, you may use the code in this book in your programs and documentation. You do not need to contact us for permission unless you're reproducing a significant portion of the code. For example, writing a program that uses several chunks of code from this book does not require permission. Selling or distributing a CD-ROM of examples from O'Reilly books *does* require permission. Answering a question by citing this book and quoting example code does not require permission. Incorporating a significant amount of example code from this book into your product's documentation *does* require permission.

We appreciate, but do not require, attribution. An attribution usually includes the title, author, publisher, and ISBN. For example: "*Learning the iOS 4 SDK for JavaScript Programmers* by Danny Goodman (O'Reilly). Copyright 2011 Danny Goodman, 9781449388454."

If you feel your use of code examples falls outside fair use or the permission given above, feel free to contact us at *permissions@oreilly.com*.

How to Contact Us

Please address comments and questions concerning this book to the publisher:

O'Reilly Media, Inc.
1005 Gravenstein Highway North
Sebastopol, CA 95472
800-998-9938 (in the United States or Canada)
707-829-0515 (international or local)
707-829-0104 (fax)

We have a web page for this book, where we list errata, examples, and any additional information. You can access this page at:

http://www.oreilly.com/catalog/9781449388454

To comment or ask technical questions about this book, send email to:

bookquestions@oreilly.com

For more information about our books, conferences, Resource Centers, and the O'Reilly Network, see our website at:

http://www.oreilly.com

Safari® Books Online

Safari Books Online is an on-demand digital library that lets you easily search over 7,500 technology and creative reference books and videos to find the answers you need quickly.

With a subscription, you can read any page and watch any video from our library online. Read books on your cell phone and mobile devices. Access new titles before they are available for print, and get exclusive access to manuscripts in development and post feedback for the authors. Copy and paste code samples, organize your favorites, download chapters, bookmark key sections, create notes, print out pages, and benefit from tons of other time-saving features.

O'Reilly Media has uploaded this book to the Safari Books Online service. To have full digital access to this book and others on similar topics from O'Reilly and other publishers, sign up for free at *http://my.safaribooksonline.com*.

Acknowledgments

Having published over 45 books since the early 1980s, I have witnessed many changes across the computer-book universe. But one beacon of quality has always burned brightly: O'Reilly. The opportunity to publish a title through O'Reilly inspires an author to produce a work commensurate with an impeccable publishing record. It was a comfort to have super-knowledgeable editors Brian Jepson and Andy Oram challenging me to compose a better book at every step. Technical reviewers Alasdair Allan and Zachary Kessin responded above and beyond the call of duty to make sure my facts were factual and the reader's best interests were being served.

CHAPTER 1

Why Go Native?

Those who frequently develop mobile web applications with HTML, CSS, JavaScript, and related technologies tend to find a way to reuse those comfortable tools for every app challenge. The iOS (formerly iPhone OS) platform has attracted much attention in the web developer community, and Apple continues to evangelize web app development for the platform.

At the same time, there's evidence of a desire among developers to adapt their web technologies to replicate the look and feel of native iPhone and iPad apps, whose look and feel users know from the built-in apps and other apps downloaded from the App Store. Perhaps you've used third-party libraries, such as iUi or jQTouch, to deploy your content and application ideas so that they look and behave like native iOS apps.

Despite advances in web technologies—especially the HTML5 and WebKit extensions to CSS and Document Object Model (DOM)—an iPhone or iPad web app lacks access to several key facilities built into iOS. You must also deal with the Mobile Safari browser address bar, especially if your users aren't experienced enough to generate a home screen icon for your app. Additionally, even though both your iPhone-specific styles and scripts target a single OS platform, you still may encounter compatibility issues with earlier versions of Mobile Safari running on iPhone and iPod touch units in the field that haven't been updated to the latest OS versions. For example, I saw from my server logs that nine months after the release of iPhone OS 3.0, some users of my native iPhone apps continued to use iPhone OS 2.2, especially with iPod touch devices (most of whose users once had to pay for major OS upgrades).

In other words, the choice to reach iPhone and iPad users through web applications, which were supposed to simplify development, introduces its own set of complications. Maybe it's time to make the leap and start developing native iOS apps. This chapter highlights iOS features you can use if you choose to develop native apps—features that are not available to web-only apps. Even if your app designs don't require a lot of native OS support, a native app still has advantages over web apps. To provide a fair and balanced picture, I'll also discuss what you lose by using a native app over a web app.

Using an App Offline

It is hard to argue with the fact that iOS devices are intended to be used in a connected world. WiFi is built into all devices by default; iPhones and iPads (and likely future devices) equipped with 3G also have cellular data connections that free users from lurking around WiFi hotspots. Unfortunately, users may be out of WiFi range, have no cellular connection, be running dangerously low on battery power, or be secured inside a jet-powered flying metal tube whose attendants prohibit radio contact with the ground. When an iOS device cannot access the Internet, a traditional web app—which resides entirely on your web server—is not accessible. Although it is possible to code a browser-based web app to be copied and stored on a device, the mechanism isn't foolproof.

A native app, however, is at least launchable even when the device has no connection to the Internet. Exactly how usable the app is while offline depends on the nature of the app, of course, but it's clear from the apps that Apple supplies on every device that an iOS device does not completely die if Internet connectivity is missing. You can still listen to music, watch previously downloaded videos, look up your contacts, and tap out notes; with an iPhone and iPod touch, you can still be awoken by an alarm or calculate a total; and with any camera-equipped device, you can take pictures. Applications you download from the App Store let you do tons more things, such as play games, read gorgeous-looking downloaded books, edit photos, figure out restaurant bill tips, look up a dictionary definition, or identify a bird in the nearest tree—all without the need for a constant Internet connection.

Many native apps also connect with the Internet for some functions. Games commonly upload scores so you can see how well you perform against other users around the world. Many apps also rely on the Internet for up-to-date information, such as email apps, news readers, weather apps, Twitter and Facebook clients, and many more. For designers of many of these types of apps, the challenge is to create an app that can perform its basic functions offline, even if it means the user needs to download some current content before cutting the wireless cord. Once disconnected from the cloud (perhaps even while flying above the clouds), the user can relaunch the app and still access fairly recent content.

Unfortunately, you cannot rely on Mobile Safari to preserve a downloaded web page's content for long. Even if the user manages to keep the Safari window open, restoring it for use sometimes causes the page to attempt to reload itself from the server. No server? No content, even though it may be in a cache someplace on the device.

Some web apps have successfully been converted to *bookmarklets*. A bookmarklet is a browser bookmark that contains a `javascript:` or `data:` URL whose code generates the HTML, CSS, image data, and JavaScript code for a web page when chosen from the browser's bookmarks list. It's true that this method allows a web app to be stored entirely on the user's device, but a web page generated in this fashion has some additional limitations over regular web pages. For example, a bookmarklet app cannot use browser cookies because of security restrictions in the browser.

Mobile Safari does support the HTML5 offline application cache. This mechanism allows web app publishers to code their pages (and configure their web servers) in a way that allows the browser to store a copy of a web page and additional resources (e.g., images) on the device. Developers deploying this technique have a variety of limits to attend to, such as a maximum of 25 KB for any resource file, including any images. Of greater concern, however, is that if the user reboots the device (completely powering down the unit), all data in this offline cache can be lost. Native apps, however, survive such system reboots every time.

There is a risk that when you have been designing Internet-based content and software for a long time, you tend to take Internet connectivity for granted—after all, you have always-on broadband at home or work. Additionally, all the buzz about cloud computing makes it sound as though every computer user on the planet has ubiquitous and nearly free access to an Internet that is as reliable as the sun rising tomorrow morning. That is not always the case for all users.

More Access to the Hardware

It doesn't take long to learn that web pages developed for general-purpose web browsers are encumbered with many restrictions. For example, a web page does not have free rein over the host computer's filesystem, making it impossible for well-meaning scripts to read or write files on the hard disk (except for closely monitored dedicated files for items such as cookies and HTML5 data storage). JavaScript is granted very limited access to even the host browser's environment or settings. Despite the possible convenience afforded by automatically adding the current web page to a user's bookmarks list, such access is out of bounds for web pages.

All of these restrictions, of course, are imposed for the sake of security and privacy. Left unfettered, a script on a malicious hacker's website could wreak havoc on every browser that lands at the site. Not many users would like unknown computers reading their recent browser histories or replacing system files with ones that could cause banking website visits to be redirected to lookalike phony sites that capture usernames and passwords. Cyber crooks are constantly on the prowl for vulnerabilities in popular browsers that they can exploit without the user's knowledge—the so-called drive-by attacks that have plagued various browsers through the years.

An application designed to run natively on popular desktop computer operating systems, on the other hand, typically has exceptionally broad freedom to rummage around the computer at will. On some operating systems that are set up for user accounts, the user must grant specific permission to the program's installer. Such permission is taken to mean that the user trusts the installer and the program(s) it installs to do no harm. Developers who publish software with a goal of building a software business avoid doing bad things to customers' computers even though users essentially hand over the key to the system. On the other hand, if a program has a hidden agenda (e.g., loading spyware onto every user's computer), the nefarious activity will likely be discovered sooner or later. News of the offenses will carry quickly across the Internet and the company's reputation will be ruined.

Apple engineers have thus far greatly restricted the hardware features available to web apps running in Mobile Safari. Despite some cool hardware, such as the digital compass in the iPhone 3GS, web apps simply have no access to most of the neat stuff. About the only hardware-based features that a web app can count on are:

- Accelerometer orientation changes (e.g., portrait or landscape)
- Gyroscope motion (iOS 4.2 or later)
- Multitouch events (e.g., two-finger pinching or stretching)
- Location services (as many as are supported by the device)

Native apps, however, have substantially more access to the hardware—although not necessarily every piece that developers might like. For example, apps built for devices containing cameras can capture images (and video, where available) to facilitate image editing tasks. Devices equipped with a digital compass expose the current heading of the device. Sound captured by the device's built-in (or plugged-in) microphone can be recorded and further processed by code inside a native app. An app can read information about the battery state and an iPhone's proximity detector (which knows when a user has the handset near her face). Native apps can also read from and write to files of their own construction (albeit within some security-driven confines of the directory structure reserved for the app).

Although Apple has begun to expose limited parts of the hardware to web apps (essentially creating objects, properties, and methods that extend the DOM), such exposure lags well behind the range of hardware features waiting to be used by native app developers. I expect more hardware access to come in future iOS versions, but web app access will likely stay several steps behind native app capabilities.

More Access to the Software

On the software side of the iOS, native app development offers a wide range of features that web app developers don't typically have available. For example, here is a list of software features introduced with iPhone OS 3.0 that are available only to native apps:

- iPod library access to read library contents and play tracks
- Displaying interactive embedded Google Maps with many of the same capabilities and identical performance to that of the Maps app
- Peer-to-peer communications for multiplayer game play
- Precise control over how cut/copy/paste works in an app

- Powerful structured data mechanisms ideally suited to displaying lists (the Core Data framework)
- Precise control over audio recording details (sampling rates, audio formats, etc.)
- Push notifications to signal users about important events that launch your app
- Creating and sending email messages from within the app
- Reading and selecting information from the Contacts app
- Very powerful OpenGL ES 2.0 3-D graphics composition platform
- In-app purchases to encourage users to add paid features or extend subscriptions

If that list doesn't send your imagination into overdrive, perhaps several new native app features of iOS 4 will:

- Playing audible media while the app is suspended in the multitasking environment
- Receiving system notifications of changing between active and suspended mode
- Posting notifications to users at predetermined times, even if the app is suspended
- Integrating with Calendar app data
- Displaying revenue-generating advertisements from Apple's iAd service

It's not uncommon for native app developers to apply several of these advanced software features (along with hardware features mentioned in the previous section) to augment their apps. For example, one of my own native apps, iFeltThat Earthquake, uses the in-app email feature to make it easy for users to contact me with questions and suggestions about the app. The app also lets users select an entry from their Contacts list to create a geographical center point around which recent earthquake activity is shown (the app uses geocoding to convert a contact's street address to map coordinates).

All of this native software goodness still allows developers to fold useful web content into a native application. iOS supplies a mechanism for displaying live web content within a native app. The "viewer" used for such web content has all the HTML, CSS, and JavaScript features of Mobile Safari (and its WebKit engine), but without the chrome of the Safari app. You simply define a rectangular viewing region on the screen and supply a URL to the web viewer. In iFeltThat Earthquake, for example, I keep users informed about news and user tips via an HTML-authored page made available from a web server. Each time the app launches, it looks to see if the news web page has been modified since the last visit; if so, it downloads the page, stores a copy on the device, and signals the user that a news flash is available for reading.

I chose to compose the news material in HTML for a couple of reasons. First, as a veteran HTML handcoder, I am, of course, comfortable generating content in that format. It allows for quick composition and easy testing of the page from a local server using Mobile Safari on an iPhone-compatible device. It also means I am free to change the styles (CSS) of the news page without having to update the entire app. The second reason for choosing HTML is that I can easily provide links to other HTML content, whether composed by me or served from a different external source. Because the news page is shown within a web viewer inside the app, links operate as they do in any browser, replacing the current page with the destination of the link. My in-app web viewer provides just a minimum of browser controls for reloading, stopping a load, and back and forward navigation.

In many ways, web development skills are powerful adjuncts to native iOS app development. Being comfortable in both environments means you can call on the right deployment tool for various parts of a native app. Hardcore Objective-C and Cocoa developers might be wary or unaware of the web powers that you have in your hip pocket. Once you master native app development, you'll have a distinct advantage over your Objective-C-only colleagues.

What You Lose

By and large, the full iOS SDK feature set offers your app designs far more flexibility and the ability to recreate the full range of user interface features you see on Apple's own apps and apps developed by third parties. But there are costs—in monetary and toil currencies—to obtain those native app powers.

Except for apps designed for in-house corporate use, native apps that run on nonmodified devices—i.e., iPhones and iPads that have not been jailbroken (hacked to allow unapproved third-party apps)—must be distributed via the iTunes App Store. This is both a blessing and, for some, a curse for several reasons.

About Jailbreaking

When the first-generation iPhone landed in developers' hands in 2007, quite a few programmers were put off by the lack of a publicly available development environment for applications. Apple granted itself the power to build native apps included with the phone, but the developer community was shunted to the web app world—with a Mobile Safari version boasting far fewer app-friendly features than today's HTML5-empowered model. Some adventurous programmers, however, found ways to gain access to the same interior programming functionality that Apple's engineers had and opened up native programming to third parties. Having pierced through Apple's restrictions, they called the technique *jailbreaking*. To run one of these independent apps, an iPhone user had to "jailbreak" the device using a software-run process that grew easier and easier over time as jailbreaking tools improved.

Several months after the initial iPhone debut—and perhaps pushed by the encroaching jailbreak programming efforts—Apple released the iPhone SDK to allow third parties to write native apps, but only with publicly documented routines. That restriction still rankles some developers, so jailbreaking is still alive today, even as Apple continually opens more internal routines to all developers. Jailbroken devices reportedly account for as much as 10% of the world's iPhone and iPad population (but a higher percentage of active tech bloggers, who make jailbreaking seem more prevalent than it is). Although

---

jailbroken devices can still download apps from Apple's App Store, a separate store, called Cydia Store, offers apps designed for jailbroken iPhones and iPads.

Some programmers believe it is almost an obligation to jailbreak their devices, lest they appear captive to the will of Steve Jobs. I personally prefer not to jailbreak my devices, for practical, rather than ideological, reasons: I want to know that when I test my App Store apps, the devices are working like the ones owned by 90% or more of my potential customer base. The ultimate choice, however, is yours.

Distribution

On the one hand, since the App Store is a single point of distribution, all users of unhacked iPhone, iPod touch, and iPad devices go to the App Store in search of apps that will help them scratch an itch. While you may have to choose your app's description keywords carefully to help potential users search for your product, at least you don't have to play search engine optimization games to get your app high in search engine results.

On the other hand, the App Store becomes the one-and-only gatekeeper between your app and the consuming public. You must submit your finished app to the App Store for approval before it appears in the store. Approval times can vary widely, often without explanation. Sometimes it's a matter of only a couple of days; other times it can take weeks. The same is true for updates to existing apps. If you need to issue an update to fix a bug, the approval time can be just as long—and, inexplicably, sometimes longer—to get that maintenance release out to the world. You can apply for an emergency update to help hasten the approval, but if you abuse that privilege, you risk upsetting the gatekeepers.

App Updates

Speaking of updates, the web app scenario is far superior to the App Store native app. You instantly deploy an update to the server that hosts the web app whenever you want, as often as you want. This encourages web app developers to issue frequent incremental updates rather than storing up fixes to submit to the App Store in less-frequent batches.

If your app updates are more content-oriented, you can still pass along those updates to a native app in a couple of ways. I described earlier how I use HTML to supply my native apps with news updates. Similarly, updated material can be supplied in other formats (e.g., property list XML files), which a native app can read whenever it launches. Users can save newly acquired material to the device so that it is available to the app even if the device is not connected to the Internet the next time the app launches. Implementing this approach to updating an app takes a bit of advance planning, so it is well worth exploring the possibility early in the design phases of any iOS app.

Apple iOS Developer Program

A prerequisite to submitting a native app to the App Store is an annual paid membership to the iOS (formerly iPhone) Developer Program. The current fee is $99.00 per year. Membership lets you obtain the necessary digital certificates that permit developers to load native apps onto test devices and to upload finished apps to the App Store for approval. You also have access to beta versions of the next version of iOS SDK and iOS software (all under nondisclosure agreements, so you can't blab about them).

In addition to paying the developer program fee, you must also complete a distribution contract with Apple. For paid applications, the contract process also requires that you establish banking relations with Apple. As with app approvals, the time required to complete the contract varies depending how busy Apple is. It's not something to leave to the last minute, because it can take several weeks to complete, even longer for developers outside of the United States. Once you pay for the iOS Developer Program, you should begin the contract process, even as you work on your first native app.

Content

As the gatekeeper to "shelf space" on the App Store, Apple's approval process also imposes restrictions on the content of native apps. Your developer agreements spell out the fundamental guidelines, but Apple inspects each app for compliance on a case-by-case basis.

Such is not the case for web apps. You can serve up whatever you want (within the confines of your own local laws, of course) because the web app is hosted on your server and the device's owner can freely decide to visit your server or skip it.

If you are already aware that web apps—indeed any content designed to be played through the Mobile Safari browser—cannot avail themselves of Flash or Java, you should also be aware that native apps don't get you any further with respect to those two software platforms. As of this writing, iOS does not natively support either runtime environment.

Authoring Platform Choices

You can write HTML, CSS, and JavaScript code with a text editor on any operating system platform of virtually any generation. Plain text editing doesn't even require a graphical user interface, which is why you can find plenty of Unix programmers composing web code in command-line interface editors, such as *Emacs* and *vi* (or variants thereof). The key to this flexibility is that conversion to machine code occurs in the web browser. Such is not the case for writing native apps.

Developing native iOS apps requires Apple's integrated development environment (IDE) called Xcode (pronounced EKS-code). Even though Windows users can sync their iOS devices to their PCs via iTunes for Windows, the Xcode IDE is available only for Macintosh computers.

Taking the Plunge

Beginning with the next chapter, you will see the changes to the development process and programming environment that you will have to adopt to develop native apps. Some of the changes are radical, so if you jump into the programming environment cold, the transition will seem overwhelming. But, just as you learned the intricacies of CSS, JavaScript, and the DOM, the same will happen with iOS SDK development with practice and experience: throughout this book, you'll learn new concepts that build upon one another. My purpose here is to help you embrace that transition by putting new items in the context of your existing knowledge.

Let's get started.

CHAPTER 2

Welcome to the iOS SDK

Even in these days of powerful high-level web authoring tools, it's still quite common for JavaScript programmers to compose or modify code with nothing more sophisticated than a text editor. Perhaps you use that text editor to work on *.html*, *.css*, and *.js* files that users access directly; or you use that text editor to write server code (in Python, Perl, Ruby on Rails, or one of several other languages), which in turn assembles HTML code served up to requesting browsers. With the browser operating as a code interpreter (even if it performs some fast precompiling behind the scenes), the write-test-debug cycle is pretty fast: make a code change and reload the browser to test the results. Egregious errors, such as JavaScript syntax errors, signal themselves while the page loads; more subtle errors, such as referencing an object that hasn't yet been created, fill the error console when the code runs.

When you switch to native app development, this comfy authoring environment and cycle go out the window. Luckily, it's replaced with an integrated and visually oriented environment that—once you learn its ways—reflects a lot of the best in modern programming environments. This is the native iOS app SDK, whose nucleus is Xcode. Among other things, Xcode helps you visualize and manage the potentially large number of files associated with each app in development.

Additionally, the tools delivered with Xcode are highly integrated. For example, you will write some code that responds to a user tapping a button in an iPhone app: the tool you use to create the user interface is aware of the code you've written and helps you connect the button in the user interface to that code. The user interface building tool is instantly aware of changes you make to the code, even though the tools are two separate programs in the Dock.

Hardware and OS Requirements

As mentioned in Chapter 1, you need an Intel-based Macintosh running Mac OS X version 10.6 (Snow Leopard) or later to use the Xcode IDE. As Apple releases new versions of the iOS SDK and Mac OS X, requirements may change.

You don't need a brand-spanking-new Intel-based Mac to develop iOS apps. There are plenty of used Intel Macs for sale on eBay and elsewhere. For the tower- or iMac-averse, laptop styles—MacBooks and MacBook Pros—are well suited for iOS development, except perhaps for a possibly small screen. If you can afford a large external LCD monitor, you will have an easier time managing your project windows. And maxing out a laptop's RAM slots will also contribute to good performance of Xcode.

Installing the SDK

To begin your exploration of iPhone development, start by signing up to become a Registered iOS Developer at:

http://developer.apple.com/programs/start/standard/

Registration requires that you have an Apple ID. If you have an iTunes account or if you have purchased from the Apple Online Store, you already have an Apple ID. Otherwise, you can sign up for one online while you register as an iOS Developer.

The free version of the iOS Developer program lets you download the full SDK from the opening page of the iOS section of the Apple Developer website. Be sure to confirm you have the minimum Mac OS X version required for the current SDK you're about to download.

The iOS SDK is huge—well over three gigabytes. Be patient with the download. It arrives as a compressed disk image, a file with a *.dmg* extension that expands into a mounted disk volume. If the completely downloaded file does not automatically expand, double-click the file to mount the disk image on your Desktop (some browsers will do this for you automatically after the download is complete). The disk image will open itself to reveal installer notes and a package file containing the SDK (Figure 2-1).

Double-click the *.mpkg* package file to run the SDK installer. I recommend following the default choices presented at each step of the installation process. Allow the SDK to be installed in a new *Developer* directory on your startup disk. If you have iTunes running, you will be prompted to quit the app before the installation will complete. After installation has finished, you can drag the disk image and compressed image file to the Trash.

About iOS Developer Programs

The free version of the iOS Developer program allows you to use the SDK to run native apps you create only on the iOS Simulator program (one of the SDK tools), which runs only on the Mac. To upload a native app to an actual device for testing (or your own use) and to submit an app for distribution through the App Store, you must sign up for the $99.00 (per year) iOS Developer Program (or the $299.00 Enterprise Program for companies planning to write apps only for employee use). This paid developer program also grants you access to an Apple-hosted online forum where you can ask for coding

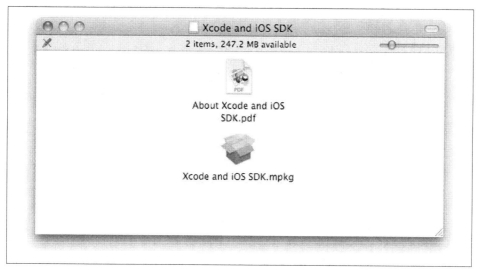

Figure 2-1. Contents of the iOS SDK disk image

help (or read how others may have already solved your problem). Additionally, when Apple releases beta versions of the next iOS version and associated SDK, paid members can download those pieces for development and testing purposes. For example, on the day that iPhone OS 4.0 was announced in April 2010, members of the developer program could download a beta version of Xcode to write apps and a beta version of the OS to install on devices to see how the new features worked.

> You will not be able to submit apps to the Store that you have built from a beta version of the SDK. Therefore, if you have one or more apps on the App Store, you should always keep a current version of the SDK on hand for building updates to existing apps. Historically, it has been possible to install both the current and beta SDK versions on a single Mac, if desired (you still need to install the beta SDK in a separate folder).

You can go pretty far toward developing your first iOS app without investing a dime in Apple developer programs. It's a free way to discover if programming for iOS in the Objective-C language is right for you. But don't wait too long to decide to sign up for the paid program. Once you sign up for that program, but before any app you create can appear on the App Store, you must still go through a contract and banking credentials process with Apple, all of which is handled online. Each developer has had a different experience with completing the contract and banking agreements. For some, the process takes only a few days; for others, it can take months. What you want to avoid is waiting to begin the contract process until you submit your first app to the App Store. In my case, the first app I submitted in early 2009 was approved in three days; the contract, however, took almost one month, during which time my approved app sat in limbo.

Inside the SDK

The *Developer* directory containing the iOS SDK is well over eight gigabytes of goodness waiting for you to explore. You will spend most of your time in four applications, three of which are highlighted in Figure 2-2.

Figure 2-2. Three primary applications of the iOS SDK (version 3.2.5 shown)

The four primary tools are:

Xcode

> This is the integrated development environment where you will write your code, keep track of external files (images and others), and build your app for testing and eventual submission to the App Store.

Interface Builder

You are not required to design your user interfaces using this graphically oriented design tool, but if your app utilizes standard iPhone or iPad user interface elements, it can significantly reduce the amount of code you write.

Instruments

After your app reaches a usable form, you will use Instruments to observe how well it uses memory and system resources.

iOS Simulator

Although the iOS Simulator app is buried elsewhere within the *Developer* directory hierarchy, you will use it often during all development phases for both iPhone and iPad testing (the tool contains simulators for both platforms). The simulator launches from your Xcode project windows.

Each time you go to work on your app, you begin by launching Xcode. You can launch all of the other supporting apps directly from within Xcode. For example, when you want to see how well the current implementation runs on the iOS Simulator, you will instruct Xcode to build the app and run it on the simulator. If the simulator is not yet running, Xcode will launch it, install the app, and launch the app on the simulator.

Viewing Developer Documentation

The first time you launch Xcode, you will see a Welcome to Xcode window with a variety of choices, as well as a list of previously opened projects (probably empty for you). Click Cancel for now. Instead, open the Help menu and choose Developer Documentation, as shown in Figure 2-3. You will be referring to documentation a lot, and this menu (or keyboard equivalent) is a quick way to open the documentation window before you open a project.

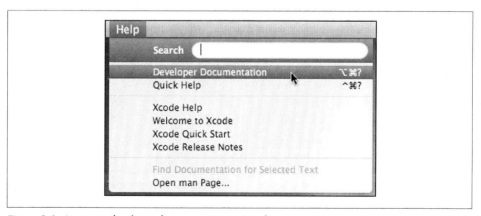

Figure 2-3. Accessing developer documentation in Xcode

The best place to begin in the developer docs is the home page for the latest iOS SDK you are using. Figure 2-4 shows where the main navigation menu is located and what the home page looks like. The Xcode documentation system can display multiple sets of documentation for different iOS versions and Mac OS X development (selectable in Xcode preferences). Figure 2-4 shows only the iOS 4.2 doc set installed.

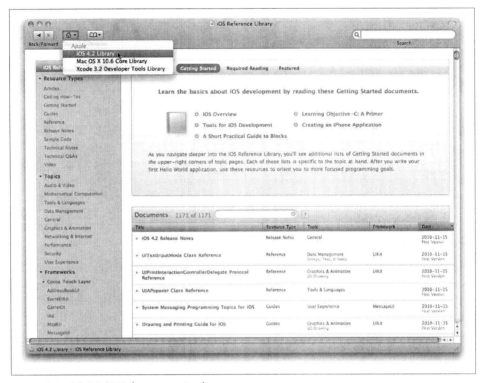

Figure 2-4. iOS 4.2 SDK documentation home page

After you've finished this book, the Getting Started section (upper right box in Figure 2-4) is the place to go next. You'll have enough links to keep you busy for quite a while.

While we're on the subject of the developer docs, let me also show you how you will interact with the iOS Reference Library while you compose your code. In particular, you will frequently need to look up how various objects work. Simply enter a term into the Search box in the upper-right corner. For example, by the time you are finished with this book, you will know that Objective-C arrays are instances of the NSArray object. To read the details of the NSArray object, simply enter the object name into the case-insensitive Search box (Figure 2-5).

The left column contains a list of documents and items within those documents that match the search string. If you have multiple documentation sets for different iOS

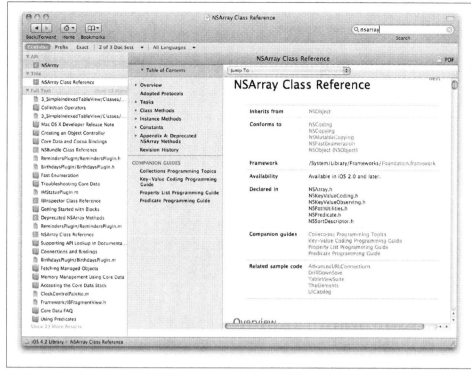

Figure 2-5. Searching for details on the NSArray object

versions installed in your copy of Xcode, the search results will show separate entries for each version—all named the same. This can be confusing at first glance, but you can hold the pointer over any item in the returned list to see the doc set to which that item belongs, as shown in Figure 2-6, which shows what the top of the search results looks like when two iOS doc sets are installed.

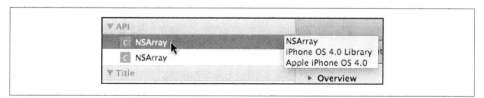

Figure 2-6. Hover over an item to reveal its doc set

As shown in the middle and right columns of results of the NSArray search (Figure 2-5), reference documents frequently include links to various programming guides and sample code projects that come with the SDK. Each programming guide is a goldmine of information, especially for programmers who are new to the guide's subject matter. Read those guides thoroughly—and perhaps multiple times—to learn the gospel according to Apple. Very often, these documents assume you have a working knowledge of Objective-C and other aspects of the iOS SDK, most of which you will be exposed to throughout this book.

Loading Code Samples

A comparatively recent innovation in the iOS SDK is a simplified way to open a copy of a code sample that you can play with at will without worrying about messing up the original. Figure 2-7 shows the result of clicking on a link to a code sample—called TheElements—shown at the bottom of the right pane in Figure 2-5. For sample code, the Table of Contents panel lists the files associated with the sample project. Direct your attention to the button on the righthand panel.

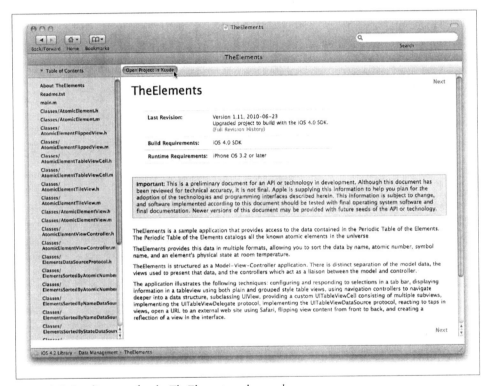

Figure 2-7. Landing page for the TheElements code sample

Use the following steps to load the sample into Xcode:

1. Click the Open Project in Xcode button.
2. Select the folder where the installer will create the project's folder (i.e., a folder named *TheElements* will be created for you, so choose where you want that folder to go).

3. Click Choose.

The installer script copies all necessary files into a folder named *TheElements* and immediately launches the project file, named *TheElements.xcodeproj*. A *.xcodeproj* file is the master hub for everything associated with the app and is the file you open whenever you want to work on an app. Figure 2-8 shows the Xcode project window for TheElements sample project.

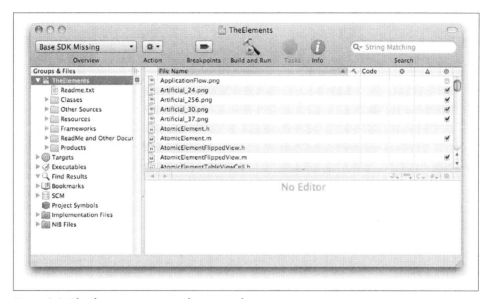

Figure 2-8. TheElements project window in Xcode

While the project window may look intimidating at first, you won't be dealing with most of what you see here on a daily basis. Your focus will primarily be on items listed in the lefthand Groups & Files section and mostly on items in the top group (above the Targets group). This is where your source code files, images, and other contributing files for the app go.

The column view of the project contents shown in the top right-hand pane is another view you won't be looking at much, if at all. Instead, drag the divider between the two right-hand panes upward all the way to give yourself a larger source code editor view (see Figure 2-9). Because no file is selected yet, the editor pane reads "No Editor."

You can now open the various group folders to expose individual source code files. When you click any source file, the appropriate editor appears in the editor pane, as shown in Figure 2-10.

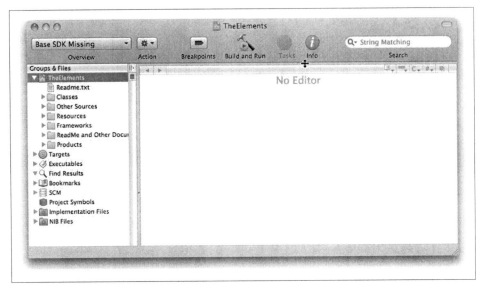

Figure 2-9. Drag the bottom divider upward to reveal more of the editor

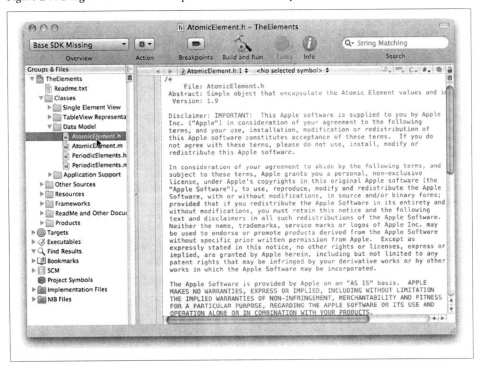

Figure 2-10. Select a source code file to view its contents in the editor

Sample source code files supplied by Apple almost always begin with a lengthy comment (in green text according to the default text-color scheme). After a brief description of the file comes a lot of legal and licensing text. The actual code comes afterward. Feel free to scroll down the editor to get a taste of what iOS SDK app source code in Objective-C looks like.

Coding Styles in SDK Samples

Different Apple engineers write code samples supplied with the SDK. You will therefore find a variety of styles in the way projects are composed. The lack of uniformity can be confusing to newcomers who desperately want to adopt a solid coding style. At best, you should look to the samples as just that: mixed samples rather than specific instructions on how to structure projects, name variables and methods, or even how to divide code into separate files. Additionally, most samples aim to demonstrate a specific concept rather than define an all-around best practice example. Pieces of some samples distant from the primary subject matter may even be less than optimal. Therefore, as you learn more about Objective-C and the SDK, don't be afraid to employ your own structure and styles that are comfortable for you.

Setting the Project's Base SDK

You probably noticed that the Overview menu at the upper-left corner of the project window says "Base SDK Missing." Before you can compile an app and run it, you need to set the SDK version Xcode should use for compilation and deployment. Because TheElements project was created when SDK version 3.0 was still available and modified to build for iOS 4.0, Xcode in the iOS 4.2 SDK doesn't recognize the setting as being valid. It's time to bring the setting up to date by adjusting what is known as the Target—a collection of specs Xcode uses to build an application around the source code of the project.

Open the target's settings by choosing Project→Edit Active Target "TheElements". You will see the Target Info window. In the first group of settings is the Base SDK, which confirms that the originally specified SDK 4.0 is not available. Click in the right column to reveal your possible Base SDK choices, as shown in Figure 2-11. Choose Latest iOS. This setting will allow the project to work in future SDK versions without further adjustment.

Close the Target Info window. The Overview menu should now indicate "4.2|Debug| TheElements" or similar indications. If the Overview menu doesn't change, close and reopen the project. In the next chapter, you will work with an additional setting that will let your app work with iPhone devices running OS versions as early as 3.0—even though the Base SDK is still set to 4.2.

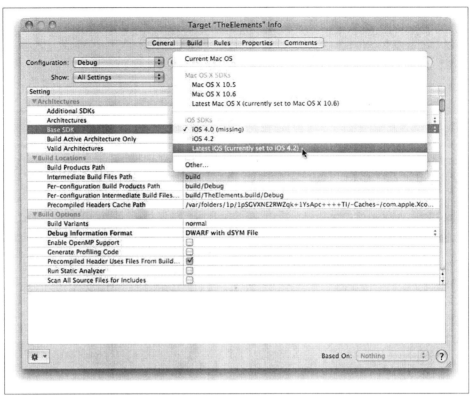

Figure 2-11. Setting the project to use the latest iOS version as the Base SDK

Trying the iOS Simulator

To make sure your Xcode installation and sample code are working properly, you should try running the sample in the iOS Simulator. The first step is to direct Xcode to build the app for the simulator rather than for a device. You don't have the necessary certificate to load this app onto an actual device, so the simulator will do for now.

Near the upper-left corner, click the Overview drop-down menu. Choose Simulator, as shown in Figure 2-12, if it is not already chosen. Then, choose TheElements - iPhone Simulator 4.2 from the Active Executable group.

Next, click the Build and Run button in the center of the top toolbar

You will see the stages of the build process displayed in the lower-left corner of the Xcode project window. After a few moments, the iOS Simulator will launch (it's a separate application from Xcode), and the TheElements app will automatically launch, as shown in Figure 2-13.

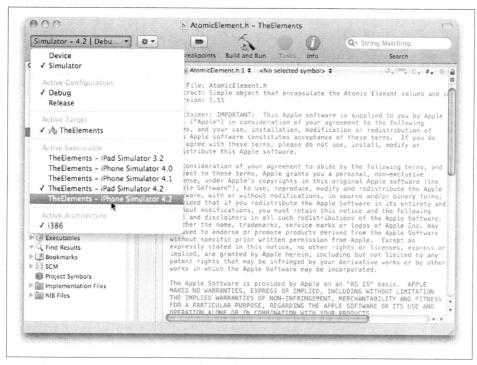

Figure 2-12. Instruct Xcode to build for the simulator running iOS 4.2

Figure 2-13. TheElements app running in iOS Simulator

Use the mouse as your finger to scroll through the list and click on buttons. Although there aren't any images to zoom in this app, if you want to use a two-finger pinch or stretch gesture, hold down the Option key while clicking and dragging inside the simulator's active app area (you'll see grey dots representing finger touch spots). When you quit the app on the simulator (by clicking the Home button at the bottom center), you will see an icon for the app on the iPhone home screen. The icon is one of the image files that came with the collection of files for the project.

Coming Up...

At this stage of your exposure to Xcode, don't bother trying to figure out the files and structure of the sample TheElements app—it has a lot of moving parts that probably won't make much sense yet. By the time you reach Chapter 8, however, you'll be ready for a more detailed walk-through of this project's component files. In the meantime, there is plenty of language material to cover. But before we get to the new language stuff, we have one more stop to make: using Xcode to create a test workbench app in which you'll be able to study how the Objective-C language and iOS features covered in later chapters work.

CHAPTER 3

Creating a Test Workbench

If there is one comfortable technique to which we HTML, CSS, and JavaScript developers have grown accustomed, it is writing some tiny code samples to test expression evaluations and execution logic. You very likely have at least one *test.html* file somewhere on your hard drive. In one of my JavaScript books, I include code for a page called The Evaluator, which allows readers (and, more importantly, me) to see values of single-line expressions and obtain property dumps of objects (lists of property names, values, and value types for any JavaScript or DOM object in the page).

It's convenient to test code snippets initially in an environment that is isolated from your major work in progress. First, you don't want other code to influence your experiment (think "scientific method"). Second, you don't want your experiments to mess up your existing working code. The Workbench app you will build in this chapter will provide you with a running iPhone environment (initially on the iPhone Simulator) in which you can easily test expressions, logic, and the like. Use it as a learning lab while you work through the remaining chapters of this book.

Figure 3-1 shows the finished app. True, it's nothing more than an iPhone screen with a button on it. You will set up this app so that you can test your code in the iPhone OS runtime environment by clicking that button. Results will appear in a separate window of Xcode, called the Console (more about that later). The purpose of the Workbench app is to provide a clean environment into which you can insert your little Objective-C experiments and other learning explorations, which all get triggered when you click that button.

In the process of building Workbench, you will be simply following my instructions. I don't expect you to understand everything that is going on, but I will explain many concepts to you as we go. For example, you'll begin to appreciate the importance of choosing good names for projects in "Naming and Saving the New Project" on page 29. Later you will get to play with Interface Builder to design the layout. If you don't fully grasp why something is the way it is, don't worry—future chapters will cover most of these concepts in more depth, while your future introductions to iOS SDK programming will cover the rest.

Figure 3-1. The Workbench app

Creating the Project in Xcode

Every iOS app you generate with Xcode is managed within a container known as a *project*. The project file (with a file extension of *.xcodeproj*) knows all of your preference settings for the particular app, maintains lists of source code and other external files associated with the project, and tracks many more pieces that most app developers don't ever touch. Each time you come back to an app you've already begun, you will open its project file to get back to work.

For the Workbench app, begin by creating a new project. Do so from the File menu in Xcode, as shown in Figure 3-2.

Selecting a Project Type

The New Project menu item presents a dialog box of choices (Figure 3-3). Because Xcode is used for both iOS and Mac OS X development, you will see options for both environments (even though you downloaded Xcode with the iOS SDK from the Apple developer site, it includes the development tools for Mac OS X as well). You obviously want to focus on the iOS section, and pay attention to the options for creating apps within that section.

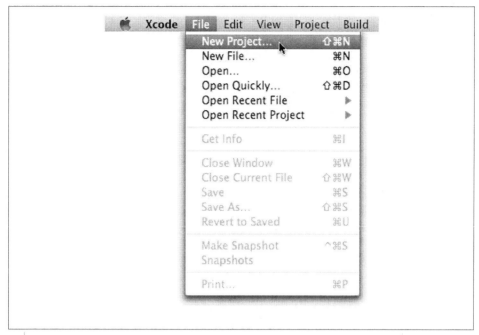

Figure 3-2. Create a new project menu choice

The type of application you choose at this juncture determines the content of the pre-written files Xcode generates for a brand new project. Apple's Developer Tools group has gone to great pains to supply as much template code as possible to help you start your way into an app. In fact, each project template is finished enough to the point that you can create an "empty" project, build it, and install it on the simulator. It won't do anything, but the fundamentals of an actual running iPhone or iPad app are supplied for you in the new project template.

Knowing how to select the right template type comes with more experience than you have at this point, so take my word for it that a view-based application is the one you want for Workbench. Although other types would also work, it will ultimately be helpful for your experiments to have the view-based infrastructure in place.

Select the View-based Application icon in the New Project window, and click Choose.

Device-Specific or Universal App?

When you select View-based Application in the New Project window, the Product menu allows you to produce the fundamental code for either an iPhone- or iPad-specific app. An iPhone-specific app will run on an iPad in a small display area (which the user can upscale to a full-screen view that is usually not very pretty), but an iPad-specific app cannot run on an iPhone. Xcode provides a starting point for a single "universal" app that contains code for iPhone- and iPad-specific areas in one final app file that you can upload to the App Store. You can see that choice in the New Project window by clicking on Window-based Application and viewing the Product menu.

Universal apps tend to have identical functionality for both versions, with its device-specific code providing tweaks that reflect the differences between the platforms in user interface design and screen sizes. An advantage to this approach is that you can use a single set of underlying code to handle data, network communications, and so on for both device families. The App Store, however, also has many examples of completely separate versions of an app, in which the iPad version offers additional features suited to the larger screen. Although it might require more work on your part to keep code shared between the two versions of the app in sync with each other as you release upgrades, it's not uncommon to find enhanced iPad versions of an app commanding a higher price on the App Store.

The choice between a Universal app and separate versions for iPhone and iPad is one of those factors that you should keep in the back of your mind as you begin planning your real apps. In the meantime, the fundamentals you'll be learning in your early days will apply equally to whichever product platform(s) you eventually choose.

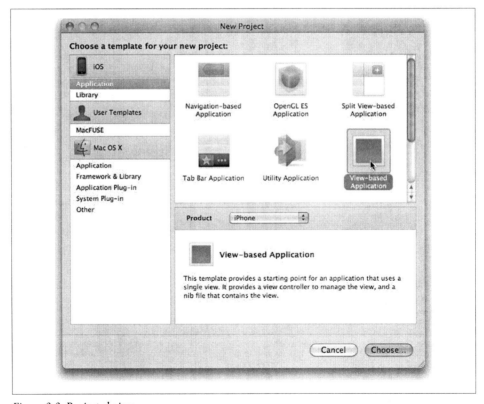

Figure 3-3. Project choices

Naming and Saving the New Project

Next you will be presented with a Save file dialog box. This is where you will specify the location for the project folder and the name of the app. These are two separate points that should be given a bit of thought.

Be aware that Xcode will create a folder for the project (using the name you will assign in a moment). In other words, the folder location you choose in the New Project file dialog box should be a kind of master folder into which you will place each of your iOS SDK project folders (one project folder per app). By default, Xcode suggests placing your apps in the user *Documents* directory. I prefer to keep all my projects for a particular minimum iOS version grouped together on my hard disk. Use an organization scheme that makes the most sense for you.

 Avoid the temptation to save your projects inside the *Developer* directory created during SDK installation. A future SDK update could invasively modify that directory's contents. Save your projects elsewhere.

The name you assign to a new project will ripple through the project's files in ways that will surprise the newcomer (you'll get to see some of the implications later in this chapter). Although the name you assign at this stage does not have to stay with the app all the way to the App Store or to the app icon's label in the home screen, I recommend not trying to be too clever while thinking up a project's name, especially if you have not yet figured out what you want to call the app in the App Store.

By convention, project file names begin with an uppercase letter, although this is not an absolute requirement. One reason for this project naming convention is that Xcode generates some project files and objects beginning with the name you assign, and those files' names typically begin with an uppercase letter.

For multiple-word project names, I recommend using CamelCase formatting rather than spaces between the words. If you use spaces, Xcode will turn those spaces into underscore characters for the filenames it generates.

For the Workbench project, assign the name **Workbench** and click Save.

Welcome to Your Project

After a little bit of churning, Xcode creates the new view-based project represented in the window shown in Figure 3-4.

Let's take a quick tour of the window, starting with important items in the toolbar at the top.

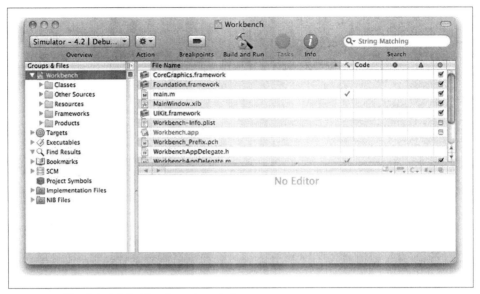

Figure 3-4. The default Workbench project window

 If you have previously customized Xcode, the makeup, order, or labels of buttons and other items in the toolbar may look different from Figure 3-4. If you clicked the clear "lozenge" in the upper-right corner, you won't see a toolbar at all. Click it again to make the toolbar reappear.

The Overview pop-up menu is where you select how Xcode should build and run the app. When it shows "Device" on the left side, it means that deployment will go to any iPhone-compatible device that is currently connected to your Mac via USB cable and designated as a development device (you will also need to be a member of the paid iOS Developer Program). During most of your development, you will be in the Debug mode, and instead of loading the app onto a device, you will direct the app to load into Simulator.

Continuing our tour of the toolbar, the Action menu contains commands that you may issue on items selected in the Groups & Files list below. Your interaction with this menu will likely be minimal, because most menu items are duplicated in the Xcode menu bar. Once you start writing code and wish to step through code while it runs, you will activate the Breakpoints button, which controls whether the next button reads Build and Run (ignoring breakpoints) or Build and Debug. Clicking the Build button in either form causes Xcode to compile your project and load the app onto a device or into iOS Simulator (depending on the Overview setting).

As you have probably experienced with JavaScript debuggers, you set a breakpoint in your source code by clicking in the column to the left of any statement. With breakpoints enabled in Xcode, program execution pauses at the designated line location. You can then step through your code while observing variable values and following logic paths in the separate Debugger window, available via Xcode's Run menu.

The lower-left pane, labeled Groups & Files, is where you organize the files of your project. Notice that the folder organization here is completely independent of the organization of actual files in your project's Finder folder. The purpose of this pane is to let you collect all of the project's external files into an organization that helps you locate the files for editing, especially as a project grows to potentially dozens of files. You can add groups (folder icons) as you go and change the organization at will; you may even nest groups to multiple levels if it helps you keep things straight. Most of your activity will be in the topmost group, whose name is that of your project. Therefore, at this stage, don't be put off by the long list of other items, many of which you won't deal with directly or regularly.

By default, the upper-right pane lists the items contained by whichever group is selected in the Groups & Files pane. If an item's name is shown in red, it means the file is expected but doesn't exist yet (or has been deleted from the project's Finder folder). For example, because you have not yet built the Workbench app, the compiled *.app* file (in reality, it's a package) does not yet exist (although it is expected to exist eventually) and is listed in red. If you select only a single file in the Groups & File list, that file is the only one shown in the upper-right pane. Don't worry about the columns at the right at this point.

Finally, at the bottom right pane is the editor window where you write and edit source code. It is more important to have a big editor window, and the upper-right pane's contents aren't that important during code creation. Therefore, drag the divider between the two right-hand panes upward so that you have only a single editor window, as shown in Figure 3-5.

Editing Your First Files

To display a source code file in the editor window, select the file from the Groups & Files pane. For Workbench, expand the Classes group and select the *WorkbenchViewController.h* file, the third one in the group, as shown in Figure 3-5 (you'll learn about classes and the meaning of the *.h* and *.m* files in a later chapter).

Xcode created all of the code you see here. The file begins with several lines of comments—yes, two forward slashes is one way to signify comments, just as in JavaScript. The comment lines include the name of the file and its owning project, as well as some identifying information, which Xcode has obtained from the system. You are free to edit comments as you wish, including adding more lines if you need them.

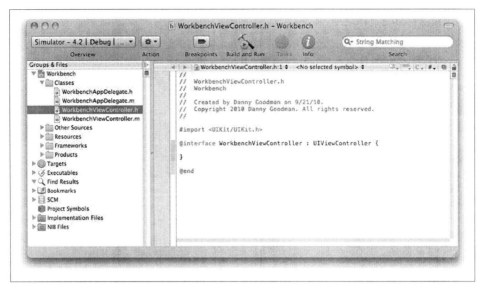

Figure 3-5. Editing the WorkbenchViewController.h file

You'll begin editing this file by specifying the syntax for the method that will ultimately be triggered when you tap the button in the Workbench app. I've named the method `runMyCode:`. Objective-C method definitions begin with either a minus sign (-) or plus sign (+). Each sign has a specific meaning (described in Chapter 4), but for this method, use the minus sign. In the *WorkbenchViewController.h* file, insert the following code after the right curly brace, but before the line containing @end:

```
- (IBAction)runMyCode:(id)sender;
```

As you type, you'll notice that Xcode tries to complete words automatically that it recognizes, such as `IBAction`. If you wish to accept the suggested autocompletion, press the Tab key, and the text insertion pointer zips to the end of the word.

 Just like JavaScript, Objective-C is case sensitive, so be careful with your typing. But unlike JavaScript, the semicolon at the end of a statement is absolutely required. Omitting a semicolon at the end of an Objective-C statement is like omitting the period at the end of an English sentence.

As shown in Figure 3-6, when you make a change to a file's contents, the icon for that file in the Groups & Files listing turns dark gray, signifying the file is "dirty." Typing Command-S saves the file and restores the "clean" icon.

Next comes editing the *WorkbenchViewController.m* file, where you'll add the code that actually runs when the method is invoked. Click the *WorkbenchViewController.m* file in the Groups & Files listing to display the file's contents in the editor pane. Then

Figure 3-6. After entering the new statement to WorkbenchViewController.h, but before saving

insert the following code below the `@implementation` line, as shown in Figure 3-7, carefully observing braces, parentheses, symbols, and quotes:

```
- (IBAction)runMyCode:(id)sender {
    NSLog(@"Button was pressed.");
}
```

Type Command-S to save the changes.

You will certainly notice a bunch of green code below the code you just entered. Each block is surrounded by /*...*/ comment delimiters, the same block comment characters used in JavaScript. Each of the commented blocks contains a separate method that Xcode provides as parts of the default template for this view type of application (Xcode templates for other application types provide other methods tailored to the app type). These methods are optional and, depending on your app design, you might not ever use them (in which case you can delete them from the source code file). On the other hand, if you need them, some of the code is already provided for you to help you save time.

If you scroll to the end of the *WorkbenchViewController.m* file, you will find a few other methods that are not commented. Uncommented methods provided by Xcode are either required or highly recommended. The methods that Xcode supplies by default contain the minimum code statements required to run without additional modification.

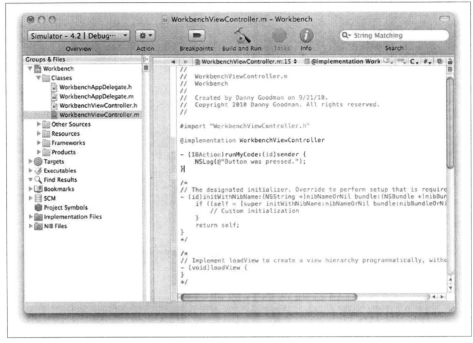

Figure 3-7. Editing the WorkbenchViewController.m file and before saving

What the runMyCode: Method Does

The format of an Objective-C method definition is clearly different from that of a JavaScript function. You'll learn more about these differences in Chapter 4 and Chapter 8. For now, I'll say that the method is defined in a way that exposes it to the Interface Builder tool, which you'll be using in a moment. The method also receives one argument, which is a reference to the button that caused the method to run.

In succeeding chapters, you will fill in different operations between the curly braces to experiment with language and other features. For this first outing, however, all the method does is display a sentence in the Console window (described in just a bit) whenever you click on the button. This will confirm the app is working as it should.

To display content in the Console window, you can use the NSLog() function, whose basic format (although not necessarily its argument) should be familiar to any Java-Script programmer. The sole parameter to this function is a string object containing any text you want to display in the Console window. To prevent the discussion at this early stage from bogging down in the fine points of Objective-C data typing, suffice it to say that one way to define an Objective-C string object is with an at sign (@) followed immediately by a quoted string. In JavaScript, this type of string is called a *string literal*; in Objective-C, it's called a *string constant*, but that term can be confused with genuine constants, so I will refer to this type of string object as a string literal. If you forget the at sign in Objective-C, the code will fail to compile.

`NSLog()` is helpful during code creation in that you can view intermediate values and results in the separate Console window in Xcode while the app is running (either in the simulator or on a device). Unlike the commonly used JavaScript `window.alert()` method, the app is not interrupted with a dialog box. For example, you can insert an `NSLog()` function call within a loop routine to show intermediate results each time through even a lengthy loop. The Console window will fill up with all kinds of data, but you'll then be able to go back and see how the execution performed during the loop process. I'll have more to say about `NSLog()` in future chapters, where you'll learn how to integrate nonstring values into results displayed in the Console.

Building the User Interface

At this point you have the working Objective-C code for Workbench, but you haven't done anything yet to generate the button that appears in the app or to connect that button to the `runMyCode:` method. You'll use the separate Xcode tool called Interface Builder (or IB) to do that.

Xcode not only generates the basic source code files for you, but it also generates the Interface Builder files you'll use. Expand the Resources folder in the Groups & Files panel, as shown in Figure 3-8. Two of the files have names ending in the *.xib* extension. Although pronounced "zib," you will more commonly hear these files referred to as "nib" files. Previous generations of Interface Builder for Mac OS development created files with the *.nib* extension, but for the current version of Xcode, Interface Builder generates files with the *.xib* extension.

About .nib and .xib Files

The name "nib" originated eons ago at NeXT Computer, the company that Steve Jobs founded in 1985. The company created a new operating system, called NeXTSTEP, and a development environment for that OS. Eventually acquired by Apple, the operating system technology found its way into Mac OS X, and the development environment, which included the NeXT Interface Builder component, grew into to-day's SDKs for Mac OS X and iOS programming. You can find plenty of NeXTSTEP heritage in today's Cocoa programming, even in the naming of various pieces. For example, the "NS" part of the `NSLog()` function described in this chapter comes from "NeXTSTEP." Lots of Cocoa identifiers begin with those same two letters.

As Interface Builder evolved over the years, the file format for *.nib* files needed enhancements to work more easily with source code management systems. Thus, Apple created an enhanced file format for Interface Builder files, and assigned the *.xib* extension to those files. But the "nib" heritage lives on to the extent that Cocoa Touch method names that invoke Interface Builder files continue to use the word "Nib" within their names, such as the `initWithNibName:bundle:` method.

Nib files store their information in XML format. While it's true that you can open and inspect a *.xib* file with a text editor to see the XML code, don't expect to modify a nib file this way. A nib file is to be edited only through Interface Builder. Not being able to see the actual code of a nib file disturbs many iOS programming newcomers, because using Interface Builder requires a leap of faith. You can't single-step through code that assembles your Interface-Builder-generated user interface elements, as you can if you manually create your user interface via Objective-C code. On the other hand, many things happen automatically through Interface Builder that lighten the coding load.

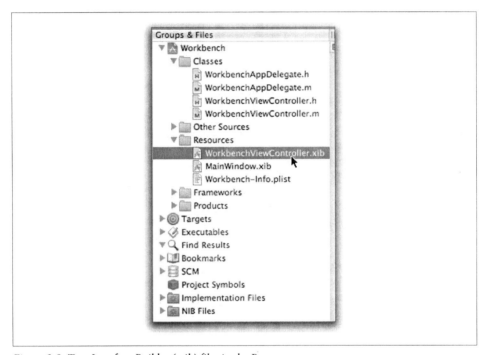

Figure 3-8. Two Interface Builder (.xib) files in the Resources group

Before you even look at one of the Interface Builder files, Xcode has already done quite a bit of work for you. You saw earlier in this chapter that Xcode generated two source code files for something called WorkbenchViewController. This is where the code that operates in response to clicking the button lives. To help you lay out where that button goes and how it looks, Xcode has prepared an Interface Builder file tied directly to WorkbenchViewController—with the identical name, but different file extension, *.xib*. All three files with the same name (but different extensions) will work together.

Double-click the *WorkbenchViewController.xib* file in the Resources group. This act launches Interface Builder (it may take a moment to get running), which then displays a few small windows for the file.

The main window representing the file is the one shown in Figure 3-9. This window, known as the *document window*, acts as a kind of table of contents for the user interface elements defined for this view controller. You can view the contents by icon, list, or tabular view. I prefer the list view in Figure 3-9, because it makes it easier to work with more complicated user interfaces later on. At the moment, the only actual user interface element defined by default is called View.

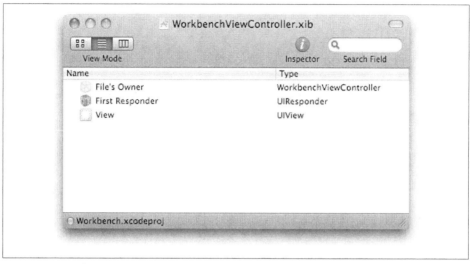

Figure 3-9. Interface Builder document window

Another window, titled View and shown in Figure 3-10, is where you will lay out a button. This window is initially sized to the maximum size of the device for which you're developing. Because you're making an iPhone-based app, the View window represents the full-size iPhone screen of 320 points wide and 480 points tall. By default, the view specifies a top status bar (with the battery icon), which is 20 points tall. If you should accidentally close the View window (or if it doesn't open automatically when you open the *.xib* file), double-click the View icon in the document window.

Before the Retina Display of the iPhone 4, screen dimensions were measured exclusively in pixels. But the Retina Display squeezes four pixels in the space where one exists in lower-resolution displays. To keep interface layouts specifications in sync across display resolutions, measurements are now calibrated in a unit called the *point* (not to be confused with the typographic unit), rather than the *pixel*.

Figure 3-10. The empty View window

Adding a Button to the View

It's now time to add a button to the View. Locate the Library palette window (or choose Library from the Tools menu if the palette isn't visible). The Library window contains all the user interface pieces that you can lay out inside a view. To simplify finding the interface element you need, choose the Inputs & Values group from the pop-up menu, as shown in Figure 3-11. You will see a variety of user controls (buttons, text fields, and other indicators) that should be familiar to you as an iPhone user.

Figure 3-11. The Library window with Inputs & Values selected from the Cocoa Touch group

Click the Round Rect Button icon and drag it out of the Library window (Figure 3-12) and into the View window. As you drag the item, it changes to just the button once you reach the View window, as shown in Figure 3-13. Precise placement of the button is not critical for the Workbench app. Once you drop the button (release the mouse button), you can click and drag the button around the view. Position the button approximately close to where it appears in Figure 3-1.

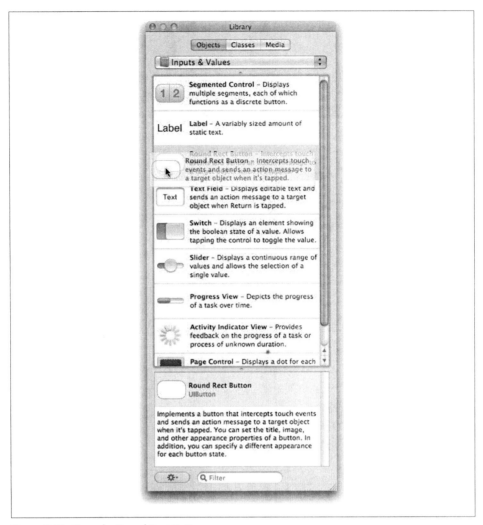

Figure 3-12. Drag the Round Rect Button

Click inside the button until you see a text cursor, then type the label **Run My Code** (shown in Figure 3-14). As you type, the button automatically resizes its width to accommodate the longer text.

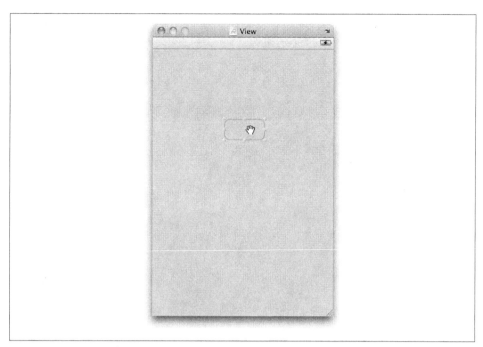

Figure 3-13. Position the button in the View window

Figure 3-14. Type a label for the button

Click outside of the button to view your handiwork, as shown in Figure 3-15. So much for the layout. Next comes the wiring that allows the button to run the code you wrote earlier.

Figure 3-15. The finished button layout

Connecting the Button

To associate the button in Interface Builder with the runMyCode: method in the view controller, you'll use the Inspector window. The Inspector window has four different modes, named Attributes, Connections, Size, and Identity. Modes are selectable by buttons at the top of the Inspector palette or from the Tools menu. Figure 3-16 shows the Attributes Inspector. As its name implies, this tool lets you determine numerous properties of a selected interface element. The composition of controls in the Attributes Inspector changes with each type of element you choose from the Library and drop into your views. For a button, you see items such as button type, title (which you filled

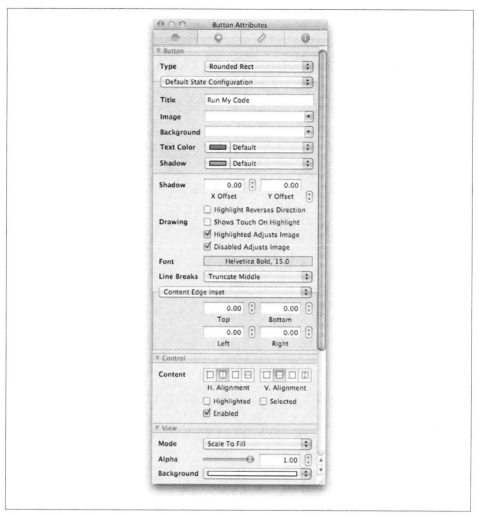

Figure 3-16. Attributes Inspector for the Run My Code button

in graphically earlier), various colors, and a bunch of visual characteristics. You're going to keep the default attributes for this button, so don't tinker with any settings here.

Your immediate task is to hook up the button to the method. Turn to the Connections Inspector, which you access by clicking the blue round icon with the arrow in the Inspector toolbar (or choosing Connections Inspector from IB's Tools menu). The job of the Connections Inspector for a button is to connect an event action to a method in the code. Figure 3-17 shows the Connections Inspector and its list of event types.

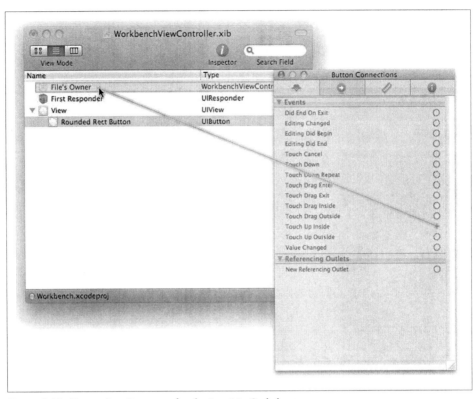

Figure 3-17. Connections Inspector for the Run My Code button

The event you're interested in is known as Touch Up Inside, meaning the event fires when a user releases his or her finger from anywhere inside the boundaries of the button. Click in the empty circle to the right of Touch Up Inside and drag the mouse to the File's Owner item in the document window, as shown in Figure 3-17. The File's Owner represents the WorkbenchViewController, where the source code for the method lives. As you drag, a blue line follows the cursor, and the intended destination highlights as shown.

When you release the mouse button, a context-sensitive menu appears, as shown in Figure 3-18. This menu offers a list of all possible method definitions from the controller code that were identified as being Interface Builder actions (IBActions). Select runMy Code:. If you look back at the code you entered for the runMyCode: method, you'll recall that it was identified as an IBAction in both the interface and implementation sections of the source code. That's where Interface Builder obtained the method name. This should also give you a clue about how tightly interconnected Xcode and Interface Builder are at all times. For instance, if you were to switch to Xcode to add a second IBAction-style method to the view controller source code (both files), and then switch back to IB and make a new connection, that second method would instantly appear in the pop-up list at the end of a connection.

What's That Method Name Colon All About?

In JavaScript, you typically refer to a function either as *functionName()* (when writing about it) or just *functionName* when referencing the function as an object in code. Objective-C method references (whether in writing or in code) convey a little extra information about the method's definition. For example, the `runMyCode:` method added to this project has a single argument, whose value is separated from the method name by a colon. If the method did not have an argument, the method reference would not have a colon. Therefore, if you define two methods in the same class file, one named `runMyCode` and the other `runMyCode:`, when you try to make a connection like the one shown in Figure 3-18, the pop-up list would show both methods. The presence or absence of the colon would help you decide which one to attach to the action. There is more about method naming in Chapter 4.

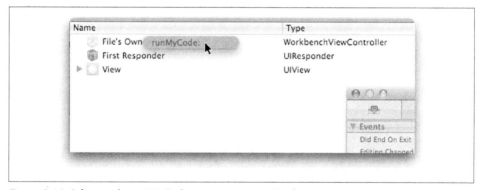

Figure 3-18. Selecting the runMyCode action written in Xcode

You can confirm that the connection has been made correctly by checking the Connections Inspector. It should show the specific connection for the Touch Up Inside event. Figure 3-19 shows the result.

Remember that you are creating and editing a file in Interface Builder. Therefore, you need to save your changes, just like any source code file. If you forget to save, Xcode will offer to save any unsaved changes when you attempt to build and run the program.

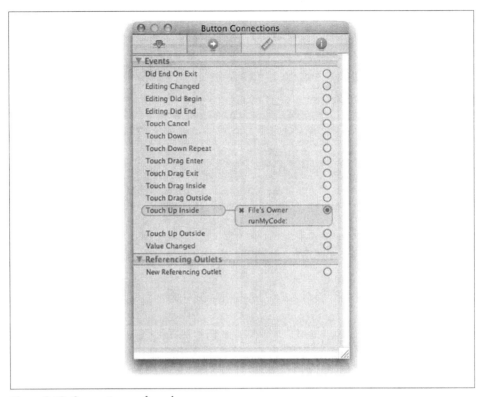

Figure 3-19. Connection confirmed

Going for a Test Ride

It's now time to verify that Workbench is working as it's supposed to. Switch back to Xcode. You'll be running the app in the iOS Simulator, and Xcode more than likely has already set up the Base SDK correctly for you. Confirm that the Overview menu has Simulator and Workbench - iPhone Simulator 4.2 checked, as shown in Figure 3-20. You will not be able to install this app on your own device without obtaining a developer certificate—something you will learn how to do in later stages of your introductory iPhone education.

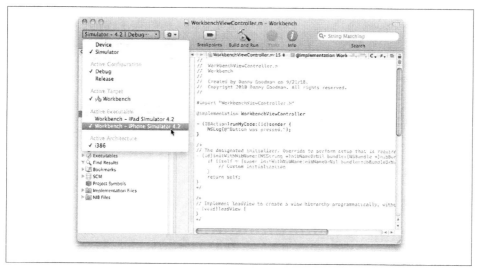

Figure 3-20. Selecting the iPhone Simulator platform to run the app

Next, open the Console window (where you can see the app is behaving correctly) by choosing Console from Xcode's Run menu (Figure 3-21). The Console window should be visible, as shown in Figure 3-22.

Figure 3-21. Opening the Xcode Console window

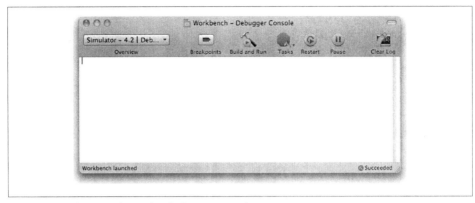

Figure 3-22. The Console window before running the app

And now the moment of truth: click the Build and Run button in any window associated with the project. The build part of the operation is Xcode compiling the code into an app file (a package with the *.app* extension) that will be installed into the iPhone Simulator and launched. If there is a problem during compilation, the process stops before ever installing on the simulator. Errors or warning notices appear in the Xcode window's bottom bar. If you encounter a problem with the code shown in this chapter, you may not understand Xcode's error messages at this stage. Therefore, go back through the steps in this chapter, carefully review the code you typed for errors (like the missing @ symbol in the NSLog() function or missed semicolons). Do the same with the steps in Interface Builder. This code should run as described here.

If the app launches successfully in the simulator, come back to Xcode before you go any further and make sure the Console window is visible at the same time the simulator is. Now click the Run My Code button in the app on the simulator. The Console window should display proof that the button is connected and the app is running as intended (Figure 3-23).

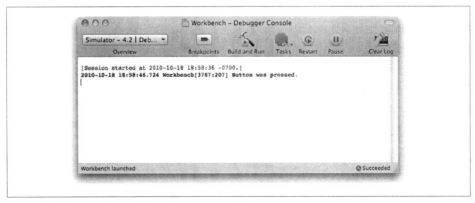

Figure 3-23. The Workbench is working and ready for more

You should save a pristine copy of this project in a separate directory. Then, in subsequent chapters you can copy a fresh version to a working directory to add the code being demonstrated.

You can exit the app by either clicking the Home button in the simulator or clicking the Tasks button in any Xcode window when it is a bright red stop sign.

Congratulations

You have just built a custom iOS app using Objective-C, Xcode, and Interface Builder. Not a scrap of JavaScript or CSS anywhere to be found. And this is not just some "Hello, world" app, but one that you will use while reading subsequent chapters and even beyond this book.

 The console always displays a timestamp, app name, and other preamble information each time NSLog() is called. In future chapters, whenever the console output is shown in the text, I'll omit the preamble to focus on the data result.

In the next chapter, we'll come back to Workbench to learn more about the pieces that go into an app and I'll provide you with the powers to do wonderful things. If you have not had formal training in object-oriented programming (OOP), you'll not only learn what that's all about, but also that your DOM scripting world has already been exhibiting object-oriented tendencies right under your nose.

CHAPTER 4

Structural Overview of an iOS App

Now that we have a working iOS app, we can look more closely at many of the details in the source code for that app and the project. Xcode will again be your gateway to the inner workings. Although the title of this chapter doesn't mention object-oriented programming (OOP), this chapter is where you will learn the fundamentals—especially the terminology, which is often quite different from what you've seen in the JavaScript world. Despite the differences in naming, you will recognize some familiar concepts.

Where It All Begins: APIs

An application programming interface, or API, is essentially a list of entities you can program and what you can ask those entities to do in a program. Designers of computers and software systems can choose to expose the inner workings of those devices and programs to third-party programmers. APIs typically shield the third-party programmer from the complex inner workings of the systems and provide him with simpler, optimized, and well-tested ways to control those systems.

APIs You Already Know

As a client-side scripter, you have already worked with a number of APIs, even if the three-letter term wasn't forced upon you. The API most obvious to you should be the DOM, which exposes every type of HTML element as an object you can script. The authors of the W3C DOM write specifications about how objects are named, what their properties and methods are, and how objects are to behave under script control. The initial audience for these standards is browser makers who implement the standards and provide the APIs that you access via JavaScript.

APIs for current programming environments rarely stand still. That has certainly been the case in the browser API world. The evolving HTML5 standard includes an API for new HTML elements that facilitate embedding audio and video into a web page, as well as other APIs for offline web applications and dynamically editable content. A browser maker can also elect to add APIs, which is what Apple has done with Mobile Safari to enable limited access to iOS location services through a web page's scripts.

The JavaScript language provides its own APIs for the core language. The way your scripts work with strings, numbers, dates, regular expressions, and operations through the Math object are all part of that API. All of those properties and methods you see in reference guides are there to provide you with easy access to what would otherwise be very complex, low-level programming.

The Cocoa Touch APIs

To allow developers to write apps for the iPhone and similar devices, Apple's engineers created a set of APIs. The historical basis for the iOS APIs was the set of Mac OS X development APIs. On the Mac, the most recent set of APIs is known as Cocoa (whose technological heritage, in turn, originated with the NeXTSTEP development environment). Although the name Cocoa was originally associated with a children's multimedia creation environment (by Apple), the name eventually shifted to the Mac OS X development world, where it has remained.

Because so many fundamentals of iOS are based on Mac OS X but implemented for purely touch-based devices, it was logical enough to call the iOS APIs Cocoa Touch. That's not to say Cocoa Touch is merely Cocoa with the addition of some touchscreen events. Cocoa Touch omits many Cocoa technologies that aren't necessary for a slimmed-down device (compared to a desktop or laptop computer) and adds gobs of technologies that Mac OS X computers may never acquire—you're not likely to rotate your MacBook display to portrait mode or demand turn-by-turn directions from an iMac.

Cocoa Touch APIs consist of specifications for objects and built-in functions that programmers can use while developing apps for iOS devices. Just as the JavaScript API in browsers supplies scriptable access to strings, numbers, and dates, the Cocoa Touch API provides Objective-C access to those same kinds of data. And, just as the DOM API in browsers specifies how JavaScript can access and control document objects, such as forms, arbitrary divs, or images, the Cocoa Touch API lets programmers access and control buttons, images, and scrollable regions within a view.

But of course, the Cocoa Touch APIs grant lots of OS-specific access to features such as the device's geographical location, the music library in the built-in iPod app, and those ubiquitous scrolling lists of items. With each new generation of iOS, Apple adds more APIs. For example, at the announcement of the iOS 4.0, Apple claimed to have added over 1,500 methods to the SDK, including access to a user's calendar data and files in the photo library and the ability to build SMS messaging into apps. For iOS 4.2, Apple added scores of APIs, including a MIDI controller and wireless printing facilities.

The job of an iOS SDK programmer, therefore, is to use the Objective-C language to manipulate data (text, graphics, sounds, etc.) with the help of the APIs built into the operating system. You'll still need good ideas about the data and how best to integrate that data into the device, but learning the broad spectrum of APIs available to you is a very important part of the learning process.

Public Versus Private APIs

If you read the fine print of your iOS SDK license agreement, you find the provision that your apps may use only "Documented APIs," which Apple defines as the APIs it reveals via its developer documentation in the SDK. Those are not the only APIs in iOS, but they're the only ones that you, as a registered developer, can use if you plan to distribute your app through the App Store.

Apple's explanation for this distinction between public and private APIs is that undocumented, private APIs are generally not yet finalized—not ready for prime time, as it were. The burden of documenting an API is that developers will use it, and it becomes nearly impossible to change that API in the future because it would break all existing apps that use the API. Additionally, there are APIs in the OS that Apple will likely never document because developers could abuse the privileges, much to the dismay of users (e.g., automatically making phone calls) or cell phone service providers (e.g., downloading movie-length HD video over a 3G connection).

Being limited to documented APIs might be frustrating at times, especially if you see Apple's own apps performing tasks that your apps cannot. In the meantime, there are enough APIs ahead of you on your learning curve to keep you plenty busy.

Frameworks

One way Apple keeps the thousands of APIs straight is to organize them into groups known as *frameworks*. You may recognize the term from your exposure to JavaScript libraries such as Dojo, jQuery, and YUI. Although there are differences between libraries and frameworks (a subject beyond the scope of this book, and usually generating programming-religious discussions), they both provide APIs that facilitate programming-specific tasks. Frameworks targeting iOS web app development include iUI and a jQuery plug-in called jQTouch. The iUI framework consists of CSS and JavaScript files you link into a web page. The JavaScript objects and functions in the *.js* file are immediately available within the scope of the current document window. For example, the iUI framework performs much of the heavy lifting in turning an HTML unordered list into a page that resembles the typical iPhone vertically scrollable table view; a tap on an item (via a touch event) causes what looks like a detail view to slide in from the right side.

You can see the three basic frameworks that are common to virtually every iOS app created with the SDK. Open the Workbench project in Xcode and expand the Frameworks folder in the Files and Groups panel on the left. There you will see entries for the Foundation, UIKit, and CoreGraphics frameworks (Figure 4-1).

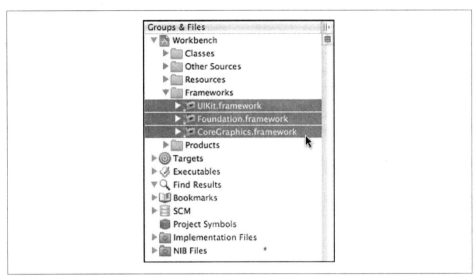

Figure 4-1. Three basic iOS SDK frameworks

You don't truly have to know what's inside each of these three frameworks, but having an overview of them from 35,000 feet will help you understand how the iOS SDK organizes its various powers. You are welcome to expand any of the framework items, but the long lists of header files might make your head explode until you progress further into this chapter. With that, let's do a quick framework survey.

Foundation Framework

The Foundation framework reveals how much iOS has in common with Mac OS X. Both environments use the same Foundation framework, although the iOS version trims off many items that don't apply or aren't yet supported. Definitions in this framework include the basics: strings, various types of data collections, dates, timers, fetching data from the network through URLs, and even XML parsing (although not in a DOM-friendly manner). The Foundation framework is all about manipulating data, and not displaying it. In that sense, you might equate this framework with the core JavaScript language, which is designed for use in all kinds of environments, including those outside of web browsers.

UIKit Framework

As its name implies, the UIKit framework is all about user interface elements—specifically, iOS kinds of user interface elements. This is where the SDK lets you create and manipulate buttons, images, scrolling thingies, text boxes, various bars, alert dialog windows, and those neat looking slot-machine-style picker controls. Most of the time you will use Interface Builder to lay out user interface elements for a screen, but under the hood, the SDK ultimately relies on the UIKit framework definitions for those elements to figure out how to draw them when the app runs. If the Foundation framework is like the core JavaScript language API, the UIKit framework is like the DOM API, including the JavaScript `style` property to control very specifically how things on the screen appear (colors, sizes, etc.).

CoreGraphics Framework

Unlike the Objective-C-based Foundation and UIKit frameworks, the CoreGraphics framework uses the C language in all of its definitions. This is one reason you need to be familiar with basic C syntax when doing iOS SDK programming. The CoreGraphics framework focuses on 2-D drawing activities, such as when you need to fill a space with a gradient or rotate a user interface control (e.g., creating a vertical slider control).

Adding Frameworks

The above descriptions are brief, to be sure, but you'll recognize that I make no mention of some of the specialized capabilities of iOS apps, such as location services, maps, or playing audio. That's because APIs for those capabilities are contained in other frameworks that are not part of the default set that Xcode automatically puts into a view-based application. If you want to get an idea of the other frameworks available to you, Control-click the Frameworks group and follow the submenus to Add→Existing Frameworks, as shown in Figure 4-2.

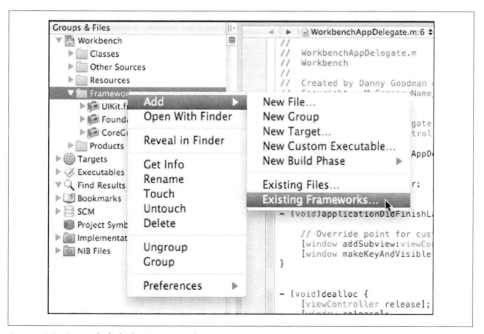

Figure 4-2. Control-click the Frameworks group

In the resulting dialog box, choose Frameworks from the top menu to limit the list to available frameworks, as shown in Figure 4-3. You can see the range of subject matter covered by Apple's documented frameworks. Don't add anything to the Workbench project now. In Appendix A, you'll learn how to use the SDK documentation to determine which framework to add to your project for a particular feature you want to add to your app.

Figure 4-3. List of existing frameworks

Frameworks Set in Stone

You may be accustomed to inspecting and even modifying the source code in JavaScript libraries that come in various web browser scripting frameworks. That's one significant difference between a JavaScript library and an iOS SDK framework. The source code that does the work of the iOS APIs is hidden away. At best, you can see lists of the API calls available within a framework, but not how those frameworks actually do their work. That also means that you cannot alter the frameworks directly. That's a good thing: given the complexity of iOS, such willy-nilly modifications could spell trouble for your app, because you never know when your code or another API relies on a mint-condition API call. Instead, Objective-C provides you with multiple ways to add to the existing functionality of an API that your program can use at will. (See Chapter 8).

Now that you've explored the Frameworks group in Xcode, it's time to head back up to the Class Files group in the Workbench project. This is where you will spend most of your coding time.

Welcome to Class Files

Most, if not all, of the code you write for an iOS app is contained in what are called *class files*. A class is an object-oriented programming term and is vital to understanding most of what goes on in iOS SDK programming.

A class is code that defines the characteristics of an object. You've worked with tons of objects in JavaScript—whether they be pure language objects, such as the Date object, or DOM objects that represent HTML elements on the page—so you should already be familiar with the concept of an object having properties (which can hold data) and methods (which perform actions). In fact, when you write the code for a JavaScript object constructor function, you are doing essentially the same job that you will be doing when you write the code for an Objective-C class definition. It's just that the format and environment for the Objective-C variety is radically different from the JavaScript constructor. To help you visualize the differences between the JavaScript object constructor and Objective-C class definitions, I'll show you a variation on a venerable JavaScript object constructor example, which I will then rewrite in Objective-C (you can even test it in Workbench by the end of the chapter). Both examples focus on using the constructor or class as a way to obtain object instances.

The JavaScript Way

I'll begin with a variation of an "old chestnut" example, one that defines an object that represents an automobile. I'll add a function to the old standard to demonstrate how an object gains a method. Example 4-1 is an HTML page with scripts that define a Car object constructor, create two instances of that object, and then assemble a text description out of properties of each object instance. The results are inserted into span elements on the page.

Example 4-1. JavaScript object constructor at work

```
<!DOCTYPE HTML PUBLIC "-//W3C//DTD HTML 4.01 Transitional//EN"
       "http://www.w3.org/TR/html4/loose.dtd">
<html>
```

```
<head>
<title>Car Object Example</title>
<script type="text/javascript">
// Constructor function
function Car(make, model, year) {
    this.make = make;
    this.model = model;
    this.year = year;
    this.getFormattedListing = function() {
        var result = "[" + this.year + "] " + this.make +
        " " + this.model;
        return result;
    }
}
// Create instances of Car
var myCar1 = new Car("Chevrolet", "Malibu", "2007");
var myCar2 = new Car("Ford", "Taurus", "2010")

// Insert Car data in display elements
function showCar() {
    document.getElementById("display1").innerHTML = myCar1.getFormattedListing();
    document.getElementById("display2").innerHTML = myCar2.getFormattedListing();
}
</script>
</head>

<body onload="showCar()">
<h1>Info About My First Car</h1>
<p>I used to drive a <span id="display1"></span>.</p>
<h1>Info About My Current Car</h1>
<p>I now drive a <span id="display2"></span>.</p>
</body>
</html>
```

After the page loads, the showCar() function fills in content of two span elements with formatted text descriptions of the two cars. The constructor function is reused, as-is, to create two instances of the Car object, each with its own details, but the function always formats the results in the same way.

The Objective-C Way

I'll begin by showing you the code for a class definition that will let you generate instances of objects representing car information. Much of what you'll see at first will likely be foreign to you, but don't fear. I will dissect and explain the code to fill in the blanks. Don't go rushing to recreate these files just yet; Xcode can do a lot of the grunt work for you, as I'll demonstrate later in this chapter.

An Objective-C class is described using two different sections of code, called the *interface* and the *implementation*. Although you can combine the two sections into a single file, the convention that Xcode follows when it generates templates for classes is to place each of these sections into its own file. The filenames are the same, but each file has its own filename extension to differentiate the two.

The interface contains a list of variables and methods that the class wishes to expose to other classes. Items are defined with just the barest minimum of detail, such as the name and type of each variable or the name of a method, which kind of data it returns, and which arguments are required. In contrast, the implementation section contains the code that executes when each method is invoked.

Example 4-2 shows the interface portion of a definition for the DGCar class. Notice that the class name (DGCar) begins with an uppercase letter—another Objective-C convention (but not an absolute requirement). Interface files always have the .h filename extension. The "h" comes from the word "header," and I will refer to .h files as *header files*. I could have named the class Car, but that is such a generic term that it could conceivably be used by the frameworks supplied in the system I'm programming (e.g., if Apple ever got into the automobile business). To greatly reduce possible confusion—since each class must have a unique name inside a project—I put my initials as the first two letters of the class name. You'll find that Apple does this all over its frameworks. Every class name in the Foundation framework begins with "NS" (revealing its NeXT-STEP heritage) and every class name in the UIKit framework begins with "UI." Other frameworks define their class names with still other prefixes. Pick a class naming prefix, and stick with it so you can always identify your custom classes and keep them separate from Apple's framework classes or other third-party classes you adopt in the future.

Example 4-2. The header file for the DGCar class—DGCar.h

```
//
//  DGCar.h
//  Workbench
//
//  Created by Danny Goodman on 4/12/10.
//  Copyright 2010 Danny Goodman. All rights reserved.
//

#import <Foundation/Foundation.h>


@interface DGCar : NSObject {

    NSString *make;
    NSString *model;
    NSString *year;

}

- (DGCar *)initWithCarMake:(NSString *)inputMake
                    model:(NSString *)inputModel
                     year:(NSString *)inputYear;
- (NSString *)getFormattedListing;

@end
```

Example 4-3 shows the implementation file for the `DGCar` class. The implementation file's extension is *.m*, where the "m" originates from "methods"—not, as some suggest, 'mplementation. Although the `DGCar` class methods file contains two method definitions, the file can also contain variables, constants, and other components that the methods use. I will refer to *.m* files as implementation files. You'll learn about method formatting (e.g., the leading hyphen and colons) later in this chapter when I show you how to create and edit these files.

Example 4-3. The implementation file for the DGCar class—DGCar.m

```
//
//  DGCar.m
//  Workbench
//
//  Created by Danny Goodman on 4/12/10.
//  Copyright 2010 Danny Goodman. All rights reserved.
//

#import "DGCar.h"


@implementation DGCar

- (DGCar *)initWithCarMake:(NSString *)inputMake
                    model:(NSString *)inputModel
                     year:(NSString *)inputYear {
    // If initialization of the superclass succeeds,
    // then assign instance variables
    if (self = [super init]) {
        make = inputMake;
        model = inputModel;
        year = inputYear;
    }

    return self;
}

- (NSString *)getFormattedListing {
    NSString *result = @"";

    result = [NSString stringWithFormat:@"[%@] %@ %@", year, make, model];

    return result;
}
@end
```

The header and implementation files work together, and their code must be kept in sync. Coming from the JavaScript world where "once is enough," you will see what appears to be duplication in the content of the header and implementation files in Objective-C. Compilers rely on the concise header section to confirm the availability of variables and methods referenced by other classes. If you have worked exclusively with interpreted languages, it may take some time to remember to make changes to both sections whenever you edit a class. If you do forget, Xcode will remind you when you attempt to build the app.

Notice that the two Objective-C `DGCar` class files correspond to the role of only the JavaScript `Car` constructor function. Instances of the objects (in both cases) are created elsewhere.

 Experienced Objective-C coders may notice the absence of memory management in the code examples for this chapter. Fear not! Chapter 6 covers the subject, and eventually this code will be outfitted with proper memory management routines.

Header File Details

When Xcode generates a class file, it starts by inserting several comment lines at the very top:

```
//
//  DGCar.h
//  Workbench
//
//  Created by Danny Goodman on 4/12/10.
//  Copyright 2010 Danny Goodman. All rights reserved.
//
```

It should be obvious that Xcode is picking up various pieces of information from the file and project names as well as the computer user's name. Xcode inserts those tidbits automatically. If the copyright line of the comments in files you create looks like the following, you need to show Xcode or the specific project how to fill in the name of your organization:

```
// Copyright 2010 __MyCompanyName__. All rights reserved.
```

One way is to make sure that your contact card in Apple's Address Book app on your Mac has a company name filled in (even if it is a duplicate of your own name). Xcode looks there for the organization by default. Or you can set the organization name separately for a specific project by opening your project in Xcode, choosing Project→Edit Project Settings, and filling in the Organization Name field near the bottom of the General tab. Changing this setting does not alter copyright attribution on source code files already generated in the project. You might want a separate organization name if you are developing an app for someone else or your contact card lists an employer's company while you develop apps on your own.

After Xcode generates these comment lines, you are free to delete or edit them as you like. The compiler ignores all commented lines when building an app.

Importing frameworks

At the top of the uncommented code in the header file comes the place where you declare which framework(s) the current class requires:

```
#import <Foundation/Foundation.h>
```

Statements beginning with the pound symbol (#) are called *preprocessor directives*. When you build (compile) an app with Xcode, source code files are initially scanned by a preprocessor, which obeys instructions in these directives. There are a limited number of preprocessor directives, but #import is one you will use frequently. It instructs the compiler to locate the file and blend it into the current file. In some ways, it works like the HTML link element, which commonly brings an external file (e.g., a *.css* file) into the scope of the current document.

An #import directive connects your program to an associated header file that has the definitions you need. The directive has two ways of referring to files that are to be imported into the class. The one shown above, with the angle brackets, typically imports standard frameworks. The other style (which you'll see in the DGCar methods file shortly) is for importing class files you bundle in your own app.

In the case of *DGCar.h*, the Foundation framework (which you can visualize as a folder) contains a bunch of header files, one of which is named *Foundation.h*. That header file itself contains a long list of #import directives that instruct the preprocessor to import the individual Foundation framework header files (such as *NSArray.h* and *NSDate.h*). You can see this for yourself in Xcode for the Workbench project by expanding the *Frameworks* group folder and then the Foundation framework "toolbox" icon and the nested *Headers* folder. Click on the *Foundation.h* file and you'll see the list of individual framework header files being imported into the DGCar class (Figure 4-4).

A class header can import multiple frameworks. For example, if the purpose of Workbench was to display and work with maps, any class file that needs to communicate with the APIs in the MapKit framework would include an #import directive for that framework:

```
#import <MapKit/MapKit.h>
```

You would also have to add the MapKit framework to the project, as discussed earlier in this chapter in "Adding Frameworks" on page 55.

How Gigantic Are Frameworks?

If you've used JavaScript or web app frameworks in the past, you are well aware that they contain a lot of code that has to be delivered to the browser. Sometimes they need to be compressed to make the download speed tolerable to users. Considering the number of things that iOS frameworks do, you might wonder what impact they have on the size of an app file that is installed on a device. The answer: none. All of Apple's iOS frameworks are built into the operating system. The compiler generates a *.app* file that knows how to pull resources from the operating system, rather than copying the frameworks into every app.

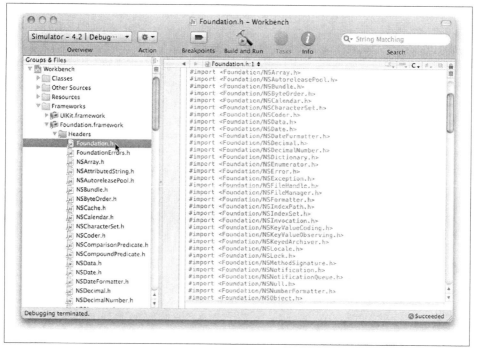

Figure 4-4. Inspecting the Foundation.h header file

Inheritance

Inheritance simply means that a newly defined class automatically gets all of the characteristics and behaviors of an existing class, and adds one or more items that make the new class something different. The new class is called a *subclass*, while the existing class from which the subclass gets its fundamentals is its *superclass*. The "child" and "parent" conceptual relationship also fits, but those terms aren't prevalent in the Objective-C language.

Before you get all tangled up in the notion of inheritance, bear in mind that DOM scripting has already warmed you up to the concept. If you were to examine the W3C standards document for the DOM, you would see that the DOM's structure is entirely object-oriented underneath, relying on relationships between superclasses and subclasses. For example, the most basic object in the DOM structure is the *node*. Every instance of a Node object has a list of attributes (more commonly called properties when being scripted) and methods that are defined for the Node. Attributes for a node include nodeName, nodeValue, nodeType, firstChild, and so on; methods include appendChild(), removeChild(), cloneNode(), and others. A node in its pure form is not specified in an

HTML document or rendered in a browser: it is merely the basic building block used to define more concrete "things" in a document.

That brings us to the DOM `Element` object, which inherits directly from the `Node` object. Thus, an `Element` object offers the same attributes and methods of a node, plus special members that apply to any kind of element, such as the `getAttribute()`, `setAttribute()`, and `getElementsByTagName()` methods. All of these are defined in the DOM Core module.

In the DOM module dedicated to HTML come definitions for objects more closely related to the items you put into HTML documents. One of the building blocks is the `HTMLElement`. It inherits all members of the `Element` and (in turn) `Node` objects, plus it acquires additional attributes that apply to all HTML elements, such as the `id`, `title`, and `className` properties. Going one step further, take the `HTMLImage` element (represented in HTML by the `<img>` tag). It inherits everything from the `HTMLElement` and adds further attributes that apply to its purpose of loading and displaying images—properties such as `src`, `height`, `width`, and `alt`. It is only by virtue of the inheritance chain—from `HTMLImageElement` upward through `HTMLElement`, `Element`, and `Node`—that an `HTMLImage` element has a `nodeName` property.

The @interface compiler directive

The identical object-oriented notion of inheritance works in Objective-C and many Cocoa Touch classes. When you name a class of your own creation (remember the initial capital letter convention!), you also specify from what other class your new class inherits in the following format:

```
@interface NewSubclass : SuperClass
```

Statements beginning with the @ symbol are called *compiler directives*. In other words, they are commands to the compiler as it processes the file. The `@interface` directive tells the compiler that this section contains declarations of the variables and methods that will be fleshed out in the companion `@implementation` section. The compiler needs to know the name of the class: `DGCar` in the example here. But to be an Objective-C class that will also be operating with Cocoa Touch classes (like arrays and strings), a custom class needs far more infrastructure than what you'll be defining in the class files. This infrastructure comes from inheriting all the characteristics of an existing object. Because the `DGCar` class is a very simple class that needs just the bare essentials, it will inherit from the most fundamental class in the `Foundation` framework: `NSObject`. As you will glean over time, most of the objects you work with from the `Foundation`, `UIKit`, and other frameworks inherit from `NSObject`, which assumes the role as the *base class*.

When you read instructions by other programmers that tell you to create a subclass of some other class, the `@interface` section begins just as above, with the name of the class you're creating, a colon, and the name of the superclass. The superclass, in turn, must belong to the framework (or other header file) imported via the `#import` directive earlier in the header file.

Using Xcode to Create DGCar Class Files

Xcode is helpful in setting up the skeletal structure of your class files, including the inheritance tree. Now is the time to follow along and create the DGCar class files (and fill them in as the chapter progresses).

Begin by selecting the Classes folder in the Files and Groups panel in the Workbench project window. Selecting this folder as a starting point causes Xcode to insert the files you're about to create within the Class group. To see the next menu, you have two options:

- Click to select the Classes folder and pull down the Action menu (the one with the gear icon).
- Use your choice of secondary click (e.g., Ctrl-click, right-click with a two-button mouse, or two-finger-click with a trackpad) on the Classes folder to reveal the context-sensitive menu.

Choose Add to view the choices of new items you can create. Select New File, as shown in Figure 4-5.

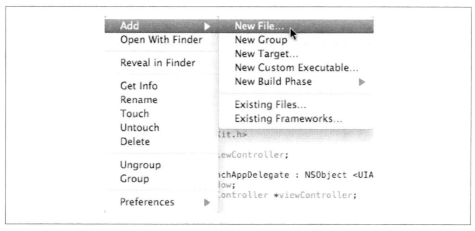

Figure 4-5. The Add submenu

A New File window opens, shown in Figure 4-6. For the simple class being created here, choose Cocoa Touch Class in the left column, then Objective-C class in the top right group. Next, make sure you specify that this will be a subclass of NSObject. This will cause Xcode to fill in as many pieces as it can into the skeleton files, including the superclass name. Click the Next button.

The final step in the creation of the set of partially prewired class files is to name the class, shown in Figure 4-7. It is here where you assign a name to the class. The default file name includes the correct *.m* extension. The name you enter into the top field becomes not only the name of the two class files, but also the name of the class, which

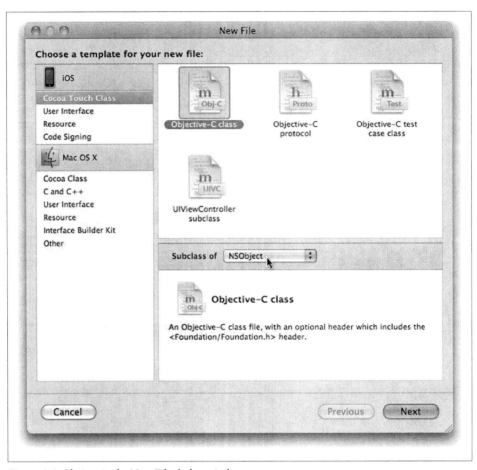

Figure 4-6. Choices in the New File dialog window

Xcode inserts into the class file templates. Xcode fills in everything else in this dialog box, but be sure to enable the checkbox next to the instruction to also create the *.h* header file for the class. Then click the Finish button.

Et voilà, your two class files are now created and inserted into the Class group, as shown in Figure 4-8. The new header file (below the comments) consists of the following code:

```
#import <Foundation/Foundation.h>


@interface DGCar : NSObject {

}

@end
```

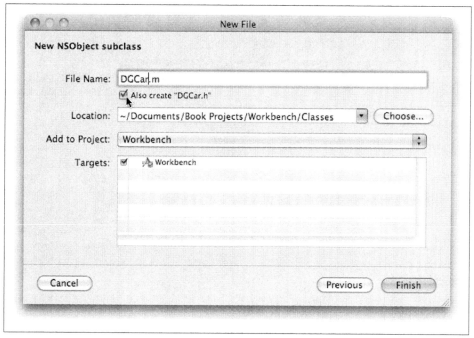

Figure 4-7. Saving the new class files

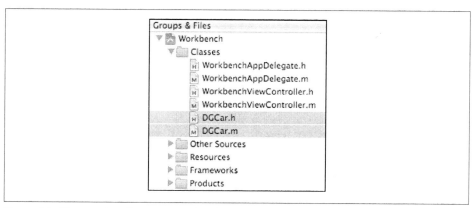

Figure 4-8. The two class files are created and added to the Classes group

Editing the @interface Section

Notice that the @interface directive is balanced by an @end directive, which is always at the end of the header file. In between are two sections for your code. The sections are labeled with placeholders in the following code fragment:

```
#import <Foundation/Foundation.h>


@interface DGCar : NSObject {

    // instance variable declarations here

}

// method declarations here

@end
```

These two sections are for declarations—almost a table of contents for the variable and method names to be assigned values and defined in detail within the companion implementation file.

For purposes of this demonstration, the DGCar class is designed to be parallel to the JavaScript Car object described earlier in this chapter. The JavaScript object has three properties and a method; the Objective-C version has three *instance variables* (also called *ivars*, pronounced EYE-varz) and two method definitions, as follows:

```
@interface DGCar : NSObject {

    NSString *make;
    NSString *model;
    NSString *year;

}

- (DGCar *)initWithCarMake:(NSString *)inputMake
                    model:(NSString *)inputModel
                     year:(NSString *)inputYear;
- (NSString *)getFormattedListing;

@end
```

You can probably recognize that the three JavaScript properties and three Objective-C instance variables serve similar purposes: when an instance of the object is created, that instance is designed to hold three values. Importantly, each instance can hold entirely different values without interfering with another—the essence of the object-oriented programming term, *encapsulation*.

There are, however, some important differences between the two environments. First, you'll notice that the Objective-C declarations define each variable as belonging to the NSString class. That is to say, each variable (when eventually initialized) will itself be an instance of the NSString class. Unlike JavaScript, when you define an Objective-C variable as a particular type of data, the data must be of that type and cannot change over the life of that variable. You'll learn more about data typing in Chapter 6.

An asterisk symbol indicates that the variable is what is known as a *pointer* to a place in memory where the object containing the value lives. The pointer notation appears with a variable when the variable is being declared, as happens in the header file. Chapter 6 has more information about pointers in Objective-C and how to use them.

Of the two methods defined in the DGCar class header file, the second one, getFormat tedListing, parallels the like-named method in the JavaScript version. The leading hyphen tells the compiler that the method is an instance method. A method declaration ends with a semicolon.

In Objective-C, all method declarations must specify the type of data returned when the method finishes running. The data type is placed inside parentheses ahead of the method name. The getFormattedListing method returns a value that is of class NSString (more explicitly, a pointer to an NSString object instance). As you'll learn later, not all methods return a value (just as not all JavaScript methods or functions return values). In those cases, place the keyword void in the parentheses where the data type goes.

Look now at the other method. Based on its name, it certainly appears to have something to do with initialization. The original JavaScript object constructor function accepts three arguments whose values are assigned to object properties at the same time an instance of the object is created. That same operation takes place in the Objective-C initialization method for this class. In Objective-C syntax, you can construct a method definition to accept arguments. Each argument must have its data type declared (again, covered in more detail in Chapter 6) and the name of a variable to which the value is assigned when the method is called (just like the parameter variables in the JavaScript constructor function's parentheses). The first argument comes after the method name, separated from it by a colon. Subsequent arguments (if any) have individual, explicit labels, which must have a space or other whitespace character (such as a carriage return) between the end of the previous argument's parameter variable and the start of the label. Thus, the second argument of the initialization method is named model and its value must be of type NSString. The way you refer to a method when writing or speaking about it is to include all of the argument labels and colons (if any). Therefore, the initialization method is technically referred to as:

```
initWithCarMake:model:year:
```

One reason the argument labels are so important is that, unlike in JavaScript, you can reuse a method's name to define a completely different method with a different set of arguments. Therefore, in this same DGCar class, you could define an additional method as the following and there would be no confusion:

```
initWithCarMake:model:year:listPrice:
```

The number of arguments and their labels in a statement that calls the method dictate the precise method being called.

Message Passing

While I'm on the subject of calling methods, Objective-C triggers the execution of methods based on a model that is different from what you use in JavaScript. Because each Objective-C object instance is conceptually a separate entity, the way objects communicate with each other is to send *messages* to each other. A message may have the feel of invoking an object's method, but there are important differences. For instance, if an object doesn't understand a message, the message is ignored and the object simply returns `nil` to the sender. Therefore, get in the habit of using the "message" terminology, such as, "Object A sends the `myMethodWithArgument1:andArgument2:` message to Object B."

One advantage of the argument labels in method definitions is that it's much easier to understand what the values being passed mean. In the JavaScript version, you just pass three strings and hope you have them in the desired order as needed by the order of the parameter variables in the constructor function. In Objective-C, however, the labels guide you to precisely how you should use each value. Importantly, the order of the labels must be the same in the method definition and the statement sending the message to that method. Just because they have labels doesn't mean you can mix up the order at will.

Speaking of labels, don't be afraid to be verbose in devising label names that really define what they're for. In fact, that goes for everything in Objective-C for which you need to assign a name. In JavaScript and web coding, you are very mindful that each character you apply to a variable or method name means a character that must make the journey from server to browser, occupying Internet bandwidth. But in the compiled Objective-C world, the compiler reduces those long names to very compact tokens. Long names in Objective-C contribute to the readability of your code (but you should not rely on them as replacements for good commenting).

Editing the @implementation Section

The implementation file, which holds the `@implementation` section, is where you write the code that executes when an instance of the class is created and thereafter. Look first at the empty *DGCar.m* file that Xcode generated for you (omitting the top comments section):

```
#import "DGCar.h"


@implementation DGCar

@end
```

Xcode automatically fills in two items. The first is the `#import` preprocessor directive. Whenever a class definition is divided into separate header and implementation files, the implementation file must instruct the preprocessor to import the companion header file. Notice that for importing class header files that are not frameworks, the header file name is in quotes rather than the angle brackets used for importing frameworks (as was done in the header file). The difference between quotes and brackets is that quotes instruct the preprocessor to start looking for the file within the same directory as the current implementation file. Since framework files are stored elsewhere, the angle brackets tell the preprocessor to skip the current directory.

If the `@interface` and `@implementation` sections were in the same file, both sections would already be together, meaning the `@implementation` section could see all the declarations in the `@interface` section and no importing would be necessary. Despite the apparent simplicity of having both sections in one file (especially if you need to make changes to method names or arguments during development), don't fight Xcode's will in generating header/implementation file pairs for your classes.

The blank `@implementation` section Xcode generates is even simpler than the blank `@interface` section shown earlier. There are no curly-braced subsections to deal with. Almost all of your code goes between the `@implementation` and `@end` compiler directives.

Adding the getFormattedListing method

Now we'll inspect the details of a method definition and see how the Objective-C form compares to what you know about JavaScript methods. The two versions described in this chapter share the same basic name, `getFormattedListing`. The Objective-C version is as follows:

```
- (NSString *)getFormattedListing {
    NSString *result = @"";

    result = [NSString stringWithFormat:@"[%@] %@ %@", year, make, model];

    return result;
}
```

Many things about this definition will look familiar to you. Compare the two language formats for method definition structure:

JavaScript:

```
function methodName() {
    // Statements
}
```

Objective-C:

```
- (returnType)methodName {
    // Statements
}
```

An Objective-C instance method definition begins with a hyphen symbol, followed by the return value type in parentheses and the method name. A block of statements to execute when the object receives a message matching the method name is contained inside a set of curly braces. Different programmers (in JavaScript, too) adhere to different styles of curly brace placement for blocks. Some place the left curly brace on the same line as the method name; others place the left brace at the start of the next line. Use the style you prefer.

Methods Other Than Instance Methods

You've seen that the hyphen signifies an instance method definition (and declaration in the header). In contrast, a plus symbol (+) signifies what is known as a *class method*. Believe it or not, your JavaScript work has probably already put you in touch with these two types of methods. The JavaScript Date object lets you create a date object instance, which contains a snapshot of time. That instance features a long list of instance methods, which you use to read and set various components of the date object instance. But you also have the power to ask the Date object (with a capital "D") to use one of its *static methods*, UTC(), to obtain the millisecond value of a particular date and time. This method is used only by way of the JavaScript static Date object, as in:

```
var UTCMilliseconds = Date.UTC(2010, 12, 25);
```

Objective-C class methods work the same way as JavaScript static methods, in that you send the message to the class rather than to an instance of the class. Definitions of class methods start with a plus symbol.

The job of the getFormattedListing method is to read the values of the instance variables, insert them into a string, and return the entire string as an NSString type. It begins by creating an empty NSString object named result. The second statement sends a message to the NSString class (not an instance) to invoke one of its class methods to plug the ivar values into placeholders within a string (more about formats in a moment). This NSString message returns a new NSString object, which is assigned to result, the value returned at the end.

Message syntax

You can see in the second statement of getFormattedListing what an Objective-C message looks like (the expression to the right of the assignment (=) operator). Forget everything you know about JavaScript method-calling syntax, and get ready for the Objective-C way of doing things. Sending a message requires at least two pieces of information:

- A reference to the intended recipient object, i.e., the message's *receiver*
- The name of method to be called (plus any arguments and passed values)

These pieces are embedded inside square brackets in the following format:

```
[receiver method]
```

To send a message containing a single argument, the syntax format is as follows:

```
[receiver method:argument]
```

Each additional argument consists of a label and a value, separated by a colon, as in the following format:

```
[receiver method:argument labelA:argumentA labelB:argumentB]
```

You can add one or more spaces around the square brackets if it helps with your code readability. I predict that until you get used to the square bracket notation, you will inevitably start writing messages without them because of your experience with Java-Script syntax. Additionally, every message includes a receiver, even if the message you're sending aims to invoke a method in the current class definition. In those cases (as you will see many times later in the book), the receiver is—you guessed it—self, as in the following message, which calls a loadNewData method defined elsewhere in the current class (and which does not return a value):

```
[self loadNewData];
```

Adding the initWithCarMake:model:year: method

Every Objective-C object derived from NSObject inherits from that base object the init method. That method is used as part of the process to generate an instance of the object (in addition to memory allocation, which you'll learn about in Chapter 6). If your custom class does nothing special when it creates an instance of itself, there is no need for you to define an init method in your class: the object will receive the init message and automatically use the init method defined for its superclass, NSObject. That's how inheritance and message passing work.

In the case of the DGCar class defined here, its code follows the model in the JavaScript version, in that whenever an object instance is created, that instance is handed three string values to be assigned to instance variables. To accommodate that, the DGCar class defines a customized initialization method, named initWithCarMake:model:year:. The definition of that method follows:

```
- (DGCar *)initWithCarMake:(NSString *)inputMake
                    model:(NSString *)inputModel
                    year:(NSString *)inputYear {

    // If initialization of the superclass succeeds,
    // then assign instance variables
    if (self = [super init]) {
        make = inputMake;
        model = inputModel;
        year = inputYear;
    }
```

```
        return self;
    }
```

The method definition signifies with the leading hyphen that it is an instance method. Initialization methods always return a value that is a reference to the object instance. You may have seen this same concept in JavaScript constructor functions that end with a `return this` statement: the constructor function returns a reference to the instance object just created. Therefore, the initialization method for `DGCar` returns a reference to the very same object instance being created. The asterisk indicates that the value is a pointer to the object instance in memory (pointers are covered in Chapter 6).

When an Objective-C method accepts arguments, each argument is assigned to a variable—the same way JavaScript function arguments are assigned to parameter variables. The difference in Objective-C is that you must specify the data type for each one. Therefore, the car make must be passed to the `DGCar` initialization method as an `NSString` type of object. The same goes for the other two arguments. Just as the method returns a pointer to the object instance, the incoming arguments are assigned to variables that hold pointers to their locations in memory. Thus, the `(NSString *)` data type designations all have asterisks. If you omit or forget the asterisks, the compiler will complain that the argument is defined with an incorrect data type.

Because the `DGCar` class has its own initialization method, the first task for that method is to send the "normal" `init` message to the `NSObject` superclass. You don't necessarily need to know everything the method does in the superclass, but it is vital to completing the object's instantiation. And, just as the `DGCar` class's initialization method returns a reference to the instance being created, so does the `NSObject`'s `init` method. The `DGCar` method needs to capture that reference and apply it to itself. The way to do that is to assign the value returned by the `NSObject`'s `init` method to a `DGCar` property that references the instance object being defined by the current class (`self`):

```
        self = [super init];
```

Notice that this action is embedded within an `if` condition. The code confirms that the root object initialization was successful before continuing with the subclass initialization. If the superclass initialization were to fail, the condition expression would evaluate to `nil`, causing the nested statements to be skipped. Performing these kinds of success tests is good practice, even if the likelihood of failure approaches zero.

When the superclass initialization succeeds, parameter variables are assigned to the three instance variables that had been declared in the class's interface. When you write the code in Xcode, the editor color codes instance variables that have been correctly declared (the default is green, but you can change color coding in Preferences). It is vital that the data types of the parameter variables match exactly the data types of the instance variable declarations. Xcode closely checks the consistency of data types as it builds an app. Mistakes will be highlighted before the app ever reaches the simulator.

The last statement of the DGCar initialization method returns a reference to the current instance—self. A return value's data type must match the data type declared at the start of the method definition. In this case, the self keyword references an instance of the DGCar class being initialized here. The returned value could also be nil, which would occur if the superclass initialization failed. As you'll see in a moment, the reference to a successfully created instance will be assigned to a variable elsewhere so that the instance can receive further messages.

Integrating the DGCar Class into Workbench

After you have entered the customized code into the DGCar header and method files, it's time to integrate the class into Workbench and see it in action. The class has already been added to the Workbench project (when Xcode created the files), so click the *WorkbenchViewController.m* file to add code to the runMyCode: method that is to act with the DGCar class when you click the button in the simulator.

The first task is to add an import directive to the WorkbenchViewController implementation. You can put it above or below the existing #import statement, because neither depends on the other:

```
#import "WorkbenchViewController.h"
#import "DGCar.h"
```

The only changes to the rest of the implementation file are inside the runMyCode: method. Replace the original NSLog() function with four new statements:

```
- (IBAction)runMyCode:(id)sender {
    DGCar *myCar1 = [[DGCar alloc] initWithCarMake:@"Chevrolet"
                                    model:@"Malibu" year:@"2007"];
    DGCar *myCar2 = [[DGCar alloc] initWithCarMake:@"Ford"
                                    model:@"Taurus" year:@"2010"];

    NSLog(@"I used to drive a:%@", [myCar1 getFormattedListing]);
    NSLog(@"I now drive a:%@", [myCar2 getFormattedListing]);
}
```

 This method also needs some memory management, but I'll reserve that discussion until Chapter 6.

Now that you have a little more experience with Objective-C methods, I can address finer details of the runMyCode: method, which you added to the project in Chapter 3. This method, you'll recall, runs in response to the Touch Up Inside event in the button that appears on the screen. Events trigger actions, and those immediate actions don't return values. Such is the case of the runMyCode: method. Normally, a method that does not return a value specifies void as the return type (in parentheses before the method name). But because we wanted to associate this method with a button in Interface Builder, we specified the return type as IBAction. From a data typing point of view,

IBAction is the same as void, meaning the method returns no value. The IBAction type (especially in the header file declaration) tells Xcode to be ready to connect with Interface Builder and offers the method as a choice when it comes time to connect the event to the code. You saw how runMyCode: "magically" appeared in the pop-up list of items when making the connection in Chapter 3 (see Figure 3-18 as a reminder).

The runMyCode: method has one argument, which is assigned to the parameter variable sender. Although I have chosen to compose this IBAction method with one argument, you can use one of three action method formats, as follows:

- (IBAction)*methodName*
- (IBAction)*methodName*:(id)sender
- (IBAction)*methodName*:(id)sender (UIEvent *)event

Your choice depends on whether you expect your action method to need a reference to the user interface control (the sender) and to more details about the event. The UIEvent object is analogous to the event object that is passed to JavaScript/DOM event handler functions. For Workbench, the sender argument is a reference to the button that the user clicks, and I chose this format for demonstration purposes. What may be confusing at first is that the data type is simply id, rather than some UIKit type, such as UIButton (the type of button used in the project). You'll learn about the id data type in Chapter 6—it's a cool feature of Objective-C.

Creating Object Instances

Each of the first two statements in the runMyCode: method creates an instance of the DGCar class (just as the JavaScript example created two instances of the car object):

```
DGCar *myCar1 = [[DGCar alloc] initWithCarMake:@"Chevrolet"
                            model:@"Malibu" year:@"2007"];
DGCar *myCar2 = [[DGCar alloc] initWithCarMake:@"Ford"
                            model:@"Taurus" year:@"2010"];
```

On the left side of the assignment operator are the variables that hold pointers to the object instances. Each is of data type DGCar. Notice that the data type of a variable being declared (as in the header file) or being assigned a value through an assignment operator is not enclosed in parentheses. The right side of the operator must evaluate to a DGCar object instance.

To reach the object instance value, the righthand expression sends two messages nested inside each other. As in JavaScript, when expressions are nested, the most deeply nested expression evaluates first. In this case, it is the [DGCar alloc] message. You can visualize that the nested message replaces itself with its result, after which the outer message executes.

The alloc method belongs to the NSObject superclass, and its job is to reserve a chunk of memory for use by the object instance. Because the DGCar class definition does not have an alloc method defined for it (Apple cautions programmers against overriding this method in custom classes), the message passes up the inheritance chain until it finds a match—in this case, one generation higher in the NSObject superclass. As you will learn in Chapter 6, whenever you allocate memory for an object via the alloc method, you are also responsible for recovering that memory when you're done with the object.

NSObject's alloc method returns a bare-bones instance of the object with a clean memory slate. To complete the instantiation, you must send the init method to this bare-bones instance so the various class members (instance variables and methods) can be written to the memory reserved for the instance. The value returned by [DGCar alloc] becomes the receiver of the initWithCarMake:model:year: message. Recall that the DGCar class sends the init method to NSObject as part of the custom initialization method. Thus, the custom initialization method of DGCar is killing multiple birds with a single call, causing the superclass's init method to be called and assigning values to the instance's three instance variables.

Once the DGCar class instances exist (myCar1 and myCar2), you can send them whatever other messages you have defined for them. You've defined only one other method, getFormattedListing, to stay in sync with the JavaScript version. To invoke that method for myCar1, the message is:

```
[myCar1 getFormattedListing]
```

For the purposes of the Workbench app, you'll display the value returned by that method to the Xcode project console window via the NSLog() function, introduced in Chapter 3. You need to plug that returned value into the argument of NSLog().

NSLog() and String Formats

Recall that the initial NSLog() statement put into Workbench was as follows:

```
NSLog(@"Button was pressed.");
```

The argument is an Objective-C string literal, which begins with the @ symbol, followed by the quoted string of characters. But if you want to combine fixed text with values stored in variables or returned by methods, you can use string format placeholders, or *specifiers*. A specifier consists of a percent symbol (%) followed by a character or symbol indicating the type of data to be sent to the console. If the value is an object, the specifier combination is %@. Values to be plugged into the specifier appear after the quoted string, separated by a comma:

```
NSLog(@"I used to drive a:%@", [myCar1 getFormattedListing]);
```

Conveniently, you can use the same format specifier to display the contents of a wide range of object types. That's because most Cocoa Touch object classes include a description method, which returns a meaningful string representing the object or its data (e.g., the contents of an NSArray object). If you're looking to get a numeric value, however, you need some of the other specifiers, such as %d for an integer value or %f for a float value. Chapter 8 dives deeper into format specifiers.

You are free to stack up multiple specifiers and their fillers in a single NSLog() argument. The following statements present an alternative version that plugs in two strings derived from the same instance methods as used earlier and includes some escape carriage return characters (\n) to make the output display on three lines:

```
NSString *myCar1Description = [myCar1 getFormattedListing];
NSString *myCar2Description = [myCar2 getFormattedListing];
NSLog(@"My cars:\nThen - %@\nNow - %@", myCar1Description, myCar2Description);
```

This is how you will use NSLog() frequently when experimenting with Objective-C and Cocoa Touch in the Workbench app—using the Xcode console window to examine results or intermediate values.

 Exercise moderation in distributing NSLog() functions throughout an app, and prepare for the day when you release the app. Although NSLog() functions don't display content visible to the casual iPhone or iPad user, too many of them in the wrong places can slow down your final app. Alternatively, search the Web for **iphone debug macro** to see many ways to customize Xcode to display log statements only while debugging a project.

Running the Code

After you have made the modifications to the runMyCode: method in *WorkbenchViewController.m* file, you are ready to build and run it in the simulator. If the console window is not open, choose Console from Xcode's Run menu. Then click the Build and Run button. When you click on the Workbench app's button, you should see the results as shown in Figure 4-9 (your timestamps will be different, of course).

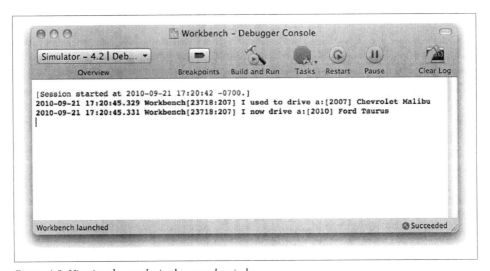

Figure 4-9. Viewing the results in the console window

What About Accessing Instance Variables?

You may be wondering how the `runMyCode:` method can get or set individual instance variables in one of the objects. In JavaScript, it's as easy as using the dot syntax to reference the object property, either for reading or assignment:

```
// setting a JavaScript instance variable
var car1Year = car1.year;
car2.year = "2009";
```

In Objective-C you have two ways to get and set instance variables: the traditional way and the modern (Objective-C 2.0) way. I'll describe only the traditional way in this chapter, while Chapter 8 will show you the modern way.

If you design a class so that other classes of objects need to access its instance variables, the traditional approach calls for creating a matching set of *getter* and *setter* methods. In other words, the methods act as gateways to reading and writing values of instance variables. Doing this, of course, requires quite a bit more source code, but the result is an instance that can potentially be more reusable in other scenarios.

To demonstrate how this works, I'll create a new class named `DGCarAlternate` (this will allow `DGCar` and `DGCarAlternate` to coexist side by side in the Workbench project without colliding with or relying upon each other). Example 4-4 shows the header file for the `DGCarAlternate` class. Six new method declarations (new items in bold) are for the getters and setters of the three instance variables (one pair for each variable). Notice that the method names for the getters are the same as the instance variable names. Additionally, notice that the setter method names begin with lowercase `set`, followed by an initial-capitalized variable name, as in `setMake:`.

Example 4-4. DGCarAlternate.h file

```
#import <Foundation/Foundation.h>

@interface DGCarAlternate : NSObject {

    NSString *make;
    NSString *model;
    NSString *year;

}

// Getters and Setters
- (NSString *)make;
- (void)setMake:(NSString *)newMake;
- (NSString *)model;
- (void)setModel:(NSString *)newModel;
- (NSString *)year;
- (void)setYear:(NSString *)newYear;

- (NSString *)getFormattedListing;

@end
```

Definitions of the actual methods are in the implementation file, as shown in Example 4-5 (new items are in bold).

Example 4-5. DGCarAlternate.m file

```
#import "DGCarAlternate.h"


@implementation DGCarAlternate

// Getter and Setter Methods
- (NSString *)make {
    return make;
}

- (void)setMake:(NSString *)newMake {
    make = newMake;
}

- (NSString *)model {
    return model;
}

- (void)setModel:(NSString *)newModel {
    model = newModel;
}

- (NSString *)year {
    return year;
}

- (void)setYear:(NSString *)newYear {
    year = newYear;
}

// Return formatted listing string
- (NSString *)getFormattedListing {
    NSString *result = @"";

    result = [NSString stringWithFormat:@"[%@] %@ %@", year, make, model];

    return result;
}

@end
```

Notice that I removed the custom initialization method from the DGCarAlternate class. Why? Because values will be assigned to the instance variables via setter methods rather than when the instance is allocated and initialized—merely a style choice for this demonstration. Example 4-6 shows the application of the DGCarAlternate class to the run MyCode: method in Workbench.

Example 4-6. The Workbench runMyCode: method designed for getters and setters

```
#import "WorkbenchViewController.h"
#import "DGCarAlternate.h"

@implementation WorkbenchViewController

- (IBAction)runMyCode:(id)sender {
    DGCarAlternate *myCar1 = [[DGCarAlternate alloc] init];
    DGCarAlternate *myCar2 = [[DGCarAlternate alloc] init];

    [myCar1 setMake:@"Chevrolet"];
    [myCar1 setModel:@"Malibu"];
    [myCar1 setYear:@"2007"];

    [myCar2 setMake:@"Ford"];
    [myCar2 setModel:@"Taurus"];
    [myCar2 setYear:@"2010"];

    NSLog(@"I used to drive a:%@", [myCar1 getFormattedListing]);
    NSLog(@"I now drive a:%@", [myCar2 getFormattedListing]);
}
...
@end
```

Notice that objects must still be instantiated via the `alloc` and `init` methods. But both messages pass up the inheritance chain through `DGCarAlternate` to the `NSObject` super-class (there is no `alloc` or `init` method defined in `DGCarAlternate` to intercept the messages).

Now that I have access to the instance variable getters, I can obtain those values individually from the `runMyCode:` method. For example, I can create a different format for the results sent to the console, as in the following:

```
NSLog(@"I used to drive a %@ %@ made in %@.", [myCar1 make],
    [myCar1 model], [myCar1 year]);
```

The setters also allow me to change the values of instance variables. Therefore, I can mix the first version of this class (with the custom initialization method that assigned values as the instance is being created) with additional code that changes one or more variables after instantiation.

Recap

We've covered a lot of ground in this chapter. The main goal was to introduce you to the different ways you need to begin thinking about objects and data in an iOS app, compared to your experiences with JavaScript. You have certainly seen some small similarities between JavaScript and Objective-C, such as assignment operators and notions of methods that optionally return values. But you have also seen that an iPhone or iPad app is largely a collection of class files, assisted by Interface Builder nib files (if you choose to go that way). Classes rule the day, and the basic structure of defining objects (through classes) entails writing more code, some of which will seem redundant based on your interpreted language experience. If you make a change to an instance variable name or method argument structure, you have to code the changes in both the header and implementation files.

The significance of the class structure should come into more focus in the next chapter. There, you'll see how you'll need to change your top-to-bottom interpretative conceptions to a completely different program execution flow model.

CHAPTER 5

App Execution Flow

Web developers are accustomed to seeing their code creations—HTML, CSS, and JavaScript—interpreted by browsers from top to bottom. As a web page loads, the browser immediately begins turning whatever it can into rendered content, applying styles, precompiling JavaScript, and, depending on the page design, executing various JavaScript pieces. A script statement that runs while the page loads and relies on a function must find that function already defined in the code load order, or a script error may block all further scripts. Your code may also be dependent upon an event such as the window object's load event, whose firing means that all of the document elements are in place. Whatever your page entails, a highly predictable sequence of events occurs during the loading stage.

When it comes to a compiled iOS app, however, source code order becomes less important. Dependencies are less about the precise order of source code files because the compiler goes through the entire project, pulling together the disparate pieces into a single application. In this chapter, you will follow the way code execution flows in the Workbench app. This experience will introduce you to some vital services within the Objective-C and Cocoa Touch environments that perform the jobs you currently associate with browser events, such as the load event. Let's face it: an iOS app needs to do a bunch of work when it starts loading to present itself to the user. You'll be amazed at how much of the activity occurs automatically, provided you know where to look for the automated triggers.

Some C Language Roots in an iOS App

If you read any tutorial on the C programming language, you soon learn that the entry point to any C program is a function named main(). In other words, the C compiler assembles all of the code into an executable file whose first job is to invoke the main() function automatically when the program starts. That function becomes the launching pad for whatever else the program does. So has it been in C programs for decades. Believe it or not, your iOS app also relies on a main() function to get things rolling when an app launches. Fortunately, Xcode does all of the work for you, writing the function in the *main.m* file, planted by default into the Other Sources group of files in your project. You will rarely, if ever, have to dig into the *main.m* file after it is created. Even so, it is instructional to learn what it does, especially if your web authoring experience makes you curious about how things work.

Example 5-1 shows the contents of the Workbench app's *main.m* file (without comments) as written by Xcode. It is, in fact, the same file Xcode writes for all view-based applications.

Example 5-1. Workbench's main.m file

```
#import <UIKit/UIKit.h>

int main(int argc, char *argv[]) {

    NSAutoreleasePool * pool = [[NSAutoreleasePool alloc] init];
    int retVal = UIApplicationMain(argc, argv, nil, nil);
    [pool release];
    return retVal;
}
```

Statements in the `main()` function rely on classes defined in both the Foundation and UIKit frameworks. Because UIKit framework classes also import the Foundation framework, there is no need to repeat that import into *main.m*.

You'll notice that because the *main.m* file does not define a class (in fact, there is no corresponding header file), the `main()` function is not specified as an instance or class method (that is, there is no leading - or + symbol). Instead, this is a plain ol' C function (except for a couple messages specific to iOS), defined simply to return an integer. Arguments for the `main()` function (a C integer and C array of characters) are passed by the application loader. You'll learn more about C functions in Chapter 7.

Inside the `main()` function, the first statement creates an instance of what is known as an *autorelease pool*. The explanation of an autorelease pool comes later in Chapter 6, but it is a Cocoa Touch class that assists with managing memory.

The real action occurs in the second statement, where the `UIApplicationMain()` function is called. Notice that I call `UIApplicationMain()` a function, even though you might expect it to be a method of some `UIKit` class because of its name. You will encounter many cases in both Cocoa Touch and Objective-C where an action maker is reminiscent of a JavaScript global function (such as JavaScript's `parseInt()` and `eval()` functions, which you can use anywhere without referencing any object). Unlike Objective-C method calls, which are formatted as messages inside square brackets along with an object that is to receive the method call, functions are written without brackets or a reference to a receiving object. A function of this kind may take arguments (depending on how it is designed), and it may return a value.

This seemingly free mixture of C and Objective-C syntax in Cocoa Touch programming probably adds to the confusion of newcomers. Just when you think you understand the Objective-C method calling style, a C function in the CoreGraphics framework hits you right between the eyes. You will encounter this duality frequently as you get to know Cocoa Touch—after all, Objective-C is a superset of C and therefore incorporates all of C within. As much as you might want to standardize on Objective-C to be all modern and hip, parts of Cocoa Touch insist on using C constructions. Experienced C programmers relish having this flexibility, but newcomers may think otherwise until they acclimate to the mixed usage.

UIApplicationMain() is the next stage in our exploration of how your application launches. The function takes four arguments. The first two arguments are the same arguments received by main(), passed straight through from the main() function's parameter variables. Whether the UIApplicationMain() function requires values other than nil for the remaining two arguments depends on how you intend your app to launch.

For all view-based apps that you create from Xcode templates, the third argument to UIApplicationMain() will be nil. This causes the app to use UIApplication as what is known as the *principal class*. This object becomes the primary environmental controller for your app, handling many essential services, such as listening for events and routing them where they're supposed to go (i.e., to code that you've written to actually respond to events). This UIApplication object is always alive while your app is running, and your code may call on it from time to time for various services, such as displaying and hiding the network activity spinner in the top status bar when your app is off doing something on the Internet. I hesitate to find an analogue to the UIApplication object in the browser scripting environment, but you could say UIApplication is like the navigator object (which represents the browser app) on steroids and without security shackles.

To sum up, when UIApplicationMain() receives nil as its third argument, the app awakens UIApplication to act as the central control for whatever follows—the fourth argument, the name of the class that is to be the application's delegate.

An Introduction to Delegates

If you delegate a task to someone else, you essentially appoint that person to perform that task on your behalf while you're busy doing something else. It's the handoff, the passed buck, the get-it-out-of-my-inbox move. To delegate successfully, you need to specify who that delegate is and what it is you want that delegate to perform for you.

In the case of the UIApplication object at launch time, one of its built-in tasks is to hand off the job of completing the rest of the app's loading to a class in your project. To trigger that job, UIApplication sends a very specific, standardized message to the object appointed as the delegate. It turns out that UIApplication—in its role as Central Control—can delegate a variety of jobs. For instance, in addition to signaling when the app is being started, UIApplication can also signal when the app is about to quit so the app can preserve its current state to restore the next time the app launches (code that you would write). Starting with iOS 4, UIApplication signals when an app is going to be sent to the background and reawakened under Fast App Switching so your code can suspend and restart ongoing processes (e.g., downloads) automatically for the user. The messages UIApplication is designed to send to its delegate are codified in a protocol named the UIApplicationDelegate protocol.

A class must declare in its header that it is available as a UIApplication delegate—it is wired to handle delegate messages that UIApplication might send. To make that declaration, the protocol is added to the class header's @interface section immediately after the class and superclass declaration, as follows:

```
@interface className : superClassName <delegateProtocolClassName> {
...
}
```

For Workbench, Xcode has prewired the *WorkbenchAppDelegate.h* file to adopt the UIApplicationDelegate protocol:

```
@interface WorkbenchAppDelegate : NSObject <UIApplicationDelegate> {
...
}
```

In other words, the class is defined as the WorkbenchAppDelegate class, which inherits all properties and methods from NSObject, and is open to receiving messages defined in the UIApplicationDelegate class object (and thus is said to conform to the UIApplicationDelegate protocol).

To receive and act on a delegate message, the current class must implement a method corresponding to the expected message. The UIApplication class (which is brought to life via the main() and UIApplicationMain() functions described earlier) sends a message named applicationDidFinishLaunching: to whichever class is designated as the UIApplication's delegate class. As you will see later in the chapter, the applicationDid FinishLaunching method for the WorkbenchAppDelegate class instantiates the single view controller, adds the view to the application window, and displays the window for the user to begin interacting with the app.

The important point to take away from this discussion about delegates is that delegate messages are often sent in response to a condition or action, and the corresponding method then picks up the ball to carry out some further operations. You could liken the unseen delegate action to system events in a scripted web page, where the window's load event fires as soon as all the content has arrived from the server; then your load event handler function carries out further initializations to set up the page for user interaction. In the case of launching an iOS app, the automatically invoked main() function calls UIApplicationMain(), which causes UIApplication to send the applicationDidFinishLaunching: message to whichever class is acting as UIApplication's delegate; then the applicationDidFinishLaunching: method carries out more initializations to build the app's user interface and prepare the app for use.

How UIApplication Appoints Its Delegate

Although the UIApplicationMain() function offers an easy way to specify the name of the delegate class (as an Objective-C-style string of the class name you want to act as delegate), the Xcode template goes through a more convoluted sequence when it generates the starting set of files in a typical project. Following the trail through a few files may not be easy, but if you join me on the trek, you'll learn a few more things about the inner workings of an iOS app and the files you see in the project.

You'll recall that in Workbench, the UIApplicationMain() function located in the *main.m* file passes nil as the fourth argument—the argument reserved for specifying the delegate class name. When UIApplicationMain() passes nil in this argument, the UIApplication object (specified as the principal class because the third argument of the function was also nil) expects to obtain a reference to a delegate by way of the main nib file for the app. In the Workbench app, Xcode automatically creates a main nib file named *MainWindow.xib*. Even though that is a common name for a main nib file, that's not what UIApplication looks for. Instead, UIApplication gets the name of the main nib file from a special file known as the *Info.plist* file.

The App's Info.plist File

Every iOS app must include a file known generically as an *Info.plist* file, which contains a variety of specifications about the app (described in more detail in a moment). Notice that the one created for Workbench is named *Workbench-Info.plist*. In the process of creating the file, Xcode also sets a property in the project that supplies the filename when it's time to build the app. Until such time as you need to create two editions of an app from the same project, you won't have to mess with the naming of the *Info.plist* file. Let Xcode's initial settings take care of it for you.

If you haven't come into contact with a property list (*.plist*) file before, you'll find it to be a very useful format for iOS app programming. A property list is an XML file for which Xcode provides a specialized editor. Figure 5-1 shows the *Workbench-Info.plist* file viewed in its Xcode editor.

 The SDK also includes a standalone Property List Editor application. For iOS app development, however, edit these files only in Xcode.

As its name implies, a property list contains a series of values, each of which is associated with a label, or *key*. Property list values can be numbers, text strings, and

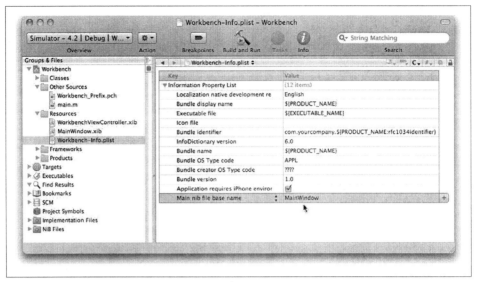

Figure 5-1. Workbench-Info.plist in the Xcode property list editor

nested collections of other values. Don't be scared off by the key names and strange values inserted by default into the *Workbench-Info.plist* file. In truth, the Xcode property list editor shields you from even scarier-looking key names by substituting more English-like labels. You'll typically modify only a handful of settings in an *Info.plist* file. Among them is the Bundle version, which corresponds to the version number of your app (version values are strings, so you can add letters, such as "d" to denote a developer version or "Beta" for a test version).

The purpose of showing you the *Workbench-Info.plist* file's values at this juncture is to let you see the last entry, whose true key is `NSMainNibFile` (or "Main nib file base name" in plain English). This is the *Info.plist* item where `UIApplication` looks for the first nib file to load.

Inside MainWindow.xib

`UIApplication` must dig into *MainWindow.xib* and find a class that adopts the `UIAppli cationDelegate` protocol. Let's see how that happens.

Back in Chapter 3, as you built Workbench, you spent a little time in Interface Builder working in a different nib file, the *WorkbenchViewController.xib* file, where you planted a button. This time, double-click the *MainWindow.xib* file in the Workbench project to view that nib file in Interface Builder. Figure 5-2 shows the *MainWindow.xib* document window (in my preferred list view format, which also shows the type for each item).

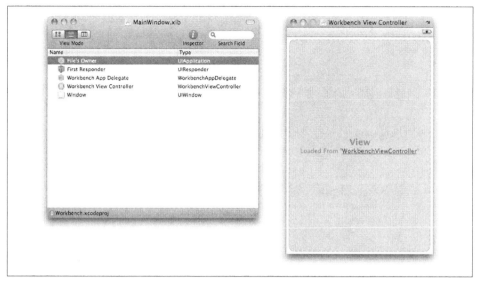

Figure 5-2. MainWindow.xib document window

Remember that Xcode filled in all this stuff for you after you specified the name of the project. For instance, the object that "owns" the *MainWindow.xib* file is of class UIAp plication—indeed, the object that UIApplicationMain() caused to be created.

To look further under the hood, secondary-click on the File's Owner item in the window. You will see a list of existing connections for the File's Owner, as shown in Figure 5-3.

Figure 5-3. Connections for the UIApplication object in the MainWindow nib file

Xcode has already made a connection for us, specifying that the item named Workbench App Delegate is `UIApplication`'s delegate. Close the connections summary window, and you'll see that the delegate is of type `WorkbenchAppDelegate`, as highlighted in Figure 5-4.

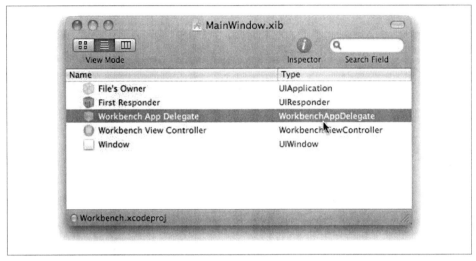

Figure 5-4. The class type of the delegate is WorkbenchAppDelegate

This connection completes the journey through the project to get an app running. The sequence of steps is as follows (and is illustrated in Figure 5-5):

1. When the app begins launching, `main()` in *main.m* executes.

2. `UIApplicationMain()` creates the principal class object, `UIApplication`.

3. `UIApplication` looks at *Info.plist* (or its designated substitute specification in the target) to find the name of the base nib file (*MainWindow.xib*) and loads the nib file.

4. The base nib file points to a delegate class, `WorkbenchAppDelegate`, and instantiates that object.

5. The `WorkbenchAppDelegate` object instance declares two instance variables, one for a window, the other for a view controller.

6. *MainWindow.xib* instantiates the window and view controller objects, which, in turn, are assigned to the `WorkbenchAppDelegate` instance variables `window` and `view Controller`.

7. Instantiating the `WorkbenchViewController` class loads the *WorkbenchViewController.xib* nib file, which creates the view's white background and button, but does not yet display them on the screen.

8. The `WorkbenchAppDelegate` class header declared support for the `UIApplication Delegate` and can therefore respond to delegate messages.

9. `UIApplication` sends the `applicationDidFinishLaunching:` delegate message to `WorkbenchAppDelegate`.

10. The `applicationDidFinishLaunching:` method runs, adding the view (with its button) as a subview of the underlying window and instructing the window to show itself and its contents.

11. `UIApplication` waits to respond to events for which user interface elements are wired (just the Touch Up Inside event of the button for Workbench so far).

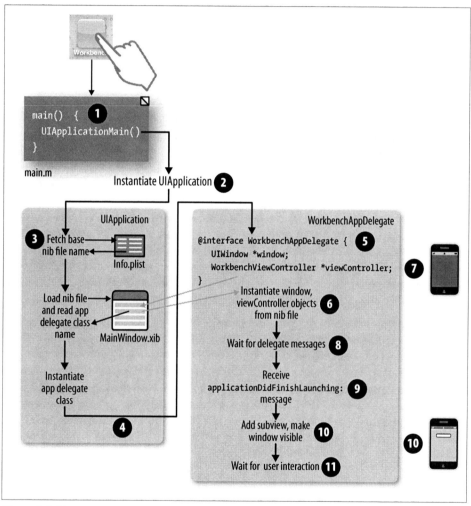

Figure 5-5. How an app starts up

Whew! The good news about this seemingly long journey is that it's rare that you need to muck with the structure established by Xcode when it assembles the first bits of your application. Generally speaking, your coding role begins inside the application DidFinishLaunching: method of the app delegate class.

Not every template is as simple as the view-based application one we used for Workbench, and yet, you can use that template for lots of app structures and designs. The templates are intended to jumpstart you down a road that lets you get something running in the simulator fairly quickly—assuming you've done your homework preplanning the app.

iPhone App Development Design Patterns

Not only is delegation powerful on its own merits, but the concept is employed widely across numerous iOS SDK frameworks. For example, if your app needs to retrieve updated data from a server, you will use a class called NSURLConnection to initiate the request. Naturally, you don't want the app to be locked up while it waits for the server to return data (especially if the wireless network is slow), so the NSURLConnection class can send an asynchronous request to the server and wait in the background for a response, whether it's data or perhaps an error. How is your app supposed to know when data has arrived so the app can work on that data? That's where the delegate model comes in: while it waits and receives data, the NSURLConnection object sends a series of messages to whichever object has been assigned as the delegate (usually the same object that issued the request). In that object's class definition are a group of methods that match the NSURLConnection messages to act on the incoming data. One of the messages signals that all data has arrived, and the matching delegate method can then send other messages to begin processing and displaying the data in the app.

Delegation is one of several *design patterns* associated with iOS app programming. In object-oriented programming, a design pattern suggests the relationships among objects and how objects should work together. Going back to the NSURLConnection class, your app uses that class without any modification; additionally, that class doesn't know or care about the specifics of the data. Instead, it just sends a message when a significant event occurs (e.g., receiving the final chunk of data) and lets your app's delegate method perform custom tasks tailored to your specific application. As you learn more about the iOS SDK, you'll be amazed at how many objects send large quantities of delegate messages while a user interacts with your app.

The Model-View-Controller Design Pattern

Another design pattern you will hear a lot about is called *Model-View-Controller*—or MVC for short. The underlying concept behind MVC is that your program should keep data (model) separate from the presentation aspects (view) of the app, and that the controller's code acts as the intermediary between the view and model.

If the idea of separating data from presentation rings bells, it's because developing web content according to World Wide Web Consortium (W3C) standards encourages the very same thing. HTML markup assigns a structure to the content in a web document, but the appearance of that content—font characteristics, alignment, and so on—is the domain of the stylesheet (CSS). In this context, the content and its HTML markup line up with the model, and the CSS handles the view. Scripting that modifies the content or changes style property assignments acts as the controller. Of course, in an HTML document, the model and view can work together without a controller to display something to the user (e.g., a CSS style applied to an HTML element); in an iOS app, however, a view and the data model *never* communicate directly with each other. Instead, a controller must act as the go-between.

Not all iOS apps have significant model components. In its current state, the Workbench app has only view and controller components. But an app that displays, say, kitchen recipes will certainly maintain a database on the device. Your job as programmer would be to define a model object class (perhaps named `Recipe`) whose properties include a name for the dish, a list of ingredients, a series of cooking instructions, calorie count, and more. Each instance of the object contains information about a specific recipe, and instances are stored on the device in a database (the properties could correspond to fields in a database table). A view controller could then ask the database for a range of `Recipe` class instances and pass property values to the view so users can read the information. If there were a "notes" field in the view, users could type in comments in a text box in the view, which the controller would write to the model object instance for permanent storage in the database.

Virtually every iOS app has both view and controller parts of the MVC pattern. The view is essentially layout information. If you use Interface Builder to lay out user interface elements, you are defining the view. A view does no practical work on its own—it's just a pretty face without much of a brain. Yet it is obviously an important part of the app because it's what users see and interact with—buttons to tap, sliders to drag, lists to flick.

The brains for a view are contained in the controller part of MVC. Look at how Xcode generated the Workbench project files and notice that it created a class named `Work benchViewController`. This is the class that contains code to control the one view we currently have, and whose layout is defined in the *WorkbenchViewController.xib* file.

 From earlier days of iPhone app programming, I developed a slightly different naming convention for a nib/controller pairing. I typically name a nib file as merely the view, as in *WorkbenchView.xib*. Its owner would be the `WorkbenchViewController` class. This scheme helped me burn the separation of view and controller parts of MVC into my brain. In the last example in this chapter, "Adding code to display the blue view" on page 105, however, you'll see why following Xcode's naming recommendation can help you use a shortcut to load a nib file with the same name.

One significant advantage to adopting MVC is that model objects are completely disconnected from the presentation of their data. As your app evolves, the details of the view may change—colors, order of property values, font characteristics—but the model doesn't have to change at all. It's very much like the way HTML tagging defines a single structure of a document, but different CSS specs can turn the same content into something that looks quite different (well demonstrated in the CSS Zen Garden website at *http://csszengarden.com*).

Other Design Patterns

Design patterns are not mutually exclusive. An environment can employ multiple design patterns at the same time if they don't collide with each other. The iOS SDK identifies a total of four design patterns in its bag of tricks. Delegation and MVC are two that we've already discussed. Notice how delegation confines itself to the realm of passing messages among objects, while MVC addresses a more global structure of an application. The other two design patterns are known as *target-action* and the *managed memory model*.

Graphical user interfaces—including modern web browsers and iOS apps—almost always have an event (or run) loop running underneath the hood. The loop constantly monitors activity in the user interface and contains instructions on where to direct execution flow when an event of a particular type associated with a user interface element occurs. In DOM scripting, you assign an event handler function to an HTML element for a particular type of event, such as when the user releases the mouse button atop a screen button. In an iOS app, an on-screen control (e.g., a button) in a view can be wired to send a message to the controller for that view when a particular event type occurs (e.g., dragging a finger on the screen). The receiver of that message (the view controller) is known as the *target* for the event, and the message is the name of the method to run when the event fires. You saw how we made that assignment for the button in Workbench through Interface Builder. After creating the `runMyCode:` method in the view controller class (defined with an `IBAction` return value), you used Interface Builder to tell the button to send the `runMyCode:` message to the view controller whenever a Touch Up Inside event occurred. That is the essence of the target-action design pattern.

The last design pattern, the managed memory model, concerns itself with how applications use and free up memory while in operation. Chapter 6 goes into more detail about memory usage, and this is one concept that is something JavaScript programmers don't have to worry about (JavaScript engines clean up after themselves automatically). For now, simply be aware that due to the limited amount of memory available to apps on the iPhone and iPad, you will have to be very conscious about how much is used and whether any memory space fails to be released when it is no longer needed. Ignoring these fine points can lead to crashes, where the app quits unceremoniously and returns the user to the home screen.

In summary, each design pattern applies to its own domain in the iOS programming world. And yet their paths cross from time to time. It's not that they interfere with each other, but you do need to keep the patterns in mind as you work your way through to your app solution.

The Importance of Views

Our journey through app execution flow has delivered us so far to the point at which the app has launched, the initial screen is on display, and the app waits for user activity to get things going. This is a good time to begin thinking about user navigation around screens within an iOS app. In the web world, and regardless of how the content is generated, the page is king—the organization of a website or app tends to be divided into distinct pages of content, with each page presenting a related activity or subject area (e.g., the home page, the support page, the contact page). A highly dynamic page, of course, can cram multiple screenfuls of functionality into a single downloadable page—the ability to view a Gmail inbox list and compose a new message on the same page comes to mind, but even Gmail's Help link takes you to a different page. And so, it is quite natural to approach a web browser programming task by thinking about page organization and how users will navigate from one page to another.

In an iOS app, however, the screen-sized view is king. Some apps, such as simple games, might keep users looking at just one view for all of the game play, but somewhere a button likely appears to show a different screen with a score history, instructions, or a list of other apps made by the same developer. The earlier you begin thinking about converting your app ideas into a series of full-screen views, the quicker you'll be able to arrive at a good navigation plan.

Everything's a View

In addition to the screen-sized views that you'll use to organize basic app navigation, virtually everything else you display on the screen is a view of some type. The `UIKit` framework defines a `UIView` class, whose child classes include all user interface controls (buttons, text entry fields, sliders, etc.), static text labels, scrollable tables, individual cells within a table, modal dialogs, and even the types of horizontal bars you see at the tops and bottoms of screens (including the status bar that displays the time and the battery icon).

When you use Interface Builder to lay out elements, you are laying out multiple views nested inside the screen-sized view. Such nested views are called subviews, and a view can have as many subviews as you need to convey your intentions. Within Interface Builder you determine the layering of subviews to the extent that the tool includes menu commands to move a view forward or back relative to its fellow nested views—just like layering absolute-positioned HTML elements in a web page.

The App Window—UIWindow

An iOS app almost always has just one view that acts as a substrate to everything that appears in the app. The substrate is of class UIWindow, but unlike windows in operating systems or a web browser, the UIWindow class is a chromeless rectangle that occupies the entire device screen (or, in the case of an iPhone-only app running on the iPad, the smaller iPhone window within the larger iPad screen).

When you let Xcode generate the starting files for an iOS app project, it takes care of creating the window in code and nib files. Turn to the *WorkbenchApplication Delegate.h* header file in the Workbench project, whose code (minus the comments) is as follows:

```
#import <UIKit/UIKit.h>

@class WorkbenchViewController;

@interface WorkbenchAppDelegate : NSObject <UIApplicationDelegate> {
    UIWindow *window;
    WorkbenchViewController *viewController;
}

@property (nonatomic, retain) IBOutlet UIWindow *window;
@property (nonatomic, retain) IBOutlet WorkbenchViewController *viewController;

@end
```

This code includes creation of Objective-C property equivalents of instance variables, which we'll cover in detail in Chapter 8. For now, you should concentrate simply on the two instance variable declarations for window and viewController. Because of the close association between the app delegate and two nib files generated by Xcode, both of these instance variables are assigned instances of their respective objects when the nib file loads.

Automatic UI element ivar instantiation (the result of a nib file loading) is often difficult for newcomers to understand. You have no code to trace to see exactly where or how this occurs. It just happens, thanks to all the outlet and reference connection settings in the nib file.

Look now at the delegate method in the implementation of this class, as follows:

```
- (void)applicationDidFinishLaunching:(UIApplication *)application {

    // Override point for customization after app launch
    [window addSubview:viewController.view];
    [window makeKeyAndVisible];
}
```

Once the application has completed all of the launch-time internal processing (well out of the reach of SDK programmers), the UIApplication object sends the applicationDid

FinishLaunching: message to allow our code to perform application-specific setup. In this case, the view belonging to the WorkbenchViewController instance is added as the lone subview of the window. Remember that the view belonging to that view controller also has a button as its subview (which we accomplished by dragging the button to the view in Interface Builder), meaning that both the view and its button subview are added to the window view hierarchy. As a final operation, the window object receives the makeKeyAndVisible message, which forces it to the front of anything else that might be on the screen (although nothing is there at this point) and makes it visible.

About the @class Directive

You may have noticed the unusual second line of the *WorkbenchApplicationDelegate.h* file:

```
@class WorkbenchViewController;
```

It is obviously some kind of reference to the WorkbenchViewController class that was created for the project and also cited as a data type for one of the instance variables in the current header file. Beyond that, however, there are no references in the header to any details of that class (e.g., no messages being sent to it or variables mentioned). The @class compiler directive tells Xcode that the current class header may contain a simple reference to another class, but not to bother looking up the class to verify anything about it. It's as if you're telling Xcode, "Trust me, WorkbenchViewController is a class that is defined in the project, so go ahead and allow it to be used as a data type." When details are needed, as in the *WorkbenchApplicationDelegate.m* implementation file, the view controller class header needs to be imported there.

Adding Another View to Workbench

Lest you get the impression that apps consist of one window and one full-screen subview, let's add a second full-screen view to Workbench that zips up from the bottom of the screen. Displaying merely a blue background and a button to navigate the user back to the primary view, it certainly won't be fancy, but it will demonstrate one of many ways you can link one view to another—all within the single UIWindow view.

To begin, select the Classes folder in the Workbench project's Files and Groups panel. Control-click (or right-click) that item to see the context-sensitive menu. Choose Add→New File to view the New File window, shown in Figure 5-6.

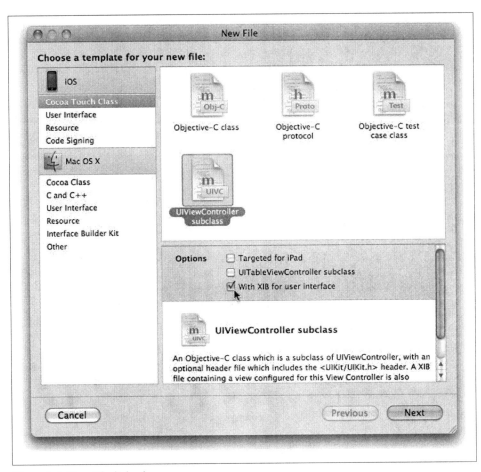

Figure 5-6. New File dialog box

Because you'll be adding a full-screen view and a controller for that view, choose a UIViewController subclass. Also be sure to enable the "With XIB for user interface" option so Xcode will generate the nib file for this view controller. Click Next to reach the dialog box where you name the view controller class as **BlueViewController**, as shown in Figure 5-7. Notice that the class name begins with the traditional uppercase letter. Make sure the option is enabled so Xcode will generate the header file along with the implementation file. Then click Finish.

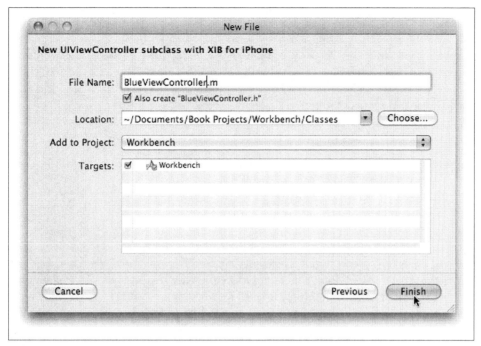

Figure 5-7. Name the class BlueViewController

With the bare code and nib files now in the project, think about the tasks needed to proceed:

1. Add an IBAction method to the BlueViewController class that will hide the view.

2. Design the view using Interface Builder.

3. Add code to the WorkbenchViewController's runMyCode: method to instantiate the BlueViewController object and display the view.

I choose this order because when laying out the elements in Interface Builder, you will need to connect its button to the IBAction method in BlueViewController—made much easier if the method already exists in the class (or is at least specified in the header file). Then you wait to add the code for displaying the blue view until the code and interface for dismissing it are already in place. If you write the code to display the view first, you will wind up at a dead end with the blue view showing and no place to go except to quit the app.

Adding the IBAction method

Click the *BlueViewController.h* header file to edit its code. Because this is a general-purpose view controller, the header file is pretty empty at this point, except that it correctly defines the class as a subclass of `UIViewController` (one of the UIKit framework classes). There will not be any instance variables for this class, so add only the following method definition:

```
#import <UIKit/UIKit.h>


@interface BlueViewController : UIViewController {

}

- (IBAction)hideThisView:(id)sender;

@end
```

Save the file when you are done. The header file, you'll recall, merely declares variables and methods. To write the code that does the work, click the *BlueViewController.m* file to edit the implementation. Xcode provides several commented delegate method templates in case you want to use them. You don't need them for this simple view controller. Instead, simply add the implementation of the `hideThisView:` method, as in the following:

```
#import "BlueViewController.h"


@implementation BlueViewController

- (IBAction)hideThisView:(id)sender {
    [self dismissModalViewControllerAnimated:YES];
}
...
@end
```

This method sends one message to its own object instance. One of the methods of a `UIViewController` class object is `dismissModalViewControllerAnimated:`. Although you don't know it yet (you will get to know these things after a little experience), you will be displaying the blue view in a modal fashion—very common in iPhone apps, less so in iPad apps—with an animated wipe from the bottom of the screen. The `dismissMo dalViewControllerAnimated:` method reverses the animation and hides the view governed by the view controller.

Creating the user interface

Before heading over to Interface Builder, I like to keep my nib files grouped together. Therefore, I recommend dragging the *BlueViewController.xib* file from the Classes group into the Resources group with the other nib files. Then double-click the nib file to open it in Interface Builder.

You'll have a little more fun in Interface Builder this time around, playing with colors and a text label, as well as the action button. This view is supposed to be about blueness, so begin by setting the background color of the view to a blue color.

Click the content area of the View window to select the View object. The background color is specified in the Attributes Inspector window, which you can reach by choosing Tools→Attributes Inspector, shown in Figure 5-8. Click in the Background menu and choose Other to see the color picker window shown in Figure 5-9.

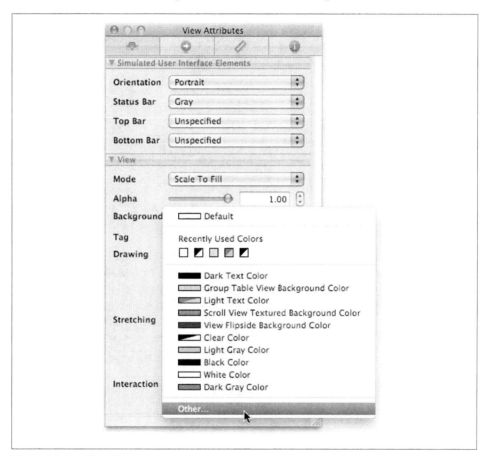

Figure 5-8. Attributes Inspector

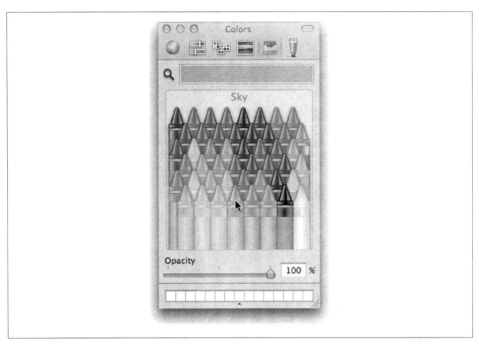

Figure 5-9. Interface Builder color picker

You have several choices in the way you select a color in the Interface Builder color picker window. Unless you have a very specific RGB, HSV, or CMYK color scheme in mind, you can use the crayon box to see a choice of colors that will always be the same whenever you want to assign a color. Lighter colors, such as Sky, make it easy to see other UI elements in their default colors. When you select a color, the background in the View window changes instantly. Close the color picker window when you are finished.

Next, go to the Library palette, click the Objects button (at the top), and choose Cocoa Touch Inputs & Values to limit your selection to interactive elements. Click the Label item and drag a label into the View (see Figure 5-10 and Figure 5-11).

You can now click the label and edit the text. Enter some text that identifies this view as the blue view. Center the label as you like, either by eye or with the help of the Layout→Alignment menu. A label element specifies how you display noneditable text in a view. Your code can change the text of a label at any time, so you can use it to display text results in your app.

The last item for this view is a Round Rect Button. Drag one from the Library to the View window. Assign the title **Go Back** to the button, as shown in Figure 5-12.

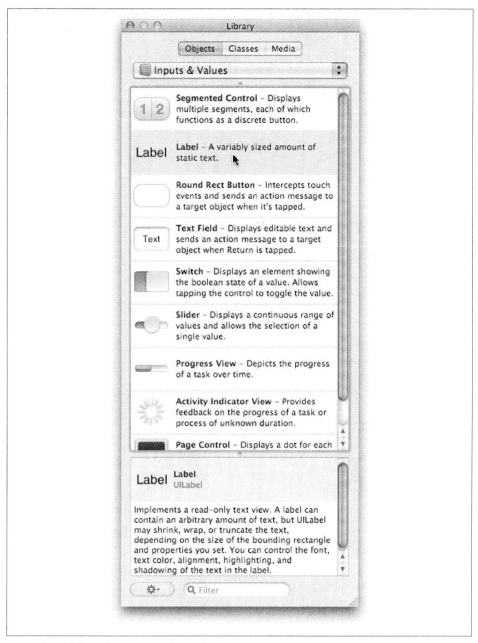

Figure 5-10. Select a label view and start dragging it

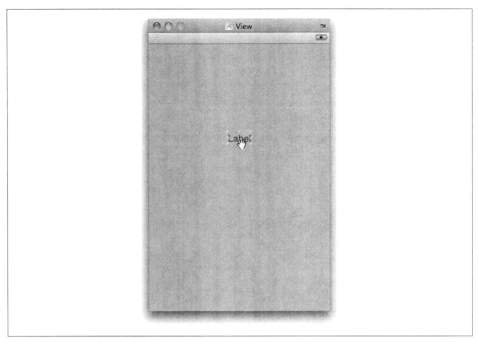

Figure 5-11. Drop the label into the View window and position it

Figure 5-12. Add the Go Back button

The final job in IB is to connect the button to the `hideThisView:` method in the view controller that owns this nib file. Click the button in the View to select it. Then choose Tools→Connections Inspector. Drag from the circle in the Touch Up Inside row to the File's Owner item in the nib's document window. When you release the mouse button from the drag operation, a pop-up list shows the one available `IBAction`, as shown in Figure 5-13 (and the reason I like to add the method to the code before working in Interface Builder). Select it to complete the connection, then save the nib file.

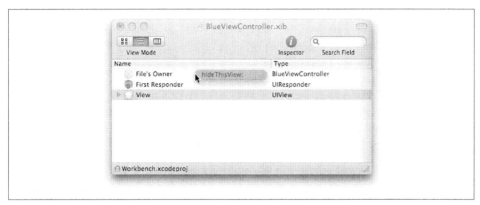

Figure 5-13. Connecting the button to the hideThisView: method

Adding code to display the blue view

You will use the original `WorkbenchViewController` button to display the blue view. You'll be adding the code to the `runMyCode:` method.

Because the new code calls upon the `BlueViewController` class to create an instance of it, the `WorkbenchViewController` must import the `BlueViewController`'s header file. You can add this to the *WorkbenchViewController.m* implementation file as follows:

```
#import "WorkbenchViewController.h"
#import "BlueViewController.h"
```

Modify the `runMyCode:` method as follows:

```
- (IBAction)runMyCode:(id)sender {
    // Create instance of BlueViewController loaded from .xib file of same name
    BlueViewController *secondViewController =
        [[BlueViewController alloc] initWithNibName:nil bundle:nil];
    [self presentModalViewController:secondViewController animated:YES];
    [secondViewController release];
}
```

The first statement creates the `BlueViewController` instance, assigning to the variable named `secondViewController` a pointer to that instance. The instance is created by nesting the `alloc` and `initWithNibName:bundle:` methods. As discussed in Chapter 4, the `alloc` method prepares memory for the object and returns an empty instance of the object. A `UIViewController` subclass has a method that completes the initialization by loading a nib file, and the method offers a special shortcut. The first argument of the initialization method normally takes a string with the name of the *.xib* file (without the filename extension) to load. But if you specify `nil` for this argument, the object looks for a nib file whose name is identical to the class name—*BlueViewController.xib* in your case. The second argument is for a reference to a *bundle*, which is the folder-like container (package) that holds all files of the compiled application. If you specify `nil` for this second argument, the object assumes you mean the bundle of the current application—virtually the only case you'll encounter.

With the instance of the `BlueViewController` safely assigned to the `secondViewController` variable, that variable is passed as the first argument of the `presentModalViewController:animated:` method. Notice that the message is directed to `self`—the instance of `WorkbenchViewController`. In other words, the message is instructing the first view of the app to display the blue view, and to do so with animation. Any view displayed as a modal view appears to rise up from the bottom of the screen. Other types of views, such as a detail view linked to a table cell, slide into view horizontally.

The final statement frees up the memory occupied by the instance of `BlueViewController`. You will learn more about memory issues in Chapter 6.

Save the changes. Make sure the iPhone Simulator is selected in the Overview dropdown menu. Then click the Build and Run button. If there are no errors in the code, the app should launch and let you show and hide the blue view.

Recap

This chapter shows two types of execution flow in an iOS app. The first deals with the steps an app follows to launch—a far cry from the top-to-bottom approach of web browser coding. You've seen how important the delegation design pattern is to getting a native iOS app going. It is the `applicationDidFinishLaunching:` delegate method that triggers further loading and initializations for your app. Also demonstrated here is one way a view can display another view as a user navigates around your app. Views take the place of web pages in the way you think about app structure.

In the next chapter, I walk you through three programming concepts that may be quite foreign to you, but whose understanding is crucial to successfully design and implement apps with the iOS SDK. You'll learn how easy you had it with JavaScript.

CHAPTER 6

Central Objective-C Concepts: Pointers, Data Types, and Memory Management

For new programmers, one of the attractions of JavaScript is that browser interpreter engines handle a lot of tedious interior management, reducing the amount of programmer planning and intervention required by compiled languages and environments. For instance, once you assign a value to a JavaScript variable, your code simply references that variable anywhere within the proper scope to get the existing value or assign a new one. Additionally, not only do JavaScript variables not care what type of data is assigned to them, but your code can assign a completely different type of data to the same variable with impunity (although it is a potentially dangerous programming practice, for maintenance purposes). Finally, JavaScript programmers don't have to think about how their code impacts memory utilization. Your code generates objects and values at will, handing over the job of allocating memory and freeing unused memory to the browser. Even if you want to free memory by removing some object, you can't force the browser to do so.

Objective-C and Cocoa Touch programming will (regrettably to some) cure you of those happy days. A variable no longer necessarily stores a value, but rather a location in memory where the data is being stored. You will need to add new sensibilities to the specific types of data being assigned to a variable or returning from a method. And you will be responsible for husbanding the exceptionally precious and limited memory available to apps running on iPhone, iPod touch, and iPad devices.

If all of these concepts are new to you, take it slow and feel reassured that you'll get more comfortable with them as you apply them in succeeding chapters. The concepts may be new to you, but they have been part of programming in other environments for decades (and thus might even seem to be archaic).

Pointers

Many code examples thus far in this book have used pointers, but you may not yet fully understand what a pointer is, how it differs from a regular variable, and when or if you should use pointers for variables, method return values, and method arguments. JavaScript, like most interpreted languages, does not use pointers, so the concept may be foreign to you.

Pointers and Memory

To begin the exploration of pointers, it helps to have a visualization of what computer memory is and how programs use it. Although there are many types of memory, the kind we are concerned with is traditionally called random access memory, or RAM for short. Some types of RAM preserve their contents when not in use, while others empty everything when power is removed. For our discussion, RAM is RAM, regardless of what happens to it when the lights go out.

Memory is divided into tiny spaces. Imagine a gigantic cabinet with gazillions of identically sized cubbyholes in it. Each cubbyhole can hold one small chunk of information. While a program runs, it uses the cubbyholes to temporarily store information. Various kinds of information require differently sized blocks of cubbyholes to hold their data—a short string of text characters uses very little space, while a two-megapixel image occupies a lot of cubbyholes, as represented in Figure 6-1.

Keeping track of where a new chunk of information goes is one of the jobs of the central processing unit, or CPU, of the device. The program (deep, deep down and with the help of the operating system) asks the CPU for a place to store information of a particular size; the CPU locates an unused block of cubbies, and stores the data in those cubbies. Of course, the program will likely need to retrieve and/or change that information over time, so the program needs to know where to get it (or, more precisely, where to tell the CPU to get it).

Helping this system along is a convention that assigns a numeric address to each cubbyhole. The numbers are all sequential, so if a 50-chunk block of data is stored in cubbyholes starting at number 100, the block of data occupies memory addresses 100 through 149. When the program declares that it's going to store data, the CPU not only locates empty space and moves the data into those cubbyholes, but the CPU also reports back to the program the address of the first cubbyhole. That address—a numeric value —is the pointer to the data. Later, when the program wants to pass the data to another function or object, it doesn't have to move or copy all of that data from memory to transfer it to another operation. Instead, the program passes only the pointer so that the other operation can use the one perfect copy of the data that exists in memory, demonstrated in Figure 6-2. The actual image, myImage, is at location 2,419,920. Another word of memory holds the value 2,419,920, and this word is labeled *myImage (with the preceding star) because the program is defining a pointer here.

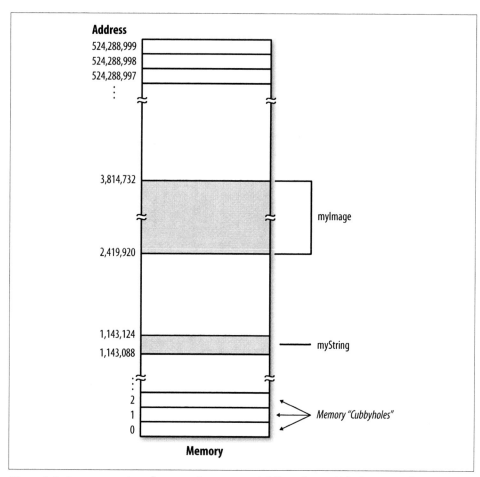

Figure 6-1. A representation of memory locations and differently sized blocks occupied by data

By passing along only the comparatively small pointer, the program uses far fewer resources in the process. Doing so also ensures the integrity of the data in memory. If the one "master" copy in memory should change between the time it is passed to another operation and the time the other operation acts on the data, the other operation will be working on the most up-to-date version.

Allow me to use one more metaphor—this time from the Web world—to help convey how a pointer can be a good thing. Let's say you create a sophisticated web page with lots of images, scripts, stylesheets, and Ajax-delivered content. You now want to share this page with several of your friends. You could save the page from your browser (with copies of all its ancillary files, as many browsers let you do these days) and email the entire package to each of your friends. Each email message would contain multiple megabytes of data representing the snapshot of the live page. Or you could send the URL—the address—of the page in an email message. As each recipient opens the

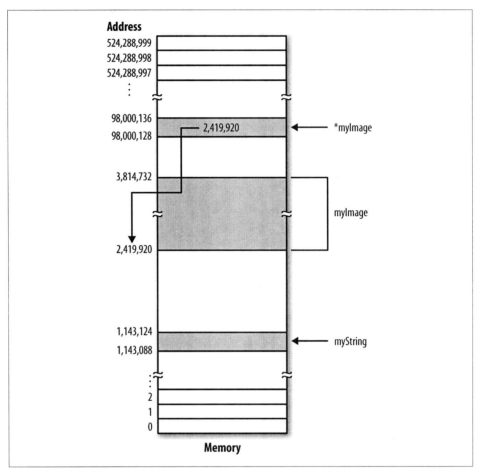

Address

```
524,288,999
524,288,998
524,288,997
    ⋮
 98,000,136
 98,000,128        2,419,920     ◀── *myImage
  3,814,732
                                     myImage
  2,419,920
  1,143,124
  1,143,088                       ◀── myString
     ⋮
      2
      1
      0
```

Memory

Figure 6-2. A pointer occupies little memory space, but can point to the start of a much larger block of data

message, he or she plugs that address into a browser to view the page as it exists on the server at that instant. You've accomplished two things. First, you saved email bandwidth by transmitting less than one hundred bytes instead of megabytes. Second, each recipient will be able to view the absolute latest version of the page. The URL acted as a pointer.

Pointers and Objective-C Variables

Compared to the basic scalar data types, Cocoa Touch objects are complex constructions. At the same time, the amount of available memory in devices using iOS tends to be much smaller than on a typical modern-day desktop or laptop computer. Therefore, every chance you have to preserve memory in an iPhone or iPad app is one that you should take. Assigning an object's pointer to a variable generally conserves memory, especially if that value is to be passed to other methods or objects.

Associating a pointer with a variable has some consequences you must be aware of. The biggest issue occurs when you need to test the equality of two variable values. You can experiment with this task in Workbench with the following replacement for the `runMyCode:` method:

```
- (IBAction)runMyCode:(id)sender {
    NSString *stringOne = [[sender titleLabel] text];
    NSString *stringTwo = @"Run My Code";
    NSLog(@"Equiv Operator:%d", stringOne == stringTwo);
    NSLog(@"isEqual Method:%d", [stringOne isEqualToString:stringTwo]);
}
```

The first statement grabs the text of the label of the button that triggers this method (the `sender` parameter variable references the button) and assigns the value to an `NSString` pointer, `stringOne`. That very same sequence of characters is assigned as a string literal to another `NSString` pointer, `stringTwo`. In the JavaScript world, even though the two strings come from different sources, a test of their equality returns a Boolean `true` because the values of the strings match. That's not the case with pointers, however. In Objective-C, a pointer variable's value is the address of the data in memory (usually expressed as a hexadecimal number). Because the two objects are different, their addresses are also different (see Figure 6-3). Therefore, a test of equivalency of their values yields a Boolean `false` (or 0 in the numeric equivalent expressed in the first `NSLog()` function):

```
Equiv Operator:0
```

To counteract this behavior—and actually test the equivalence of the characters in the strings—you can use an `NSString` instance method that compares the values of the data to which the pointers point. That method is the `isEqualToString:` method. Send the message to either of the two string pointers and name the other pointer as the argument. Now the result shows that the two strings have the same value for their data:

```
isEqual Method:1
```

If you have routines that branch based on the equality of string values, be prepared to use the `isEqualToString:` method frequently. Several other classes have class-specific equality-testing methods available for them.

Pointer Notation

It's difficult to discuss pointer notation thoroughly without also knowing about this chapter's next major concept, data types. For now, however, let me formally introduce you to the star operator (*), which denotes that a variable is being defined as a pointer to a value. You have seen the operator used in many statements that assign string objects to variables, such as the following:

```
NSString *myString = @"Hello, world!";
```

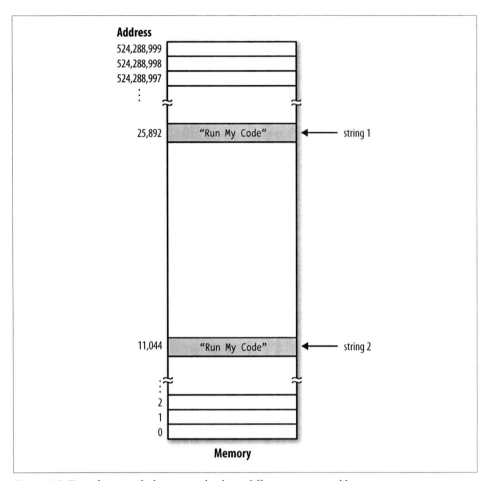

Figure 6-3. Two objects with the same value have different memory addresses

You will sometimes see examples that place the star in a different position, such as the following:

```
NSString * myString = @"Hello, world!";
NSString* myString = @"Hello, world!";
```

All variations are acceptable, but I stay with the way that Xcode templates generate pointer variables: with the star one space to the right of the data type and adjacent to the variable name.

For method declarations and definitions, if the method's return value is a pointer, the pointer star goes with the data type in parentheses before the method name, as in the following method, which we've seen before in the DGCar class:

```
- (NSString *)getFormattedListing {...};
```

Parameter variables follow the same format when specifying their data types:

```
- (DGCar *)initWithCarMake:(NSString *)inputMake
                     model:(NSString *)inputModel
                      year:(NSString *)inputYear {...}
```

We'll revisit the notation and syntactical sequences in the section "Data Typing" on page 115.

Once you define a pointer variable, you no longer use the star notation to read the variable's value. You still must match pointers with pointers. Fortunately, the iOS SDK documentation supplies tons of information about which value types are required in which places.

Determining Pointer Usage

A large percentage of your coding will involve objects that are either instances of framework objects or your own subclasses of those objects. The SDK documentation provides all the details you need to determine return value types for methods and method arguments. These predefined data types will govern a great deal of your coding.

To demonstrate the power of the documentation, let's take a look at an object class with which we have not yet worked. An app can access an Internet URL and accumulate the data supplied by the server as it arrives. This is how an app can retrieve XML data for updates. To initiate that connection, you use the NSURLConnection class. If you search the SDK documentation for this class name, you will find the class reference document. One of the instance methods initiates an asynchronous connection, and is defined in the docs as shown in Figure 6-4

```
- (id)initWithRequest:(NSURLRequest *)request delegate:(id)delegate
startImmediately:(BOOL)startImmediately
```

Figure 6-4. NSURLConnection's initialization definition from Xcode documentation

The method returns a generic id data type, but as an initialization instance method, it means that you'll use it with an alloc message on the NSURLConnection class:

```
NSURLConnection *myConnection = [[NSURLConnection alloc] initWithRequest:...];
```

But take a closer look at the arguments and their parameter variables to see what kinds of values our code must supply. The two easy ones are the delegate and startImmediately arguments. The delegate argument always points to a class to which delegate messages will be sent. Most of the time, the same class containing the initialization is also the one set up to handle delegate messages. Thus, the argument value will be self. The startImmediately argument asks for a Boolean value. In Objective-C, the preferred convention is to use the constants YES and NO (unquoted) for those values. Because you normally want an asynchronous download to begin right away, the value passed to the startImmediately argument will be YES.

To get to the value of the first argument, you'll have to go on a small expedition. The data type is declared to be of class NSURLRequest (notated as a pointer). Assuming you don't know anything about that class, you must discover how to create a value of that type. The SDK documentation comes to the rescue. In the documentation viewer, the class name (NSURLRequest) is already a clickable link (Figure 6-4), but you can also search for NSURLRequest to reach the same destination: the NSURLRequest Class Reference. There you will find four different ways to create one of these objects. For the sake of simplicity, I'll choose a class method, requestWithURL, which is defined as shown in Figure 6-5.

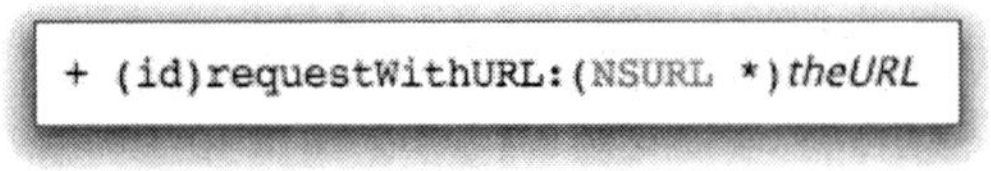

```
+ (id)requestWithURL:(NSURL *)theURL
```

Figure 6-5. Xcode documentation entry for the class method to create an NSURLRequest object

Your hunt is not over, because this method requires an argument whose data type is a pointer to an NSURL object. Off you go again to the documentation for that class, where you find one of its class methods that creates the desired object, shown in Figure 6-6.

```
+ (id)URLWithString:(NSString *)URLString
```

Figure 6-6. Xcode documentation entry for creating an NSURL object

You have finally reached a data type you recognize, NSString. You can now work backward through the sequence to generate the necessary first argument to get the connection going:

```
// Create NSURL from a string constant
NSURL *theUrl = [NSURL URLWithString:@"http://dannyg.com/dl/demo.plist"];

// Use NSURL to create NSURLRequest
NSURLRequest *theRequest = [NSURLRequest requestWithURL:theUrl];

// Use NSURLRequest as first argument to initialize NSURLConnection
NSURLConnection *myConnection = [[NSURLConnection alloc]
                              initWithRequest:theRequest
                                     delegate:self
                              startImmediately:YES];
```

All of the objects being created in this sequence are complex objects and their instance creators return pointers to their objects. Those pointers then become arguments of further methods in the sequence.

Getting used to thinking about pointers and using their notation can be a significant hurdle for JavaScript programmers who have not used other languages that require pointers. It takes a little practice (and several compilation errors) to get used to it. Eventually, you will automatically add a pointer star to your variable declarations without thinking about it (and may occasionally and accidentally add a star to scalar data types that don't use pointers—only to have the compiler remind you).

Data Typing

JavaScript is known as a *loosely typed* or *weakly typed* language because it is pretty forgiving about the types of data being stored in variables or returned from functions. In JavaScript, you do not have to declare ahead of time whether a variable you're creating will be holding a number, string, array, function reference, or other type of data. The language even goes out of its way at times to make variables of incompatible data types work together (although not always with the results you desire). For example, if you try to add a string and a number, the language converts the number to a string, and concatenates the two values:

```
// JavaScript
var a = "100";
var b = 20;
var result = a + b;
    // result == "10020"
```

Such conversions are not always successful. Change the operator above to division, and you get a very different result, because that operator absolutely requires two numeric operands:

```
// JavaScript
var a = "100";
var b = 20;
var result = a / b;
    // result == NaN
```

As forgiving as this system might be, it can impose a burden on the scripter to keep track of value types that are stored in variables. For example, if a JavaScript variable you create to hold an array inadvertently gets assigned a string, you will encounter a runtime error if you later attempt to invoke an array object method on that string variable.

In contrast, Objective-C (thanks to its C heritage) requires that you explicitly declare the type of data that is to be assigned to every variable, assigned to every method argument, and returned by every method—including one special type, called id, that can represent more than one type (more about this later in the chapter). The number of possible type declarations can be mind-boggling at first—especially when you bring all the Cocoa Touch framework classes into the picture—but you may eventually grow to like the discipline that typing instills in your coding. By validating specific data types, the compiler acts as an early warning system if your code goes astray.

Objective-C Data Types

The first batch of Objective-C data types you need to know are numeric (and come from C). You are probably familiar with the distinction between integers and floating-point numbers from your exposure to JavaScript's parseInt() and parseFloat() global functions. Those functions convert string versions of numbers to actual numeric values for all kinds of math operations. An integer is a whole number (positive, negative, or zero) without any decimal places; a floating-point number can have a decimal and numbers to the right of the decimal to designate fractional values between integers. Objective-C has many additional numeric data types, but the differences among them concern themselves with precision and the size of memory reserved for their values. Table 6-1 lists the three basic data types (also called *scalar* types) you will encounter most frequently in iOS SDK development.

Table 6-1. Common basic data types

Data type designation	Value
int	Integer between −2147483648 and 2147483647
float	Floating-point number between 1.17549435e−38 and 3.40282347e+38
double	Floating-point number between 2.2250738585072014e−308 and 1.7976931348623157e+308

The C language defines many other basic data types, all of which are usable directly in the Objective-C world of the iOS SDK. But for the most part, you will be using the huge library of Cocoa and Cocoa Touch data types in their place.

 Objective-C floats suffer from the same type of floating-point errors that JavaScript float values do. Use caution when performing arithmetic on floats if deep precision is needed; consider using a double instead. For the most part, however, you will use floats to supply values of fairly shallow precision as arguments to methods.

Cocoa Touch Data Types

You can divide Cocoa-based data types into two broad categories. The first includes data types for fundamental values used by many Cocoa classes and functions; the other contains the enormous range of classes defined throughout the Foundation, UIKit, and other frameworks that you import into your app project.

Two of the most common basic Cocoa data types are the CGRect (plus its component data types) and NSRange. The "CG" part of CGRect stands for Core Graphics. CGRect values assist with the creation and layout of rectangular objects (mostly views) on the screen. A CGRect is a C language *structure* (described more fully in Chapter 7) whose members define an origin point (the coordinate of the top-left corner of the rectangle) and the size (width and height)—everything a rectangle needs to know with respect to its placement and dimensions. Figure 6-7 illustrates the components of a CGRect within

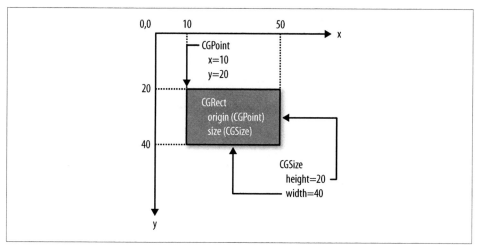

Figure 6-7. Visualization of a CGRect value

a coordinate space. If you choose to manually code the creation of UI elements (views, controls, and such), you commonly need to supply what is called a *frame*, which is merely a `CGRect` data type with the needed values.

An `NSRange` data type is another C structure, but one that defines the boundaries of a section within a series of items. For instance, a substring can be defined with the help of a range whose two members specify the offset from the beginning of the main string where the range starts (known as the location, zero-based) and the length (number of characters) of the substring. Figure 6-8 shows how you can apply a range's values to a string of text. An `NSRange` is useful in other cases, such as selecting a contiguous group of items from an array to copy into a subarray. Yet the principle is the same: an offset location and a length.

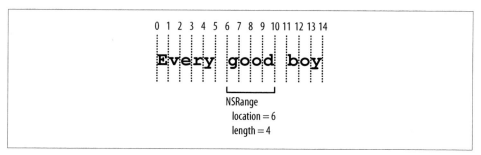

Figure 6-8. NSRange values applied to a text string

Cocoa Touch classes provide the bulk of the data types you specify throughout your code. Most of the class data types you use come from the frameworks, but your own classes will become data types as well. Such was the case in Chapter 5 when you defined variables that held instances of the `DGCar` class—each defined as a `DGCar` data type.

Objective-C Variable Declarations

The syntax for declaring a basic variable type is simple:

```
dataType variableName;
```

Or you can declare a variable and assign an initial value:

```
dataType variableName = expressionReturningDataTypeValue;
```

As described earlier in this chapter (in the section "Pointers" on page 108), there are times when you either want or need to turn a variable into a pointer. You signify creation of a pointer variable with an asterisk (or "star"). Therefore, the syntax for declaring pointer variables is as follows:

```
// Declare only
dataType *variableName;
// Declare and initialize
dataType *variableName = expressionReturningPointerToDataTypeValue;
```

As with JavaScript, you can declare a variable in one code statement and assign a value to it in another statement. But once you assign a data type to an Objective-C variable, it maintains that data type throughout its life. If you attempt to assign a value of a different data type to an existing variable, you will receive a compile-time error. Such errors are your friends because they alert you to inadvertent mistakes of mismatched data types before the code can be fully compiled into an app.

Here are some examples of variable declarations and initializations showing how data types are applied:

```
int myAge;
float pageWidthInInches = 8.5;
CGRect newFrame;

// NSMakeRange function returns an NSRange value
NSRange subStringRange = NSMakeRange(2, 10);

// Objective C string literals return a pointer to the string value
NSString *country = @"France";

// Righthand expression returns a pointer to
// an instance of BlueViewController class
BlueViewController *secondViewController =
        [[BlueViewController alloc] initWithNibName:nil
                                     bundle:nil];
```

Objective-C Method Declarations

Every Objective-C method is defined to return a value, even if that value is empty (void). Importantly, the data type of the value is declared even before you reach the name of the method. The format is as follows for an instance method (which begins with a hyphen):

```
    - (dataType) methodName {...}
```

If the method returns a pointer to a value, add the pointer star character as follows:

```
    - (dataType *) methodName {...}
```

Remember that instance methods—those that will be invoked from outside a current instance—need to be declared in the class header file. You must include the return data type in those declarations, too.

The syntax gets a little more complex when a method receives arguments. Each argument must specify a data type. Here's the format:

```
    - (dataType) methodName:(dataType)parameter1VariableName
        anotherArgumentName:(dataType)parameter2VariableName {...}
```

As before, if any of the data types are pointers, you include a star after the data type:

```
    - (dataType *) methodName:(dataType *)parameter1VariableName
        anotherArgumentName:(dataType *)parameter2VariableName {...}
```

To see these forms in action, look again at the custom DGCar class introduced in Chapter 4. Example 6-1 shows the header file.

Example 6-1. DGCar.h

```
#import <Foundation/Foundation.h>


@interface DGCar : NSObject {

    NSString *make;
    NSString *model;
    NSString *year;

}
- (DGCar *)initWithCarMake:(NSString *)inputMake
                     model:(NSString *)inputModel
                      year:(NSString *)inputYear;
- (NSString *)getFormattedListing;

@end
```

Three instance variables are declared as being pointers to NSStrings. The first method, initWithCarMake:model:year:, returns a pointer to the very same class we're defining here, and takes three arguments, each of which is a pointer to an NSString. For the sake of improved human readability, it is common practice to format potentially long, multiargument methods on multiple lines, aligning the colons that precede arguments. The second method takes no arguments, but returns a pointer to an NSString. Example 6-2 shows how the two methods are implemented.

Example 6-2. DGCar.m implementation

```objc
#import "DGCar.h"


@implementation DGCar

- (DGCar *)initWithCarMake:(NSString *)inputMake
                     model:(NSString *)inputModel
                      year:(NSString *)inputYear {
    if (self = [super init]) {
        make = inputMake;
        model = inputModel;
        year = inputYear;
    }

    return self;
}

- (NSString *)getFormattedListing {
    NSString *result = @"";

    result = [NSString stringWithFormat:@"[%@] %@ %@", year, make, model];

    return result;
}
@end
```

Let's start with the simpler, second method. The method is defined to return a pointer to an NSString object. Therefore, the value in the final return statement must be of that data type. A variable, result, is declared in the scope of the method and is initialized as a pointer to an NSString. Its initial value is an empty Objective-C string (remember that Objective-C string literals begin with @ ahead of the quoted text). It is often helpful to initialize a returnable variable with a value: if some further processing fails, at least a valid value is returned at runtime. The result variable is assigned the value returned by an NSString class method, stringWithFormat:. You'll see later in the chapter how to uncover in the Xcode documentation that the stringWithFormat: method returns a pointer to an NSString object, thus matching the declared type for result.

For the initialization method, you see that it returns a pointer to an instance of the current DGCar class. If the implementation file did not import the *DGCar.h* file, the compiler would complain because it wouldn't know about the DGCar class. This method does not define a variable for a return value because it's using a special property of an object, which is a reference to itself (self). The value of self comes from the return value of the init method of the superclass. The rest of the method transfers the argument values to instance variables. Notice that these three assignments are to the ivars declared and typed in the header file. If you were to omit the ivar declarations in the header and declare these variables inside the method, like so, the variables would be local to the method (more specifically, local to the if block), and would die even before the method returned:

```
- (DGCar *)initWithCarMake:(NSString *)inputMake
                    model:(NSString *)inputModel
                     year:(NSString *)inputYear {
    if (self = [super init]) {

        // Uh oh!
        NSString *make = inputMake;
        NSString *model = inputModel;
        NSString *year = inputYear;
    }

    return self;
}
```

This would cause the `getFormattedListing` method to fail compilation because the compiler could not see the variables needed for the string formatting method. Variable scope is discussed in more detail in Chapter 7.

You can mix and match pointers and basic value types in a method definition. Therefore, a method could accept two `NSString` pointers as arguments but return an integer—or any combination of data types. Example 6-3 shows both the interface and implementation files for a variation of **DGCar** whose **year** property is an integer. Changes from the original are highlighted in bold.

Example 6-3. A version of DGCar with one int instance variable

```
// DGCar.h
#import <Foundation/Foundation.h>


@interface DGCar : NSObject {

    NSString *make;
    NSString *model;
    int year;

}

- (DGCar *)initWithCarMake:(NSString *)inputMake
                    model:(NSString *)inputModel
                     year:(int)inputYear;
- (NSString *)getFormattedListing;

@end
//==========================================
// DGCar.m
@implementation DGCar

- (DGCar *)initWithCarMake:(NSString *)inputMake
                    model:(NSString *)inputModel
                     year:(int)inputYear {
    if (self = [super init])
        make = inputMake;
        model = inputModel;
```

```
        year = inputYear;
    }

    return self;
}

- (NSString *)getFormattedListing {
    NSString *result = @"";

    result = [NSString stringWithFormat:@"[%d] %@ %@", year, make, model];

    return result;
}
@end
```

Required changes are minimal, mostly affecting the data type specifications for one ivar and the third argument of the initialization method. Notice, however, that you also have to change the string format specifier in getFormattedListing to accommodate the integer value (%d).

The only other change to make this version work is to the values passed to the initialization method when an instance of DGCar is created. Here is the modified runMyCode: method of the WorkbenchViewController class:

```
- (IBAction)runMyCode:(id)sender {
    DGCar *myCar1 = [[DGCar alloc] initWithCarMake:@"Chevrolet"
                                            model:@"Malibu" year:2007];
    DGCar *myCar2 = [[DGCar alloc] initWithCarMake:@"Ford"
                                            model:@"Taurus" year:2010];

    NSLog(@"I used to drive a:%@", [myCar1 getFormattedListing]);
    NSLog(@"I now drive a:%@", [myCar2 getFormattedListing]);
}
```

Results displayed in the console window are identical to those from the earlier example in Chapter 4.

The id Data Type

The runMyCode: method has one argument, which is assigned to the parameter variable sender. For Workbench, the sender argument is a reference to the button the user clicks. What may be confusing at first is that the data type is simply id (without a pointer star) rather than some UIKit type, such as UIButton (the type of button used in the project). That's because Objective-C offers some uncommon versatility when it comes to specifying data types for objects.

The id data type is, in a sense, a generic data type. It can stand in for Objective-C basic data types (e.g., various types of numbers) or Cocoa Touch objects (e.g., buttons, arrays, and views). In fact, a variable defined as an id data type can even change the type of data it holds during the execution of a method. This flexibility is a hallmark of Objective-C, called *dynamic typing* (also known as *late binding*). The idea behind dynamic typing is that a variable doesn't need to be prewired for only one data type; instead the data type (a class) is assigned at runtime, and the system keeps track of the type as needed (and thus knows to which class it should send messages).

As an illustration of dynamic typing and the id data type, consider an app that defines three very different classes named Leg, Glass, and Meeting. Each class has a method named break, which performs a class-specific breaking action on an instance of that class. As the app runs, a variable of type id could contain an instance of any one of those classes, depending on user interaction or another situation. But when a statement sends the break message to the variable, the actual class of the variable at that instant determines which method executes. Importantly, the compiler can't know whether a class assigned to the variable has a break method defined for it, because at compile time the class of the variable is indeterminate.

Before you draw the conclusion that you can simply adopt the id data type for everything and treat all Objective-C variables as loosely typed JavaScript variables, hold your horses! The compiler will let potential data type incompatibilities slide by if you are sloppy with typing. Errors will occur at runtime and conceivably generate crashes that can be challenging to repair even with the Xcode debugger. You are often better off finding data type inconsistencies at compile time rather than at runtime. The Xcode compiler supplies many clues (albeit not all of them immediately clear to newcomers) about data type issues. It's true that accurately typing your variables and methods may be frustrating to work with at first—you'll feel as though you're doing a lot of the work the compiler should be doing—but the code will be easier to maintain over time.

Despite these cautions, don't be afraid of dynamic typing—Cocoa Touch frameworks use it extensively. It will just take some time working in Objective-C before you recognize places where dynamic typing can contribute to your code's flexibility.

Converting Objective-C Data Types

With variables being so highly tied to their data types—and Objective-C operations being exceedingly picky about the types of data they work on—there will be many times when you need to convert one data type to another. This happens largely in the realm of numbers and strings, but you also have the added complexity of specific number types being incompatible with each other. You can't send an int to do a float's job.

For simple conversions of basic number values, you can use a technique called *casting*. A cast forces a value to perform a conversion based on strict rules established for the C language. Most of the rules dictate how conversions between numeric types (e.g., long and short versions of int and float types) are to behave during such conversions.

Specify a cast by placing the desired output data type in parentheses before the original value. For example, the following changes an int to a float:

```
float myValueAsFloat = (float)myValueAsInt;
```

One of the rules that could impact you is that when a float or double is cast to an int, the numbers to the right of the decimal (and the decimal) are stripped off. No rounding occurs. You can see how casting works for yourself in Workbench by modifying the runMyCode: method as follows:

```
- (IBAction)runMyCode:(id)sender {
    double a = 12345.6789;
    int b = (int)a;
    float c = (float)b;
    NSLog(@"\ndouble = %f\nint of double = %d\nfloat of int = %f", a, b, c);
}
```

When you click the button in the running Workbench app, the console reveals the following log result:

```
double = 12345.678900
int of double = 12345
float of int = 12345.000000
```

Take special notice that the placeholders in NSLog() specify integer (%d) and floating-point (%f) values where needed. If you try to assign a value of one type to a % placeholder of a different type, you will receive unexpected or erroneous results.

Casting also works with complex classes. For example, you can cast the runMyCode: method's argument from an id type to a UIButton type as follows:

```
UIButton *myButton = (UIButton *)sender;
```

At compile time, Xcode will validate subsequent messages sent to myButton against the list of methods defined for that class.

To convert a string type to a number type, you can use one of several NSString methods, each of which returns a number of a very specific data type (doubleValue, floatValue, intValue, integerValue, longLongValue, and boolValue). For example, in the following code, a string object is created so that it begins with numerals but ends with nonnumeric characters. Then the doubleValue method returns as much of a double type number as it can pull from the string (much like JavaScript's parseFloat() function does):

```
NSString *myString = @"123.45abc";
double a = [myString doubleValue];
NSLog(@"double = %f", a);
```

Due to the precision of a double to six decimal places, the result in the console is as follows:

```
double = 123.450000
```

To convert a numeric data type to a string, you can create a string via the same type of format specifier you've been seeing in NSLog() throughout the preceding chapters. The format expression is an argument to the stringWithFormat: class method of NSString. Most commonly, you will need to integrate a calculated value into a longer string. In the following example, an integer is plugged into a format specifier within a string:

```
int myAge = 34;
int until100 = 100 - myAge;
NSString *result =
    [NSString stringWithFormat:@"You have %d years to go to reach 100.", until100];
NSLog(@"%@", result);
```

As you will learn in Chapter 8, Cocoa Touch provides the NSNumber class, which lets you express any of the basic numeric values as full-fledged Objective-C objects. Such numeric objects are essential if you need to store a number in an Objective-C collection, such as an NSArray. For general math operations, however, basic values are easier to work with and are memory-efficient. And if you need to migrate a value between an NSNumber object and basic value, the NSNumber class offers a full set of methods that let you jump from one form to the other.

Memory Management

This chapter has been hinting (not very subtly) at the need to pay attention to an iOS app's memory usage. The emphasis on pointers in most of the frameworks is one of Apple's contributions to help you be frugal with system resources.

An iOS device has a fixed amount of operating room in memory. This portion of memory is separate from the storage space reserved for music, video, and other files (where all the gigabytes of the device specifications lie).

Operating memory is measured in the hundreds of megabytes. The precise size is not important, except to say that not all devices are created equal in this respect. The iPhone 3GS, third-generation iPod touch, and first-generation iPad have twice as much memory available to apps than earlier models, while the iPhone 4 doubles even that amount. That's why newer devices can accommodate the more memory-intensive features of iOS 4.0, such as multitasking, while older models cannot.

This stratification of available memory in devices also suggests that you should keep an older-model device on hand for testing when you get your app running on devices. A memory-hungry app that runs fine on an iPhone 4 can bring a second-generation iPod touch (a very popular model) to its knees. Also be aware that the simulator application does not simulate the constricted memory space of actual devices. Testing a developing app on real iOS devices is absolutely essential to spot critical memory issues and performance bottlenecks.

Cleaning Up After Yourself

Some operating systems and program-running engines have a feature called *garbage collection*. Garbage is memory space that is no longer needed. For example, you may have instantiated an object to perform a limited task, such as downloading data from a server. Once the data is received, the object that performed the data retrieval is no longer needed and simply takes up memory space. A garbage-collected environment monitors these conditions and recognizes when an object is no longer being used so that it can return the object's memory blocks to the CPU to be available for other needs. JavaScript interpreters have garbage collectors built into them. Cocoa programming for Mac OS X has garbage collection. Cocoa Touch programming for iOS does not.

As potentially burdensome as this may sound, you don't have to micromanage the memory of absolutely every object your code creates and tosses aside. Only objects created in a few well-documented ways require manual memory release. The others are grouped together to be released in the next system run loop, but not in a garbage-collected manner.

Any object that your code creates via a method whose name starts with "alloc" or "new," or whose name contains "copy" must also be released by your code. Of these possibilities, you will likely encounter the `alloc` message most often, especially in combination with an initialization message. Recall from the creation of a new view controller instance in Chapter 5:

```
// Create instance of BlueViewController loaded from .xib file of same name
BlueViewController *secondViewController =
    [[BlueViewController alloc] initWithNibName:nil bundle:nil];
[self presentModalViewController:secondViewController animated:YES];
[secondViewController release];
```

Notice how creating that instance involves the use of the `alloc` method. This means the memory occupied by the `secondViewController` object is now your responsibility. The object's pointer is passed as an argument to the `presentModalViewController:ani mated:` method. After that, the current method has no further use for the object and sends it the `release` message. Importantly, the `release` message is sent to a variable that is still in scope (i.e., within the method).

Look now at another instance where you used `alloc` in an earlier chapter. Specifically, recall the creation of instances of the `DGCar` class in Chapter 4:

```
- (IBAction)runMyCode:(id)sender {
    DGCar *myCar1 = [[DGCar alloc] initWithCarMake:@"Chevrolet"
                                          model:@"Malibu" year:@"2007"];
    DGCar *myCar2 = [[DGCar alloc] initWithCarMake:@"Ford"
                                          model:@"Taurus" year:@"2010"];

    NSLog(@"I used to drive a:%@", [myCar1 getFormattedListing]);
    NSLog(@"I now drive a:%@", [myCar2 getFormattedListing]);
}
```

Both instance creation statements send the `alloc` message to `DGCar` and assign object pointers to variables whose scope is local to the current method. If the code stays as it is, each time the user taps the button to run this method, two more objects are created in other memory locations. So the memory for the previous ones continue to reserve their space, even though there is no way to reach them from previous executions of the method. That is a classic case of what is called a *memory leak*. Overall memory allocated for the app continues to grow with each tap of the button and, because the code does not have a way to reference the variables once the method ends and free up the space, the memory cannot be reused by other operations in the app. Tap the button enough times (okay, *lots* of times for these relatively simple objects) and the app will crash.

To fix the problem, you must send `release` messages to both objects from inside the current method. Of course, you don't want to release them before they're used, so add the two `release` calls to a point *after* the objects complete their operations:

```
- (IBAction)runMyCode:(id)sender {
    DGCar *myCar1 = [[DGCar alloc] initWithCarMake:@"Chevrolet"
                                    model:@"Malibu" year:@"2007"];
    DGCar *myCar2 = [[DGCar alloc] initWithCarMake:@"Ford"
                                    model:@"Taurus" year:@"2010"];

    NSLog(@"I used to drive a:%@", [myCar1 getFormattedListing]);
    NSLog(@"I now drive a:%@", [myCar2 getFormattedListing]);

    // Release the objects
    [myCar1 release];
    [myCar2 release];
}
```

When the scope of object creation and release is limited to a single method, managing the memory is relatively simple (provided you remember to do it). But what about instance variables that live a long time and may be touched by multiple methods? That's where you have to learn how iOS keeps track of an object's memory usage.

The Retain Count

For every object you create in an app, iOS keeps a tally of how many times the object is retained and which object has ownership of that object. The tally is known as the *reference count* or *retain count*. If an instance of a class object has an instance variable whose value is assigned via an `alloc` method call, not only is the ivar owned by the current instance, but the ivar's retain count is incremented by one when it is allocated. The owner (who allocated the ivar) has the responsibility to release this object at some point. Sending the object a `release` message decrements the retain count by one. This makes the object's retain count zero, which means that the object is ready to be freed—deallocated—in memory.

Whenever an object is ready to be deallocated, the system sends the object a `dealloc` message. If the object implements a `dealloc` method, this is where the object has one last chance to release any objects that it owns. Failing to release those objects will cause their memory to leak. The owner object must also deallocate itself by passing the `dealloc` message to its superclass. Therefore, it's common to see Xcode class file templates (like the `WorkbenchViewController`) supply the following skeleton `dealloc` method:

```
- (void)dealloc {
    [super dealloc];
}
```

This template stands ready for you to insert **release** messages sent to objects that need to be freed before the current object is deallocated. In other words, the message to **super** is the final statement of the **dealloc** method. The [**super dealloc**] message is the only time your code ever explicitly sends a **dealloc** message—the system sends all other **dealloc** messages automatically.

There may be times when you need to retain an object manually to increment its retain count. Consider an ivar setter method we could design for the **DGCar** class to assign a value to the model instance variable:

```
- (void)setModel:(NSString *)newModel {
    model = newModel;
}
```

This works fine if you plan to make only one assignment per instance of **DGCar**. But if this setter could be called multiple times to change values, you should manually manage retain counts in the setter method:

```
- (void)setModel:(NSString *)newModel {
    if (model != newModel) {
        [model release]; // Retain count decremented by 1
        model = [newModel retain]; // Retain count incremented by 1
    }
}
```

If the **NSString** object passed as an argument points to the same object that the **model** ivar points to, they both point to the same value and there is no need to alter the value of **model**. The other case—where **newModel** is a different **NSString** object—requires special handling. The **model** object holding the old value is no longer needed, so it is released, thereby causing the object's retain count to decrement by one. The new value is sent the **retain** message to increment its retain count for assignment to the **model** ivar. The **model** ivar object's retain count is raised from zero to one so the **DGCar** object will keep the value alive, and a subsequent call to the getter method results in a valid value. The important point to take away from this exercise is that every **retain** (or **copy**) method call should be balanced with a **release** call.

 I should clarify the need to balance **retain** and **release** messages in the context of the **setModel:** method example. You see in the example that a **release** message appears before a **retain** message. This is because we want to release the old value and retain the new one.

This still leaves the mystery about the first time the setter runs, when **model** has not yet been assigned any value—**model** is only declared in the header, and it is still **nil**. Is it legal to send a **retain** message to a **nil** object? In Objective-C, the answer is yes. Messages sent to **nil** objects are ignored.

Notice in the setter method that the **retain** message is the last one sent to **model**. To clean up correctly, the **DGCar** object must release the **model** ivar when **DGCar** is finished with it. When does that happen? When DGCar receives the dealloc message from the system. Therefore, you need to add a dealloc method to the DGCar class:

```
- (void)dealloc {
    [model release];
    [super dealloc];
}
```

It's worth repeating that your code never sends the dealloc message to one of your own classes (except to the required call to the superclass as the final statement of an object's dealloc method). When the Workbench app determines that it no longer needs a DGCar object (either under the instruction of another class that releases the object or the system when the app quits or runs low on memory), the system calls the DGCar's dealloc method. That method is where you add release messages to objects retained by the DGCar class (you should, of course, also add release messages for the other retained ivars in this class).

If the business of manually retaining ivar objects is still a little fuzzy, you can take some comfort that Objective-C has a feature called a *property* that handles interim memory management chores for you (except for the release messages you add to the dealloc method). Chapter 8 covers properties (and their freakishly JavaScript-like usage syntax).

Autorelease Pools

You might wonder what happens to all of those objects that are created without the aid of the alloc message. After all, assigning an Objective-C string constant to an NSString variable creates an object in memory. The same is true for the many other objects that have class methods returning full-fledged initialized objects. You saw a case of that earlier in this chapter in the creation of an NSURL object:

```
// Create NSURL from a string constant
NSURL *theUrl = [NSURL URLWithString:@"http://dannyg.com/dl/demo.plist"];
```

This message actually creates two objects: an NSString to be passed as an argument and the NSURL object. How do you free memory occupied by these objects when they're no longer needed?

The short answer is that you don't—at least, not directly. Objects created in this fashion are known as *autoreleased* objects. References to these objects are automatically stored in an NSAutoreleasePool object. If this name seems familiar, take a look at the *main.m* file in Workbench, whose main() function is as follows:

```
int main(int argc, char *argv[]) {
    NSAutoreleasePool * pool = [[NSAutoreleasePool alloc] init];
    int retVal = UIApplicationMain(argc, argv, nil, nil);
    [pool release];
    return retVal;
}
```

The operation that launches the app is wrapped inside two statements. The first creates an NSAutoreleasePool object named pool. After the app quits, that pool object receives the release message. When an NSAutoreleasePool object receives the release message, the pool deallocates all objects in the pool. Pulling the drain plug on a swimming pool is an apt metaphor for what happens.

Although the NSAutoreleasePool object in the main() function handles the most global collection of autoreleased objects, you can also create additional pools inside your code to deallocate batches of autoreleased objects that may collect in loops or other constructions while your program is still running. Left to accumulate in memory, these kinds of objects can grow to alarming numbers and even send your app crashing on devices with smaller available memory.

Despite its scary-sounding name, an NSAutoreleasePool object is easy to deploy. For example, if you have a repeat loop that performs a substantial amount of processing on elements of a large array, each time through the loop could entail dozens of statements that generate autoreleased objects, such as NSStrings or temporary subarrays. But you can prevent your app from building up a huge collection by wrapping the statements inside the loop within the NSAutoreleasePool creation and its release:

```
for (int i = 0; i < [hugeArray count]; i++) {
    NSAutoreleasePool *arrayProcessPool = [[NSAutoreleasePool alloc] init];
    // Your involved array element parsing statements here
    ...
    [arrayProcessPool release];
}
```

Each time through the loop, the autoreleased objects created in that one loop are released before the next time through the loop. Memory requirements of your program will remain at a safe level. In more complex code arrangements, you can nest pools as needed. Autoreleased objects generated inside the scope of each pool are released when its pool is released.

Observing Memory Usage

Apple supplies a number of extra tools in the iOS SDK. One of them, called Instruments, lets you run your app in the simulator or on a device while observing real-time memory usage and the occurrence of memory leaks. For example, you can watch how many objects are being allocated in memory while a program runs. If a particular user operation triggers a significant repeat loop that does not employ an NSAutoreleasePool object, you will likely observe the number of object allocations and overall memory usage continue to creep upward while the loop works. If so, you've spotted a candidate for wrapping inside an autorelease pool.

To run your app through Instruments, first make sure that it is in a usable state on the simulator. Then choose Run→Run with Performance Tool→Leaks from the Xcode menubar. Your app will probably run slower than usual as Instruments gathers runtime system data and displays it both in a running graph and a table.

Instruments is an incredibly rich development and testing tool. Explaining how to exploit all its powers would take a separate book. Although the iOS SDK documentation set includes an *Instruments User Guide* (search for "Instruments"), the guide is not necessarily for the newcomer to the platform. You can, however, get some individual help by asking questions at Apple's iOS Developer Center forums (iOS developer membership required).

One other helpful tool is available to all users of the SDK. Xcode includes a *static analyzer*, which goes through your source code in search of problems the compiler does not always locate. For instance, the analyzer (built from an open source tool called CLANG) will spot potential memory leaks in your code. The first time you run your code through CLANG (choose Build→Build and Analyze), you may be shocked at the number of potential leaks (generally unresolved retain counts) it displays in the Build Results window (choose Build→Build Results to show the window). CLANG can display occasional false positives for problems, but you should study each reported issue carefully.

Recap

I hope this chapter does not send you running for the hills because of so many concepts that might be strange to you. From here you'll move on to what may be more familiar territory, learning how to transfer your JavaScript and DOM scripting knowledge to Cocoa Touch ways. Many JavaScript constructions and syntax formats will be usable as-is (or very close) in your iOS app code. But where differences occur, you'll need to learn the new ways by trying them in Workbench. That's what the remaining chapters will demonstrate.

CHAPTER 7

C Language Fundamentals

The C programming language may date back to 1972, but it is very much alive today in both its original form and in many object-oriented languages based on it, such as C++, C#, and Objective-C. The Objective-C used in the iOS SDK is not a different language from C, but rather a large set of extensions to C. You can use C syntax and constructions within any Objective-C program, blending the old and the new, even in the same statement. Additionally, parts of the Cocoa Touch set of frameworks—parts you will use frequently—rely on C constructions. Therefore, it is vital that you have a firm footing in C, especially those facets that permeate iOS app development.

This chapter intentionally does not show you everything about the C language. Some language features—especially data collections—are better served in their Objective-C-based Cocoa Touch forms, and are therefore reserved for the next chapter. Rather than burden you with C language niceties you will rarely, if ever, use in app development, this chapter hits the things you really need to know. You also get the benefit of learning where C is identical to what you already know from JavaScript and where you'll have to adapt some of your existing JavaScript experience to the C world. From time to time I will supply code snippets to insert into the `runMyCode:` method of the Workbench app so you can see firsthand how the language feature works. I also encourage you to experiment with variations of what I supply to gain more experience and test boundaries.

Variable Names

Your first lesson in C is a fairly easy one, because you will carry over almost everything from JavaScript intact. For example, the rules in naming variables are nearly identical; Table 7-1 summarizes them.

Table 7-1. Variable naming rules in C and JavaScript

Rule	C	JavaScript
Case-sensitive	Yes	Yes
First letter	Letter or underscore	Letter, $, or underscore

Rule	C	JavaScript
After first letter	Letters, numbers, underscore	Letters, numbers, $, or underscore
Keywords prohibited	Yes	Yes

The only JavaScript feature you have to give up (if you use it at all) is employing the $ symbol in variable names. You should also know that Apple advises against using the underscore character for the first character of variable names because Apple tends to use that style for (noninstance) variables within code it uses to create the frameworks. Collisions between your instance variables and the frameworks' private variables would be rare, but it's best to avoid all possible problems.

One other convention that Apple recommends is to begin variable names with lower-case letters and use CamelCase form for multiword names. This helps with readability in separating variable names from initial-uppercase class names.

Another common feature for variable naming is that you cannot use a reserved word for a variable name. Although there are many reserved words in common between JavaScript and C/Objective-C, the lists are not identical. Table 7-2 shows reserved words to avoid for variable names (including parameter variable names in method definitions). Most originated in the C language, but Objective-C adds several (shown in bold).

Table 7-2. Reserved words for JavaScript and C/Objective-C

JavaScript	C/Objective-C
	_Bool
	_Complex
	_Imaginary
abstract	
	auto
boolean	
break	break
	bycopy
	byref
byte	
case	case
catch	
char	char
class	
const	const
continue	continue

JavaScript	C/Objective-C
debugger	
default	default
delete	
do	do
double	double
else	else
enum	enum
export	
extends	
	extern
final	
finally	
float	float
for	for
function	
goto	goto
if	if
implements	
import	
in	in
	inline
	inout
instanceof	
int	int
interface	
long	long
native	
new	
	oneway
	out
package	
private	
protected	
public	
	register

JavaScript	C/Objective-C
	restrict
return	return
	self
	short
	signed
	sizeof
	static
	struct
	super
switch	switch
this	
throw	
try	
	typedef
typeof	
	union
	unsigned
var	
void	void
	volatile
while	while
with	

Variable Scope

JavaScript offers two scopes for variables:

- Global within the current window (defined with or without **var**)
- Local within the current function (must be defined with **var**)

Function statements can get and set all global variables, but can get and set only local variables defined within the same function. The system is pretty simple, if loose. If you forget to use the **var** keyword while defining a local variable, it becomes a global variable. Even an external JavaScript library can define a global variable as it loads into the browser. But when you load a new page into the browser, all variables from the previous page are gone and scripts in the new page start over.

The scope situation becomes a bit more complex in C and Objective-C because programs usually consist of multiple files, many of which are capable of generating object instances that are intended to encapsulate their data (with the help of instance variables).

Instance Variables

An instance variable defined in a class header file is visible to all statements and methods defined in the same class. It's not global as in "global for the entire application code," but certainly for all code in the same class. If you create a subclass, the subclass also inherits the instance variable, which is therefore accessible to methods defined in the subclass.

It's important to remember from your JavaScript object creation experience that an instance variable has scope only within its single instance. If you define two instances of the same class, each instance maintains separate values for its instance variables without colliding with another instance. You saw that in Chapter 4, where two instances of DGCar maintained distinct values for their variables—each with specifications for a different vehicle.

In Chapter 8, you will learn how to turn instance variables into Objective-C class properties. A property has the same scope as an instance variable.

Local Variables

As with JavaScript, a C/Objective-C variable declared within a method has scope only within the method. You must exercise the same care in avoiding the accidental reuse of an instance variable as a local variable (or method parameter variable). If you try to use the same variable name in both spots, the compiler will alert you to the potential problem when you next build the app: the compiler complains that the local variable declaration "hides" the instance variable.

Parameter variables are treated just like local variables (as they are in JavaScript). For example, if your app displays a UIPickerView (the interface element with the slot-machine-style spinners), you need to implement a delegate method that responds to a user selection. Checking the UIPickerViewDelegate class reference, you find the prototype of the desired method as follows:

```
- (void)pickerView:(UIPickerView *)pickerView
        didSelectRow:(NSInteger)row
        inComponent:(NSInteger)component
```

This method has three parameter variables. Although the parameter variables are named here merely as suggestions, you can use those names as-is if they don't collide with instance variables for the class in which you are using this method. You can minimize the possibility of collisions by being more verbose or explicit in naming your custom instance variables.

Local Variables in Control Structure Blocks

As you will learn later in this chapter, C and JavaScript have much in common when it comes to control structures (repeat loops, `if`s, `switch`es, etc.). But the impact of these structures on local variables is quite different. The looseness of JavaScript will potentially trip you up in the C/Objective-C world.

Consider the following JavaScript function (artificially constructed to demonstrate a point):

```
function localTest(input) {
    for (var i = 0; i < 25; i++) {
        if (i == input) {
            var woohoo = i;
        }
    }
    return woohoo;
}
```

The first declaration of the `woohoo` local variable is nested inside an `if` construction, which, in turn, is nested inside a `for` loop. Yet the function returns the value of that nested value. A nested variable in a JavaScript function is said to be *hoisted* to the scope of the function, as if it were declared at the beginning of the function without an assigned value.

Although the function as shown will definitely return a value, the `if` condition might be built to test the loop counting variable against some external value (e.g., a number entered into a text field by a user). Under those circumstances, it is very conceivable that the `if` condition might fail for every iteration through the loop and never assign a value to `woohoo`. Yet the final `return` statement attempts to return something called `woohoo`. What happens in this case is that the value returned by the function is `undefined`, which is the value implicitly assigned to `woohoo` when JavaScript creates the variable. If the statement that calls `localTest()` expects a numeric value, your scripts will crumble into a heap. On the one hand, JavaScript gives you wide latitude when it comes to scoping your variables; on the other hand, this can get you into trouble if you don't test for all value possibilities and guard against unusual results.

If you were to compose the equivalent Objective-C method, it would look like the following:

```
- (int)localTest {
    for (int i = 0; i < 25; i++) {
        if (i == 22) {
            int woohoo = i;
        }
    }
    return woohoo;
}
```

But building this method triggers a compiler error (actually, a few errors all tied to the same problem). The issue is that in C, a variable's scope is local to the control block in which it is declared. Declaring the woohoo integer variable in the nested if construction means it can be used only in that block or any further nested block within the if construction. The return statement cannot "see" the woohoo variable, and to the compiler, woohoo is an undeclared variable within the scope of the return statement.

To repair the problem, declare the variable in the same scope as the return statement:

```
- (int)localTest {
    int woohoo;
    for (int i = 0; i < 25; i++) {
        if (i == 22) {
            woohoo = i;
        }
    }
    return woohoo;
}
```

Another common JavaScript usage with a loop-counting variable is to rely on its value following a nested break statement, as in the following:

```
function breakTest() {
    for (var i = 0; i < 25; i++) {
        if (i == 22) {
            break;
        }
    }
    return i;
}
```

This works in JavaScript because a local variable declared anywhere within a function is visible to any other statement in the function. Thus, the i loop counter is still within scope for the return statement. But the following Objective-C equivalent fails:

```
- (int)breakTest {
    for (int i = 0; i < 25; i++) {
        if (i == 22) {
            break;
        }
    }
    return i;
}
```

The compiler error again points to scoping as an issue because the loop counting variable is defined within a for loop block and not at the same or higher level of the return statement. Again the fix is to declare the variable in the proper scope:

```
- (int)breakTest {
    int i;
    for (i = 0; i < 25; i++) {
        if (i == 22) {
            break;
        }
    }
    return i;
}
```

Be careful not to declare a loop counter variable at the top of the function and again inside the **for** loop control expressions. The compiler lets you do it, but it can only lead to disaster. Instead, simply declare the variable early in the function and reference it as needed throughout the function, as shown above.

Static Local Variables

You get a lot more variable features in C than in JavaScript. Imagine defining a local variable in a method that remembers its value between calls to the method—for instance, a variable that keeps track of how many times the method is called. That's the power of a *static variable* in C.

To define a variable that behaves in that fashion, precede the first assignment statement with the **static** keyword:

```
static int methodCounter = 0;
```

Notice two points. First, you must always include a data type when you define any variable. Second, a static variable requires that you initialize it with a starting value in the same statement that declares it.

You can see the difference in behavior between a standard local variable and static inside the same method. Replace the `runMyCode:` method in the *WorkbenchViewController.m* file with the following:

```
- (IBAction)runMyCode:(id)sender {
    int myLocal = 0;
    NSLog(@"myLocal = %d", myLocal++);

    static int myStatic = 0;
    NSLog(@"myStatic = %d", myStatic++);
}
```

When you run the app and click the button several times, you see the following sequence in the console window:

```
myLocal = 0
myStatic = 0
myLocal = 0
myStatic = 1
myLocal = 0
myStatic = 2
```

The local variable stays the same because it is deallocated at the end of each call and reallocated at the start of the next call, while the static one remembers its value between calls to `runMyCode:`.

Global Variables

Using the term "global variable" can be a little dangerous until you have a clear idea of how you define "global" in an iOS app. For example, you can define a variable to have

---

global scope within a class so that any statement in that class can freely reference (get and set) the value of that variable. Such a variable is defined in the class file implementation (not the header), and outside of any method definition. It is also fairly common practice to signify that a variable is a global by preceding its name with a lowercase "g," as in:

```
int gMasterCounter = 0;
```

But a definition like this in a class file has an additional implication: each instance of that class shares the same variable and its value. In other words, the global scope in this case encompasses all instances of the class. Even if you define getter and setter instance methods for the class, the methods all read and write the same single variable. This can lead to immense confusion if you're not careful. Use global variables with extreme caution in class definitions.

If you truly must use a global variable that is accessible across a wide span of code in your project—potentially by multiple instances of multiple classes—you can define such variables in a centrally located file, and let those other files access the global as an *external global variable*. Variables you define in the fashion of global variables are already external variables, so you do nothing special when creating them. But when you want to get or set that variable in another file, you must tell the compiler that you want to use an external global variable that lives in some other file (wherever it may be):

```
    extern int gMasterCounter;
```

If this **extern** declaration occurs within a method, the scope of usage remains within the method, just like any local variable declaration.

Of course, in the memory-constrained world of iOS devices, you shouldn't be carrying around huge amounts of data in a global variable of any kind. If your need for the information is only intermittent, you have the option of saving the data to a file (even a temporary file that is deleted when the app terminates), and reading the data only when needed.

Constant Values

Following close behind the notion of a variable is that of the constant. Both entities reference values, but only a variable's value can change during its lifetime. Once a constant has a value assigned to it, the value becomes read-only.

JavaScript lets you define a true constant as follows:

```
    const constantName = foreverValue;
```

The C language offers the identical declaration, although you must also include the data type:

```
    const dataType constantName = foreverValue;
```

You have an alternative technique available to you in C, and one that is very popular. The technique employs the compiler—via the `#define` directive—to substitute C values and expressions for occurrences of macro names within a file. It is commonly used for numeric values that permeate a class or project. If you need to change that value during the development of your app, you have to do it only once in the directive. For example, if you design an app that displays lots of moving graphic images on the screen, you might want to keep those images all the same size when they are created. You define the macro names and values like the following:

```
#define kSpriteHeight 24
#define kSpriteWidth 24
```

Although these statements can go anywhere in a file, they are traditionally positioned at the top (just after `#import` directives). Also notice that these macro expressions do not end with a semicolon.

With these macros defined, when you want to employ the values anywhere in the file, insert the macro name. The following statement creates a rectangle (destined to become the frame of a `UIImageView` that displays character icons):

```
CGRect spriteFrame = CGRectMake(0, 0, kSpriteWidth, kSpriteHeight);
```

Imagine the size of the frame is utilized in several statements of a class. If you later decide to change the sizes, simply change the values of the `#define` statements, rather than search around for all instances of the hard numbers.

You can even go further by defining expressions that rely on others. For example, if you establish a ratio between sprite width and height that is to be maintained regardless of overall size, you can express the one based on the value of the other:

```
#define kSpriteWidth kSpriteHeight * 0.8
```

Now you only need to change the value of `kSpriteHeight` to affect both values.

Projects that employ a large number of `#define` statements typically gather the statements all together into a single file. Every file that relies on one or more macros imports that file into its header file.

As for macro naming styles, you will typically encounter three variations. One precedes the name with a lowercase "k" (for "constant"). Another uses "g" (for "global"). The third employs all uppercase letters, with underscores separating multiple words. Choose your favorite style and stick with it.

Functions

In Chapter 6 you were introduced to Objective-C methods and how they differed from JavaScript functions. Now I get to blow your mind by showing you C functions, which look and work a lot like JavaScript functions—except for the mandatory return type and data typing of parameter variables. As with an Objective-C method, a C function is not obligated to return a value, but its definition should specify a return type (not in parentheses), even if it is void.

Arguments, if any, are grouped within parentheses and comma-separated (just like JavaScript) and must also specify data types. Prototypes for three styles follow:

```
void functionName() {
    // statements
    ...
}
void functionName(arg1Type arg1Value) {
    // statements
    ...
}
returnType functionName(arg1Type arg1Value, arg2Type arg2Value) {
    // statements
    ...
    return returnValue;
}
```

It wouldn't surprise me if a lot of newcomers to iOS programming come to this discussion and throw their hands up in the air, wondering why there simply can't be one C or Objective-C style of function/method and be done with it.

You can take comfort in knowing that you will rarely need to generate your own C-style functions. You'll be creating most of your custom action code in the form of Objective-C methods. Your need to know about C functions is predominantly to know how to use those parts of the Cocoa Touch frameworks that have not been modernized to Objective-C (and may never be). You will encounter C constructions in several places within the iOS SDK documentation—notably portions of the Foundation framework and most definitely throughout the CoreGraphics framework. At that point, your only job is to ask yourself whether what you're seeing is a C function or Objective-C method and employ the type being shown to invoke that function or method with the appropriate syntax.

I have alluded to the possibility of mixing C and Objective-C previously, such as when you use code to create a user interface element. Follow along on a journey to see how this works in the real world.

The task at hand is to create code (inside the Workbench runMyCode: method) that creates a UILabel element to display fixed text on the screen below the Run My Code button when a user clicks the button. I'm not avoiding Interface Builder just for demonstration purposes: you often want to use code to add to a screen whose primary content is generated in Interface Builder but needs some dynamic tweaking after the app loads.

I need to find out how to create an instance of UILabel in code, so I start by searching for UILabel in the Xcode documentation. As I begin reading the UILabel Class Reference document, I see from the summary of methods that none of the headings relate to creating an instance of the class. This absence means that the creation method(s) must come from a superclass. Zipping to the very top of the Class Reference document, I see the inheritance chain, as shown in Figure 7-1

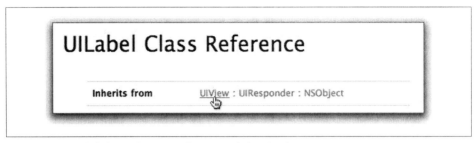

Figure 7-1. UILabel class inheritance chain revealed in the documentation

The immediate superclass of UILabel is UIView. When I click that link, I reach the UI-View Class Reference document. Scrolling down, I see a section pointing to a creation method, shown in Figure 7-2.

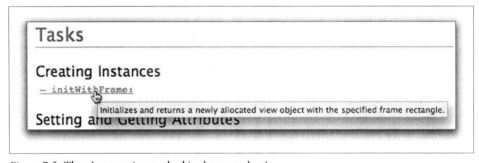

Figure 7-2. There's a creation method in the superclass!

Following that link, I land at the description of the initWithFrame: method, which leads off with a summary of the syntax for the method, shown in Figure 7-3.

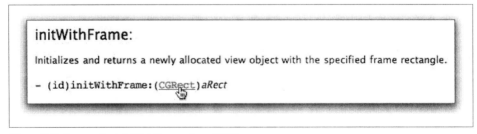

Figure 7-3. Syntax for initWithFrame: for a UIView

The method takes one argument, a value of the type CGRect. I make a mental note that the argument is a value, not a pointer (there is no star mentioned in the argument data type). Time to click on the CGRect link to see how to generate that value, as shown in Figure 7-4.

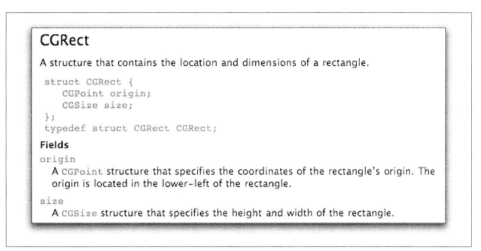

Figure 7-4. Composition of a CGRect value

You haven't met the struct yet (it's coming later in this chapter), but it's a way to package a collection of related values together, with each value capable of storing a value of a different type. The CGRect structure, for instance, has two fields named **origin** and **size**. You can see that both of those values have their own CoreGraphics ("CG") data types, but I'll hold that discussion for later. What I want to know now is how to create one of these CGRect values to apply to the UILabel's initWithFrame: method (which it inherits from UIView).

The definition of the CGRect type is in an Xcode documentation file called CGGeometry Reference. If I scroll up to its syntax summary, I find a group titled "Creating a Geometric Primitive from Values," featuring three items that appear to make the stuff needed, including one that goes all the way to generate a rect, shown in Figure 7-5.

Clicking on `CGRectMake`, I reach the definition of this function, as shown in Figure 7-6.

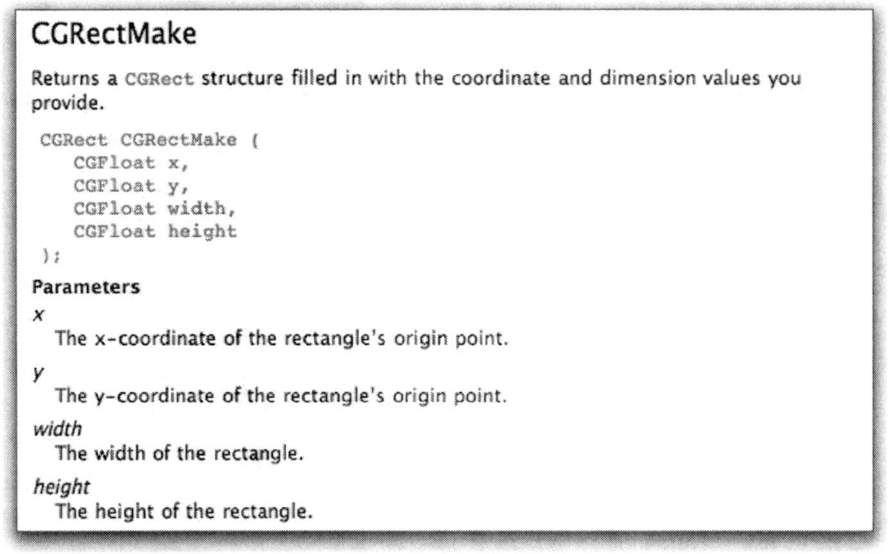

CGRectMake

Returns a `CGRect` structure filled in with the coordinate and dimension values you provide.

```
CGRect CGRectMake (
    CGFloat x,
    CGFloat y,
    CGFloat width,
    CGFloat height
);
```

Parameters

x
  The x-coordinate of the rectangle's origin point.

y
  The y-coordinate of the rectangle's origin point.

width
  The width of the rectangle.

height
  The height of the rectangle.

Figure 7-6. Official description of the CGRectMake() function

Aside from the fact that this definition occurs in a section referred to as "functions," the dead giveaway that this is a C function is the set of parentheses following the function name. Notice that the docs show the equivalent of a header declaration of the function, not the code that runs inside the function (no curly braces or `return` statement). All I have to do to obtain a `CGRect` value is call this function and supply four `CGFloat` values in the designated sequence.

What's a CGFloat?

In Figure 7-6, the `CGFloat` types are not linked to any further information. A scan through Apple-supplied sample code indicates that values you are to apply to these arguments (especially within the range of values you are likely to specify for a rectangle) are simple floating-point numbers (which can be whole numbers). A little digging through Apple's online developer docs turns up information that a `CGFloat` offers more precision (similar to a double), which can only help argument values remain true to their intended values, rather than suffering from floating-point errors. `CGfloats` are common argument value types for functions in the CoreGraphics framework.

It has been a bit of a journey, but the next time I'll know to go straight to the CGMakeRect() function definition in the docs for a reminder of the arguments and their order. For now, however, I can begin writing the code to create the UILabel. Thumbing through other parts of the UILabel Class Reference document, I found some methods that let me set the text of the label and the alignment of that text within the label. The finished runMyCode: method is given in Example 7-1. Add it to your copy of Workbench and try it out.

Example 7-1. A UILabel creator in Workbench

```
- (IBAction)runMyCode:(id)sender {
    // Create rect for label
    CGRect labelRect = CGRectMake(60, 240, 200, 24);

    // Generate label with rect specifications
    UILabel *customLabel = [[UILabel alloc] initWithFrame:labelRect];

    // Customize label text and alignment within the label
    [customLabel setText:@"A human-made label!"];
    [customLabel setTextAlignment:UITextAlignmentCenter];

    // Add the label as a subview to this controller's view
    [[self view] addSubview:customLabel];

    // Superview has retained label, so we're ready to release
    [customLabel release];
}
```

When I build and run Workbench, then click on the button, the screen gains the new label, as shown in Figure 7-7.

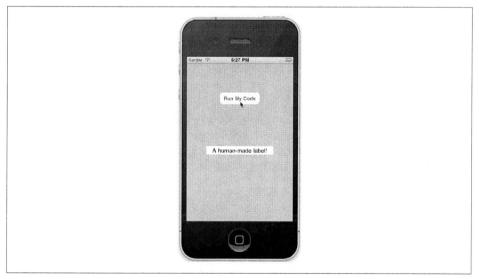

Figure 7-7. A click of the button adds the label

Of course, there is one thing about this example that needs attention if we want to implement it in a real-world app. Each time a user clicks the button, a new label is created and added to the view. You can't see the multiple views, because they're right atop each other, but as you click the button, the label views accumulate. The method needs to add an identifier (called a tag) to the label, test for the existence of such a tagged subview, and either remove it from the superview before creating another or simply bypass the creation of an additional label. Example 7-2 shows the modifications (in bold) to Example 7-1 that implement this change.

Example 7-2. A smarter UILabel creator for Workbench

```
- (IBAction)runMyCode:(id)sender {
    // Establish an identifying tag number for a label
    int labelTag = 42;

    // Create new label only if it hasn't been created earlier
    if ([self.view viewWithTag:labelTag] == nil) {

        // Create rect for label
        CGRect labelRect = CGRectMake(60, 240, 200, 24);

        // Generate label with rect specifications
        UILabel *customLabel = [[UILabel alloc] initWithFrame:labelRect];

        // Customize label text and alignment within the label
        [customLabel setText:@"A human-made label!"];
        [customLabel setTextAlignment:UITextAlignmentCenter];

        // Assign tag identifier to label
        customLabel.tag = labelTag;

        // Add the label as a subview to this controller's view
        [[self view] addSubview:customLabel];

        // Superview has retained label, so we're ready to release
        [customLabel release];
    }
}
```

The point of this demonstration is to show you how you will most likely work with C functions while developing iOS apps. Simply be on the lookout for the possibility of those types (especially when dealing with graphics tasks) and switch your brain into C mode temporarily while handling the requirement.

C Structures

Earlier in this chapter, you had a peek at a C structure, which is a collection of named values. Because of the powers of numerous Objective-C and Cocoa Touch data collections (such as NSArray, NSDictionary, and NSSet classes), it's unlikely you will find yourself needing to compose structures in your code. But you do need to understand how to use the ones that Cocoa Touch uses in some of its own classes. In the course of this discussion, you will see syntax that is reminiscent of functionless JavaScript objects, but structures are not objects in the true sense.

To get a sense of how to use a structure (also known as a *C struct*), look at the following triumvirate of related CoreGraphics framework `structs` that Cocoa Touch uses for geometric measurements:

```
struct CGPoint {
    CGFloat x;
    CGFloat y;
};
typedef struct CGPoint CGPoint;

struct CGSize {
    CGFloat width;
    CGFloat height;
};
typedef struct CGSize CGSize;

struct CGRect {
    CGPoint origin;
    CGSize size;
};
typedef struct CGRect CGRect;
```

If you search the SDK documentation for any of these data types, you'll see corresponding `struct` definitions, each of which reveals important information about the names of the values you will be getting or setting. The `typedef` statement at the end of each `struct` turns the `struct` into a data type of the same name as the `struct`. Therefore, Cocoa Touch provides the `CGPoint`, `CGSize`, and `CGRect` data types, which you can use to assign as data types to variables holding compatible values. The `CGPoint` and `CGSize` `structs` each have named two members that are `CGFloat` types, while the `CGRect`'s members are one each of the `CGPoint` and `CGSize` types.

A `CGPoint` represents a point within a coordinate space. Just as you determine CSS coordinates in an *x,y* coordinate space, a `CGPoint` works the same way (although some coordinate systems use the top-left corner as 0,0, while others use the bottom-left corner as 0,0—but that's irrelevant to this discussion).

You have three ways to create a `CGPoint` value, each of which requires assignment of two component values for the `CGPoint`'s members. The long way is to declare a variable of the `CGPoint` type and assign each value by name:

```
CGPoint myPoint;
myPoint.x = 20;
myPoint.y = 40;
```

Notice the dot syntax notation to reference the member of the value. It's just like JavaScript property notation. And the syntax you use to read the value of a member is as you'd expect:

```
double somePointXCoord = myPoint.x;
double somePointYCoord = myPoint.y;
```

The short but not particularly readable way to assign values is to list the values in a comma-separated list inside curly braces:

```
CGPoint myPoint = {20, 40};
```

The third way is to use the convenience functions that the CoreGraphics framework provides for creating CGPoint, CGSize, and CGRect values:

```
CGPoint myPoint = CGPointMake(20, 40);
```

In the case of the CGRect struct, the values are other structs. It's not a problem for assigning values via the CGRectMake() function:

```
CGRect myRect = CGRectMake(20, 40, 300, 24);
```

In fact, one of the advantages of using the creation function is that you can insert the function in place of a value, such as an argument for a method. For example, the UIView class has an initialization method that requires a CGRect value as an argument. Feel free to substitute the creation method where the argument value goes:

```
UIView *myView = [[UIView alloc] initWithFrame:CGRectMake(10, 10, 200, 100)];
```

Reading individual values from an existing CGRect value requires the exercise of dot syntax through multiple levels. For example, a CGRect's origin value is a CGPoint, whose members are x and y. To read the y value, the reference would be:

```
double originY = myRect.origin.y;
```

You can modify individual values of an existing CGRect by assigning new values to the specific member:

```
myRect.size.width = 320;
```

The other common structure you will encounter is NSRange, defined as follows:

```
typedef struct _NSRange {
    NSUInteger location;
    NSUInteger length;
} NSRange;
```

Ranges are commonly used to specify the offset and length (both integers) of a substring within a larger string, or any subgroup. For example, a method of the NSMutable String class performs string replacement within a specified range of the string:

```
- (NSUInteger)replaceOccurrencesOfString:(NSString *)target
                              withString:(NSString *)replacement
                                 options:(NSStringCompareOptions)opts
                                   range:(NSRange)searchRange {...}
```

To specify that the search range should be the entire string, pass an NSRange value encompassing the entire message receiver, use the following:

```
int replacementCount = [myString replaceOccurrencesOfString:targetString
                        withString:replacementString
                        options:NSCaseInsensitiveSearch
                        range:NSMakeRange(0, [myString count])];
```

In Chapter 8, you will see how Cocoa Touch provides a robust object, NSDictionary, which allows you to create a data-intensive object with values and labels (called keys). In the meantime, you should now be able to interpret iOS SDK documentation when it describes values as C structures.

C Arrays

The C language offers arrays that syntactically resemble JavaScript arrays. Except for the occasional need to pass a C array of values to CoreGraphics framework methods, you won't use C arrays much for your app data because Cocoa Touch provides a far more robust version in the NSArray class (described in Chapter 8). I include C arrays here to make sure you understand the syntax you will see from time to time while perusing the iOS SDK documentation, or if you need to create a small array of values for graphics method arguments.

The data typing situation in creating a new array may seem odd at first, because the data type you declare is the data type of the elements of the array—which means that all elements of a C array must be of the same type. For example, if you wanted to generate an array that is to hold up to 10 integers, the declaration would be:

```
int myArray [10];
```

From there you can assign values by referencing spots in the array through array indices (zero-based), similar to the way you do it in JavaScript:

```
myArray[0] = 10;
myArray[1] = 20;
...
myArray[9] = 100;
```

Although JavaScript would merrily let you add more items to the array by continuing to use higher and higher index numbers, a C array maxes out at the number of elements specified in its declaration. You are free to iterate through arrays in for loops, but obtaining the number of elements in a C array for the conditional expression in a for construction takes a little extra work (there is no simple equivalent to the JavaScript length property of a C array). The C sizeof operator returns the number of bytes occupied by the operand. If you divide the total bytes of an array by the bytes of one element, you have calculated the array length. Other than that issue, looping through an array and using the loop counting variable as an array index value inside the square brackets should look familiar to you:

```
int arrayLength = sizeof(myArray)/sizeof(myArray[0]);
for (int i = 0; i < arrayLength; i++) {
    // do something with myArray[i]
}
```

Multidimensional arrays are also allowed, using two sets of brackets. The following statement initializes an array that has 10 elements, each of which can hold up to 100 integer elements:

```
int myMultiArray [10] [100];
```

You will occasionally see array variables (including parameter variables) defined as type char. Each member of the array stores one text character value—more precisely, the integer ASCII value. In your coding, however, you'll be using NSString types for your text.

Enumerated Types

In your tour of Cocoa Touch frameworks, you will encounter many collections of values known as *enumerated types*. Defined in C with the enum statement, the construction is a collection of convenient names representing integer values. It's easier to show you than explain it.

You are probably familiar with the Maps app, which lets you select from three different map styles: standard, satellite, and hybrid. If you add a map view to your app, your code can change the style by sending the setMapType: message to an instance of MKMapView. Acceptable values are integers: 0, 1, and 2 to denote standard, satellite, and hybrid, respectively. To help make your code more readable, these values have been assigned to names that act as constants for their designated data type (i.e., they can't be used in other places). Because the values are all related, they are grouped into an enumerated list and assigned a type definition. The three map style values are defined in the mapping framework as follows:

```
enum {
    MKMapTypeStandard,
    MKMapTypeSatellite,
    MKMapTypeHybrid
};
typedef NSUInteger MKMapType;
```

By default, an enum type assigns integer values (beginning with 0) to the constant names in the group. It is also possible to assign explicit numbers to each constant name or assign a different starting point for the items by assigning a nonzero value to one item (in which case, subsequent items have incremental integer values). For your coding, you don't concern yourself with the integer values, but with the constant names associated with the data type. Therefore, to change an existing MKMapView object to satellite view, the message will be as follows:

```
[myMapView setMapType:MKMapTypeSatellite];
```

You will see these enumerated lists fairly frequently in the SDK documentation, along with a brief (often too brief) description of what each constant represents.

Operators

Your knowledge of JavaScript operators sets you up perfectly for C/Objective-C operators. A few JavaScript operators don't apply (`function()`, `typeof`, `void`, and `delete`), but the rest are in play and with the same general precedence rules.

You do need to be cautious when applying your knowledge of JavaScript comparison operators to Objective-C. JavaScript attempts to find common ground in comparing string and numeric values. For example, consider the following JavaScript function:

```
function comparisonTest() {
    fiveString = "5";
    fiveNumber = 5;
    return fiveString == fiveNumber;
}
```

Even though the `==` equality comparison operator compares a number against a string, JavaScript returns `true` for this function. Only by substituting the strictly equals operator (`===`) would the value types be taken into account (in which case the function returns `false`). In Objective-C, such disparate value types would never be considered to be equal. But numeric types are not as strict, so the integer 5 and the float 5.00, for example, are considered equal.

The C language adds typecasting as an operation to take into account when determining how an expression evaluates. Typecasting (e.g., converting a float to an integer by preceding the integer's value with (`float`)) has a high precedence, ahead of common arithmetic operators. This allows a value to be cast into the desired type before math operations apply to the value.

Program Flow Constructions

When it comes to program flow controls, your JavaScript experience gets you almost all of the way there. The following C/Objective-C prototypes should all look familiar to you (showing the multiple-line statement version with curly braces and optional items in brackets):

```
if (conditionExpression) {
    statementsIfTrue
}

if (conditionExpression) {
    statementsIfTrue
} else {
    statementsIfFalse
}

result = (conditionExpression) ? expression1 : expression2;

while (conditionExpression) {
    statementsIfTrue
```

```
    }

do {
    statements
} while (conditionExpression)

for (initializationExpression; conditionExpression; updateExpression) {
    statements
}

switch (expression) {
    case labelN:
        statements
        [break;]
    ...
    [default:
        statements]
}
```

Because the comparison operators you use in C/Objective-C are the same ones you know from JavaScript, you already know what to do with all of the *conditionExpres sion* placeholders. The only construction you need to watch carefully is the for repeat loop. Be sure that the counter variable you initialize in the *initializationExpression* has a data type associated with it. You can specify the data type in a separate statement above the for loop or in the expression itself:

```
int i;
for (i = 0; i < maxValue; i++) {...}

for (int j = 0; j < maxValue; j++) {...}
```

Bear in mind the discussion earlier in this chapter about scope with regard to the loop counting variable. If you need the variable value after the loop completes, be sure to declare the variable before the loop.

You can use a for-in construction, but only with Cocoa Touch objects that implement a special protocol (called NSFastEnumeration). The NSArray, NSDictionary, and NSSet classes automatically support the protocol, which means that all instances you create do as well.

The one JavaScript flow control structure you don't have directly in C/Objective-C is try-catch for handling exceptions. These are handled as compiler directives (@try and @catch), but Apple strongly recommends using other approaches to handling errors. Search the Xcode documentation for "error handling" when you're ready to learn more.

Boolean Values

The single binary digit representing values 1 and 0 has had a long history of also representing the two states of a Boolean value. For the sake of code readability, many languages equate the constants true and false to those numeric values, respectively. That's how JavaScript does it, and so does current C language practice.

But in the Objective-C world of the iOS SDK, you will more commonly use the constants YES and NO to represent Boolean values. In Chapter 5 you saw how a Boolean value was passed as an argument to the method that displayed a second view. In that case, the method required a Boolean value to signify whether the transition should be animated:

```
[self presentModalViewController:secondViewController animated:YES];
```

If you define a method that returns a Boolean value, the return type is specified as (BOOL). You can extract the BOOL value from an NSString or NSNumber object via the boolValue method of those classes. Although you can get away with continuing to use true and false or 1 and 0, it's a good idea to make your code as Objective-C-compliant as possible. Finally, if you wish to view a Boolean value in a format string (as in NSLog()), use the %d format specifier, which will display the integers 1 or 0, or create a conditional operator statement that returns more readable words, as in the following:

```
NSLog(@"flagValue = %@", (flagValue ? @"YES" : @"NO"));
```

Math Object Equivalents in C

The core JavaScript language has a static Math object, which features a number of methods and properties that act as constants. For example, if you want to determine the next lesser integer for a floating-point value, use the floor() method of the static Math object, as follows:

```
var floorValue = Math.floor(myValue);
```

The C language doesn't have a dedicated object of that type. Instead, it implements a series of functions, which you can call directly in your statements. For example:

```
double floorValue = floor(myValue);
```

Table 7-3 lists the JavaScript Math object functions and the corresponding C functions. The standard C language offers far more variations of these functions (in the *math.h* and *stdlib.h* libraries automatically incorporated into every iOS app), offering differing levels of precision. For Table 7-3, I have chosen the versions that return values of the double data type. Also pay special attention to the required data type of values passed as arguments to the C functions.

Table 7-3. Math functions comparisons

JavaScript	Description	C/Objective-C
Math.abs(x)	Absolute value	double fabs(double x);
Math.acos(x)	Arc cosine	double acos(double x);
Math.asin(x)	Arc sine	double asin(double x);
Math.atan(x)	Arc tangent	double atan(double x);
Math.atan2(x, y)	Angle of polar coordinates	double atan2(double y, double x);

JavaScript	Description	C/Objective-C
`Math.ceil(x)`	Next greater integer	`double ceil(double x);`
`Math.cos(x)`	Cosine	`double cos(double x);`
`Math.exp(x)`	Euler's constant to xth power	`double exp(double x);`
`Math.floor(x)`	Next lesser integer	`double floor(double x);`
`Math.log(x)`	Natural log	`double log(double x);`
`Math.max(x, y)`	Greater of x or y	`double fmax (double x, double y);`
`Math.min(x, y)`	Lesser of x or y	`double fmin (double x, double y);`
`Math.pow(x, power)`	X to power of y	`double pow (double x, double power);`
`Math.random()`	Random number	`int arc4random();`
`Math.round(x)`	Round to nearest integer	`double round(double x);`
`Math.sin(x)`	Sine	`double sin(double x);`
`Math.sqrt(x)`	Square root	`double sqrt(double x);`
`Math.tan(x)`	Tangent	`double tan(double x);`

The C language offers a few choices for random number generation. For Table 7-3, I chose the `arc4random()` function. This more modern variant of the traditional `rand()` function is automatically seeded so that it does not reproduce the same sequence of random numbers each time an app launches. The function returns a signed integer between –2,147,483,648 and +2,147,483,648. If you want a random integer between zero and some positive integer, use the modulus operator (%). For example, the following produces random positive integers between 0 and 9 (inclusive):

```
int oneRandomInt = arc4random() % 10;
```

Or, to obtain a positive random integer across the entire range of values, use the following variant:

```
int oneRandomInt = (arc4random() % ((unsigned)RAND_MAX + 1));
```

In place of the JavaScript `Math` object's constant values, the C language offers a series of macros that are created in the *math.h* library as `#defines`. Table 7-4 lists the JavaScript and C versions of these constants.

Table 7-4. Math constants comparisons

JavaScript	Description	C/Objective-C
`Math.E`	Euler's constant	`M_E`
`Math.LN2`	Natural log of 2	`M_LN2`
`Math.LN10`	Natural log of 10	`M_LN10`
`Math.LOG2E`	Log base-2 of E	`M_LOG2E`
`Math.LOG10E`	Log base-10 of E	`M_LOG10E`
`Math.PI`	π	`M_PI`

JavaScript	Description	C/Objective-C
Math.SQRT1_2	Square root of 0.5	M_SQRT1_2
Math.SQRT2	Square root of 2	M_SQRT2

To demonstrate the differences in the two languages, the following versions show the calculation of the area of a circle whose radius is in the variable `circleRadius`:

```
// JavaScript
var circleArea = Math.pow(circleRadius,2) * Math.PI;
```

```
// C/Objective-C
double circleArea = pow(circleRadius, 2) * M_PI;
```

If you are curious about additional math function variations available in the C language, enter any of the functions from Table 7-3 into an edit window in Xcode. Then, secondary-click the word. Look in the context menu for the Jump to Definition choice. A window appears with the header file in which the term is defined. Scroll around the header file to explore other options.

Inserting Comments

Your JavaScript experience equips you with everything you need to know about adding comments to an iOS SDK source code file. Inline comments begin with two forward slashes (//). These can appear at the beginning of a line or following the end of a statement line.

Comment blocks are contained by the /* and */ delimiter sequence. Comment blocks may be any number of lines. See the tops of any class file generated by Xcode for examples.

One significant advantage to a compiled language is that you can type comments into your source code until your fingers bleed, and they have no bearing on the size of your application binary. Additionally, unlike comments added to client-side JavaScript, your app source code comments will not be visible to consumers of your app.

Recap

As you can see, except for the data typing business and pointers, JavaScript isn't too far distant from the C language pieces you will likely encounter while developing iOS apps. There is certainly far more to the C language not covered here because the combination of Objective-C and Cocoa Touch frameworks provide more robust and convenient alternatives. That's where the next chapter picks up the story.

CHAPTER 8

Objective-C/Cocoa Touch Fundamentals

Cocoa Touch is an extremely rich set of frameworks that define everything from handling strings to creating scrollable tables and sophisticated view navigation systems. This chapter focuses on the more mundane—but vitally important—parts of Cocoa Touch. You will use a variety of classes to manage temporary data in your app and pass it around from place to place. You will see some similarities between the Cocoa Touch ways of handling things and what you know from JavaScript. By the end of this chapter, I don't expect you to have fully mastered all aspects of strings or data collections. But you will have examples that you can use as templates for your deployment of these items in your code until you are comfortable enough with them to rattle them off on your own. Before we get to those details, however, it's time to get a better sense of how classes work and how to start thinking about your app's requirements in terms of class structure.

More About Classes

In Chapter 4 and Chapter 5 you had a chance to see how important classes are to iOS programming (and most object-oriented programming). You will use classes in three basic ways within your code:

1. Creating objects (instances of classes) for temporary processing
2. Subclassing framework classes
3. Defining your own custom classes

Each deployment style has its own requirements.

Temporary Objects

It is very common to use several Objective-C statements to assemble objects that eventually get passed as arguments to methods. You saw this in Chapter 6, where it took a couple of statements to generate an NSURLRequest object needed to eventually instantiate an NSURLConnection object:

```
// Create NSURL from a string constant
NSURL *theUrl = [NSURL URLWithString:@"http://dannyg.com/dl/demo.plist"];

// Use NSURL to create NSURLRequest
NSURLRequest *theRequest = [NSURLRequest requestWithURL:theUrl];

// Use NSURLRequest as first argument to initialize NSURLConnection
NSURLConnection *myConnection = [[NSURLConnection alloc]
                             initWithRequest:theRequest
                                    delegate:self
                             startImmediately:YES];
```

Many of the Cocoa Touch framework classes offer two ways to create instances: via the alloc and init combination or via class methods. The first two statements in the example above utilize class methods of their respective object classes (NSURL and NSURL Request) to create the object instances.

You can discover what's available in the way of creation and initialization methods by looking up the reference document for the class you're interested in using. Every Cocoa Touch class has a class reference document in the SDK documentation. Near the top of the document (after some introductory material whose length varies widely) comes a summary of all methods you can use for the class. At the top of that list are creation and initialization methods available for that class. Figure 8-1 shows the combined object creation and initialization choices for the NSURL class.

Figure 8-1. NSURL class object creation methods from NSURL Class Reference

You will usually find one or more instance methods (preceded by -) for the class. Instance initializer methods must be used in concert with the `alloc` method, which means that you are also responsible for releasing the object to prevent a memory leak. In contrast, class methods (preceded by +) instantiate autoreleased objects.

Therefore, to create an instance of an `NSURL` object, you can use either of the following instantiation methods:

```
// Autoreleased version
NSURL *theUrl = [NSURL URLWithString:@"http://dannyg.com/dl/demo.plist"];

// Managed Memory version
NSURL *theUrl = [[NSURL alloc] initWithString:@"http://dannyg.com/dl/demo.plist"];
```

Although functionally identical, for the second version you also have to include a `[theUrl release]` message in the code after the value has been assigned as an argument to another object's instantiation method.

 The Apple documents are not consistent in their organization. Some class descriptions offer separate listings for creation (via class methods) and initialization (via instance methods to be used with `alloc`), while documents for other classes combine the two groups. Let the method symbols (- or +) be your guide.

Subclassing Framework Classes

You will likely begin your iOS SDK journey by focusing on writing subclasses for view controller classes, where your code will manage the operation of the user interface and data (the View and Model parts of MVC). Creating a subclass means creating a new pair of class files named for the class you create. The new class must inherit from another existing class.

When you use Xcode to create a new class file, you are presented with a limited range of choices in the New File dialog window. Figure 8-2 shows the choices for creating a subclass of nonview controller classes. The default choice is to inherit `NSObject`, but you can also have Xcode preconfigure subclasses that inherit `UITableViewCell` (for a class that will lay out elements of a customized table cell) or `UIView` (a generic rectangular space that typically acts as a container for additional user interface control subviews).

In contrast, Figure 8-3 demonstrates the path you take to create a view controller subclass. Your choices are to inherit the generic `UIViewController` or the substantial `UITableViewController` class. In addition to preconfiguring the header file to name the desired superclass, Xcode will also populate the class files with many delegate and data source (for `UITableViewController`) methods it anticipates you will want to code (or may be required to code).

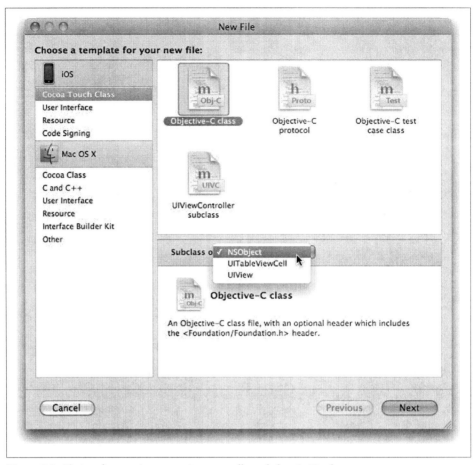

Figure 8-2. Choices for creating a nonview controller subclass in Xcode

Regardless of the route you follow to create a new subclass, the header file contains the class inheritance chain in the `@interface` compiler directive in the following format:

```
@interface SubclassName : SuperclassName { ... }
```

Remember that the subclass inherits not only the methods of the superclass, but also of superclasses further up the inheritance chain, if any. Use the SDK class reference documents to see the inheritance chain of any framework class—sometimes the method you wish a class had is already supported, but is "disguised" by being implemented in a superclass and therefore does not appear in the class reference you're reading.

Defining Your Own Custom Subclasses

In Chapter 4, you followed along with the creation of two custom classes, `DGCar` and `DGCarAlternate`, both of which inherited `NSObject`. Because these two classes have

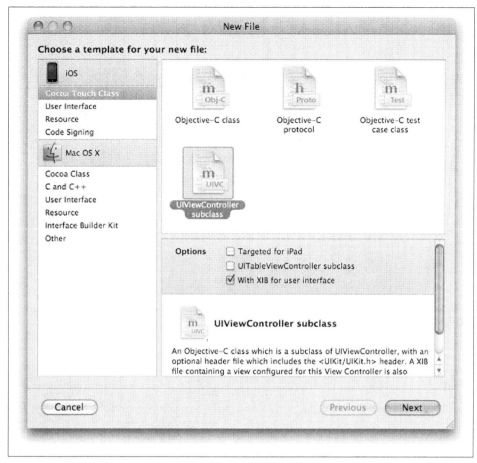

Figure 8-3. Choices for creating a view controller subclass in Xcode

similar characteristics—in fact, they both feature the same set of instance variables and implemented a method that returns data in the identical format—it was wasteful to duplicate functionality in the two class definitions. The proper way to handle the job is to make `DGCarAlternate` a subclass of `DGCar`. `DGCarAlternate` gets everything that `DGCar` has, plus whatever is unique to `DGCarAlternate`.

As a reminder, Example 8-1 shows the header files for both classes as defined in Chapter 4.

Example 8-1. Original interfaces for DGCar and DGCarAlternate classes from Chapter 4

```
#import <Foundation/Foundation.h>


@interface DGCar : NSObject {
```

```
    NSString *make;
    NSString *model;
    NSString *year;

}

- (DGCar *)initWithCarMake:(NSString *)inputMake
                     model:(NSString *)inputModel
                      year:(NSString *)inputYear;
- (NSString *)getFormattedListing;

@end

#import <Foundation/Foundation.h>


@interface DGCarAlternate : NSObject {

    NSString *make;
    NSString *model;
    NSString *year;

}

// Getters and Setters
- (NSString *)make;
- (void)setMake:(NSString *)newMake;
- (NSString *)model;
- (void)setModel:(NSString *)newModel;
- (NSString *)year;
- (void)setYear:(NSString *)newYear;

- (NSString *)getFormattedListing;

@end
```

Making DGCarAlternate into a subclass of DGCar requires two minor changes and some excisions. The important point to notice is that no changes whatsoever are made to the superclass, DGCar. That's what subclassing is all about—creating a class that leverages off an existing class and limiting the subclass code to only those things that differentiate it from the superclass or enhance what's in the superclass. Example 8-2 shows the modified *DGCarAlternate.h* header file (changes in bold).

Example 8-2. DGCarAlternate.h defined as a subclass of DGCar

```
#import "DGCar.h"

@interface DGCarAlternate : DGCar {

}

- (NSString *)make;
- (void)setMake:(NSString *)newMake;
```

```
- (NSString *)model;
- (void)setModel:(NSString *)newModel;

- (NSString *)year;
- (void)setYear:(NSString *)newYear;

@end
```

Let's now look at how these two classes might be used in the Workbench to show that they do what's expected of them. Example 8-3 shows the upper portion of the *WorkbenchViewController.m* file.

Example 8-3. Modified WorkbenchViewController.m employing the two custom classes

```
#import "WorkbenchViewController.h"
#import "DGCarAlternate.h"


@implementation WorkbenchViewController


- (IBAction)runMyCode:(id)sender {

    DGCar *myCar1 = [[DGCar alloc] initWithCarMake:@"Chevrolet"
                                             model:@"Malibu"
                                              year:@"2007"];
    DGCarAlternate *myCar2 = [[DGCarAlternate alloc] init];

    [myCar2 setMake:@"Ford"];
    [myCar2 setModel:@"Taurus"];
    [myCar2 setYear:@"2010"];

    NSLog(@"I used to drive a:%@", [myCar1 getFormattedListing]);
    NSLog(@"I now drive a:%@", [myCar2 getFormattedListing]);

    [myCar1 release];
    [myCar2 release];…

}
```

The implementation begins by importing the *DGCarAlternate.h* header file. Because that header imports *DGCar.h*, Workbench automatically gains access to both classes. The runMyCode: method creates two custom class instances, one of each class. The first is a DGCar class, which must be instantiated via its custom initialization method to feed its instance variables with values. The DGCarAlternate class is not encumbered by that requirement, but you could apply that approach if you wanted to, because its superclass supports it. Instead, Example 8-3 initializes the DGCarAlternate object through the standard init method, which it actually inherits from the NSObject class at the top of the inheritance chain. The myCar2 object can also use the setter methods of the DGCarAlternate class, but no instance of the DGCar superclass may do so.

Once the ivars for the two instances are set, the getFormattedListing message may be sent to both objects to yield the result as defined in the DGCar class. And finally, because both instances had their memory slots created by the alloc method, the objects must be explicitly released once they are no longer needed.

I should also point out that if you want DGCarAlternate to return a slightly different version of the formatted listing for instances of that class, you are free to *override* the getFormattedListing method just for DGCarAlternate instances. The message to the instance will be captured by that object and not passed up the inheritance chain.

The more you get to see how Cocoa Touch uses subclassing for its own class definitions, the more you'll see how subclassing is most often used to create more specific versions of a well-defined, tested, and generic class. For instance, the Foundation framework defines the NSArray class for creating robust array objects. But there is also a more specific variation, called NSMutableArray, which allows elements to be added or deleted from a previously established array. An NSMutableArray has all the powers of NSArray, plus extra methods that let you change the contents of an array on the fly.

Adding to a Class Without Subclassing—Categories

Objective-C 2.0 in the iOS SDK provides a mechanism called *categories*, which allows you to add methods (but not instance variables) to an existing class without creating a subclass of that existing class. This feature will remind you of using the JavaScript prototype property of an object to extend that object's capabilities so that all instances of that object gain the new capabilities. In fact, you can use categories in Objective-C to add customized methods to foundation classes if you like, including NSString. Then all NSString instances will have the customized methods available to them. Using a category, rather than subclassing, is the preferred approach to extend the functionality of a Cocoa Touch framework with new (i.e., not overridden) methods.

Defining a category is fairly easy, but as of version 3.2.5 of Xcode, the IDE doesn't provide a template for the necessary header and implementation files (or combination file). Instead, you can generate a class that inherits from NSObject and manually edit the code as needed. To see how to create and use categories, you'll create a category for the DGCar class that adds a new method to provide a different type of output of instance variable values in three lines with labels.

Begin by creating a new class file for the Workbench project. Select a plain Objective-C class that inherits NSObject. Apple recommends following a naming convention for categories that places the name of the class being extended first, followed by a plus sign and some identifying name for the category. Unlike class names, the category name is primarily intended to help you know what the category does when you come back to the code six months from now. I named the files *DGCar+ThreeLineOutput*. Example 8-4 shows the modifications you should make to the header file. Items to be deleted are in strikethrough, while additions are in bold.

Example 8-4. Converting an Xcode template class file to a category header file

```
#import <Foundation/Foundation.h>
#import "DGCar.h"


@interface DGCar-ThreeLineOutput : NSObject {

}

@interface DGCar (ThreeLineOutput)

- (NSString *)threeLineDisplay;


@end
```

You must import the header of the class you are enhancing. Next, the @interface section is very different from that of a class file; you name the class being enhanced first, followed by an arbitrary name for the category (which you will repeat in the implementation file in a moment) in parentheses. There is no implied or required link between the name of the category you put in parentheses and the category's filename. Notice that there are no curly braces in the category definition. This is because you cannot add to the original class's instance variables. Categories are for adding methods only. For this category, you're adding a single method, which you define just as you would for a method in any class header file.

Switching to the implementation file, Example 8-5 shows how to modify the Xcode template file for use in a category.

Example 8-5. Converting an Xcode template class file to a category implementation file

```
#import "DGCar+ThreeLineOutput.h"


@implementation DGCar-ThreeLineOutput DGCar (ThreeLineOutput)

- (NSString *)threeLineDisplay {
    NSString *result = [NSString stringWithFormat:@"\nYear:%@\nMake:%@\nModel:%@",
                        year, make, model];
    return result;
}

@end
```

Most of the changes to the implementation file are additions. Notice that the sequence following the @implementation directive is the same as that following the @interface directive in the header file. You also add the new method definition here, which accumulates the three instance variables in a different output format, placing each name/value pair on its own line (as in JavaScript strings, \n is an escape sequence signifying a new line character). It's important to understand that code in the category has full access to instance variables and other methods of the original class, even though they're nowhere to be found in the category code.

You can now invoke the new method on any object that is an instance of `DGCar` or one of its subclasses (`DGCarAlternate`). Add the following two statements to the `runMy Code:` method of *WorkbenchViewController.m*, after the previous `NSLog` statements:

```
NSLog(@"myCar1 Details:%@", [myCar1 threeLineDisplay]);
NSLog(@"myCar2 Details:%@", [myCar2 threeLineDisplay]);
```

When you build the project, you see two compiler warnings that the two instances may not recognize the `threeLineDisplay` method. Although the methods will work fine, you should always try to eliminate compiler warnings. The solution here is to import the category header file (*DGCar+ThreeLineOutput.h*) into the *Workbench-ViewController.m* file so the compiler is aware of the definitions in the category.

Real Classes in Real Action

You can learn a lot—and I mean *a lot*—by examining the sample apps that come with the iOS SDK. Many of the samples focus on illustrating a particular aspect of the SDK or frameworks, which means they may not be sterling examples of complete apps. But some samples give you a sense of the way you should start breaking your app idea into classes and groups of classes—a very important skill to develop in an object-oriented programming world. In Chapter 2, you loaded TheElements project into Xcode. Let's take a closer look at the source file structure for that app to see how the author divided the work among class files. I don't expect you to understand all of the inner workings of the app at this point. The goal here is to give you a preview of what lies in store for you when it comes time to develop a real app rather than merely a simple demo app.

TheElements Overview

As sample apps go, TheElements is relatively complex. It demonstrates a number of user interface features and view classes, such as the tab bar interface (with buttons along the bottom of the screen that change modes) and tables. Assuming you set the Base SDK to Latest iOS as shown in Chapter 2, build and run the app in the simulator now to get more acquainted with the app's structure from a user's perspective (Figure 8-4).

The app opens to one of four table views. As you tap on different buttons in the bottom tab bar, a different table view appears with a unique sorting order. If you tap on an element, you see a detail view, which shows only the atomic number, name, and symbol. But tap on that block, and the block animatedly flips to reveal more details about the chosen element. The Back button from either detail view returns you to the table view.

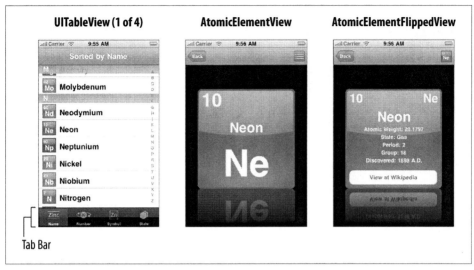

Tab Bar

Figure 8-4. TheElements app user interface

Deploying for Older iOS Versions

In Chapter 2, you saw how to set a project's target to use the most recent iOS SDK as the Base SDK for building the app. Without additional settings, this means the app will run only on the simulator (or on an actual device when you apply the requisite provisioning profile) that runs the latest iOS version supported by your SDK. If you wish to deploy to a wider audience of users who have not upgraded to the latest iOS version (such as users of the first-generation iPhone), you must set the target's deployment platform separately from the Base SDK. In other words, the Base SDK remains set at, say, 4.2, but your deployment target can be for earlier versions.

To change the deployment platform, choose Project→Edit Active Target to display the project's Target Info window. Click the Build tab and enter **deployment target** into the Search box. One of the results is named iOS Deployment Target. Click in the righthand column to view your choices, as shown in Figure 8-5.

If you choose iOS 3.0 as shown, Xcode will still use the latest Base SDK, but the app will be compiled to run on devices using iOS 3.0 or later. If your code uses APIs that are new with iOS 4 or later, you will receive compiler errors accordingly.

Tables, of course, are the central user interface elements of many iOS apps. The `UITableView` class and two supporting protocols (UITableViewDelegate and `UITableViewDataSource`) greatly simplify the display of scrollable lists and handling what happens when a user taps on one of the items. A table's *data source* is essentially an array of objects (from the Model part of MVC) whose properties furnish details for the individual cells of the scrollable table. As the user scrolls through the table, the table view iterates over the data source to generate visible cells. The array of data may originate

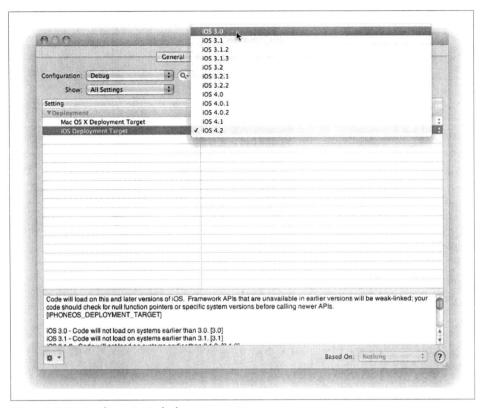

Figure 8-5. Setting the project's deployment target

from a fixed file delivered with the app, a user-expandable file stored on the device (if the app allows users to add data), and even data retrieved from the network—or combinations of all three.

As the table assembles its content for display, the UITableView class sends many messages (usually to a view controller) to find out how much data there is (how many cells will be in the table), what the cell heights are, and what the cells look like. Ever mindful of memory consumption, the UITableView class keeps the number of "live" table cells down to only the number currently visible on the screen. As the user flicks the table to scroll, another flood of messages assembles new cells to replace ones no longer visible, pulling data from the data source array for each cell—it's quite an amazing mechanism. Then, when a user taps on a cell (or a control in the cell), the UITableView sends messages to its delegate, signifying which row of the table has been tapped so your code can navigate to either another table or a detail view that expands on the summary shown in the cell.

One other point about TheElements before getting into the file structure: originally created when Xcode was still quite young, the designers created user interfaces—the views—in code, rather than in Interface Builder. This is always an option for a developer. It's not uncommon, of course, to take a hybrid approach in which developers build parts of the interface in Interface Builder and then customize or enhance it through code.

TheElements Class File Structure

Now take a look at the class file structure of the project in Figure 8-6. One feature you'll notice immediately is that the author divides the classes into groups. Remember that group folders do not represent Finder folders, but rather a separate organization scheme within Xcode to help you organize files that live elsewhere in your project's folder.

The designer groups classes into four subgroups:

- Single Element View
- TableView Representations
- Data Model
- Application Support

We'll dissect the files that comprise each group.

Single Element View classes

The single element views represent the detail view that shows information about a single element. That group is further subdivided into two groups:

- View Controllers
- User Interface Elements

One view controller class (`AtomicElementViewController`) handles the detail display of information. It takes a bit of study of this class to determine that although the behavior makes it appear as if there are two separate detail views (with a flip animation between them), there is only one full-screen container view (created in the view controller class code) with the colorful squares (both the big one and a smaller one at the right of the top navigation bar) managed as smaller subviews within the full-screen view. The view controller not only handles the flip animations of those smaller views, but also hands the necessary data to those views so they display the details associated with the element tapped in the earlier table view—thus keeping the data model separate from the views in which the data appears, along MVC lines.

Code for creating the big square subviews is contained in the User Interface Elements group, where you see one set of class files each for the regular view and "flipped" view (the one that displays more details). Each big square instance also creates a separate view rectangle that holds the reflected image below the big square. If you dig deeper

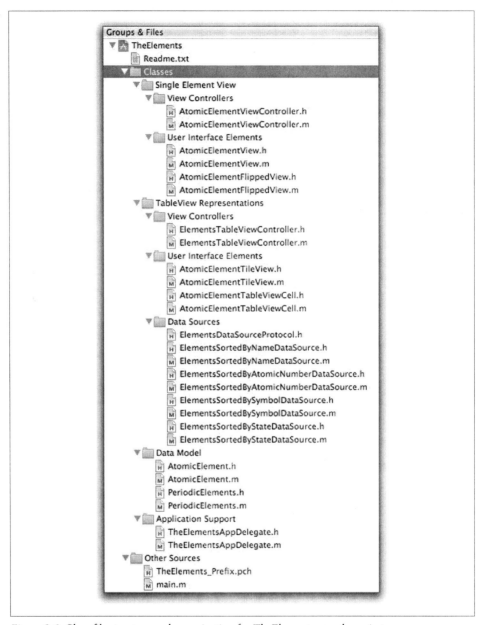

Figure 8-6. Class file structure and organization for TheElements sample project

into these view classes, you'll see that the `AtomicElementFlippedView` class is a subclass of `AtomicElementView`. The flipped view is focused on the different layout of more detailed data points about the atomic element. But the flipped view utilizes the reflected image creation method of its superclass.

TableView Representations

When the app launches, it displays a scrollable table of elements sorted according to the selected tab bar button. Unlike many apps that use a tab bar to lead users to distinctly different views (e.g., a data table view, a settings view, a help view), the views associated with each tab all show a UITableView. The main feature distinguishing one UITableView from the others is the sorting order of the elements in its list. This order has a great bearing on the class structure for the app.

The UITableView Class

One of the most popular user interface classes across iOS apps is UITableView. It is the recommended way to present long lists of text and/or images. The iPod app, for example, uses numerous tables to display lists of albums, playlists, and songs. Each item occupies a table cell. Typically, a tap on a table cell leads either to a detail view of the item tapped or to a sublist, also implemented as a UITableView in a separate underlying view that swoops in from the side.

Cocoa Touch provides a huge amount of infrastructure to ease the creation of simple tables. For example, you can create the window's primary subview as a subclass of UITableViewController (rather than the generic UIView you used in Workbench). That view controller class becomes the delegate, and it's in the delegate methods—most of which Xcode provides when you use its template—where most of the magic occurs.

A table needs information to display in cells—a data source. For a simple list of text, the data source can be an array of strings. As the view controller needs to fill visible cells with data, one of the delegate methods is called repeatedly and rapidly, each time receiving a row number. A row number corresponds to a data source array index, and you can assign the array entry to the cell's label for that row. A sophisticated mechanism reuses cells as the user scrolls the table to minimize memory usage. Numerous Xcode sample apps demonstrate how to implement tables.

Inside the TableView Representations group are the following three subgroups:

- View Controllers
- User Interface Elements
- Data Sources

As with the Single Element Views group, this group has one view controller class. The app makes four instances of this class—one for each sorted version of the table. In other words, four instances of ElementsTableViewController are generated when the app launches. Each one of those table view controllers has its own data source, provided (in part) by the four sets of classes contained in the Data Sources group. All four of those classes implement a customized protocol, named ElementsDataSource (defined in the *ElementsDataSourceProtocol.m* file). Defining your own protocols (for delegate mechanisms) is an intermediate to advanced subject, so I won't be able get into the details here. It's more important at this stage for you to observe how the designer of this app parceled out capabilities among class files.

The classes for the table view user interface elements define views for table cells. Each cell also has a nested tile view, which shows the colored square for each atomic element. You can design table cells in Interface Builder (I do it for some of my apps), but this app's designer opted to do it all in code. Each time a table needs to create a cell, it generates an instance of `AtomicTableViewCell`, which, in turn, creates an instance of `AtomicElementTileView` to work as a subview within the cell. Despite the number of atomic elements, however, the memory conservation mechanism of `UITableViewController` creates only as many cell instances as are in view at any moment. A cell that scrolls out of view is reused, stuffed with information for a different element.

Data Model

Two classes are defined in the Data Model group. These classes define the Model part of MVC. The `PeriodicElements` class acts as the primary data wrangler—reading the data from a *.plist* file contained in the app bundle and generating the collections of `AtomicElement` class objects that are stuffed into the sorted lists. It is the `AtomicElement` class whose instance variables contain specifics about each element (atomic number, symbol, year of discovery, and so on). In other words, one `AtomicElement` instance is created for each atomic element in the *.plist* file (all 117 elements). Pointers to those objects are stored in the sorted data source lists.

Bear in mind that as data model components, these class instances know only about their data and nothing about how that data is going to be displayed. It is the job of view controllers to pass along the data to the views. Sometimes the view is a table cell; other times the view is a big colored rectangle in the detail view.

Application Support

Just one class occupies the Application Support group: the app delegate class. This is where the `applicationDidFinishLaunching:` message goes (following instructions in the *main.m* file because this app doesn't use nib files).

Unlike the simpler apps you've seen until now in this book, the app delegate class for TheElements triggers a cascade of activities to get the app ready for human consumption. Among the tasks are setting up the tab bar interface, which, in turn, creates all four table view controllers. Each table view controller, of course, requires its own data source, and these data sources are built inside their respective view controllers. There aren't many classes of the project that aren't involved in setting up the app.

Other groups and files

The rest of the groups in this project contain files that are not classes. A few of these files, however, are worthy of note. The Resources group contains all of the images used throughout the app. If you click on any image in the project window, you get an uneditable look at the image in the editor pane. The designer made four sets of colored element background images sized to meet specific requirements for full-screen, navigation bar, and table cell displays. This approach offers better quality control, as opposed to scaling one image for all uses.

You can also see the *Info.plist* file, which I introduced back in Chapter 3. Another property list file, *Elements.plist*, holds the actual data that gets displayed throughout the app. One instance of the `AtomicElement` class is created for each entry in the *Elements.plist* file before the sorted data sources are assembled.

Two important image files are included here. Although the images are not required during app development, you will need to add them to the project before submitting the app to the App Store. *Icon.png* is the image for the icon that appears on the iPhone or iPad desktop (the file must be named *Icon.png*, with an initial uppercase "I," unless you specify a different icon filename in *Info.plist*). The operating system provides the rounded corners and shine effect for icons, so you don't have to do that yourself. Icon measurements for iPhone/iPod touch versions are 57×57 pixels, 72×72 pixels for iPad apps, and 114×114 pixels for the iPhone 4 Retina Display. You will also eventually need a 512×512 pixel icon for submission to the App Store, so it is usually a good idea to begin your icon design in that size and derive your various smaller app icon files from that large master.

The other image, *Default.png*, is what an iPhone or iPod touch shows the user while the app is performing its initial loading. This image is a static image (i.e., it cannot be animated) and you should size it to fit the entire screen. For an iPad app, Apple encourages developers to produce at least two versions, one for portrait and one for landscape (named *Default-Portrait.png* and *Default-Landscape.png*, respectively). Your choice for the launch image design can range from an empty regular user interface shot of your app (Apple's preferred approach, as evidenced by its own apps) to a full-blown splash screen with custom graphics.

For details about specifications for app icons and launch screen images, consult the iOS Human Interface Guidelines in the iOS SDK documentation. To find this document quickly, open the documentation window in Xcode, choose the latest iOS version in the Home menu (upper left), then filter for the word "human," as shown in Figure 8-7.

Class Properties

I've waited to describe properties until now because I wanted you to have a good working knowledge of instance variables and companion getter and setter methods in their traditional sense. Introduced to the Objective-C language as recently as 2007, properties provide a compact (in terms of source code) way of writing getters and setters (collectively known as *accessor methods*) for your instance variables. Of interest to those with JavaScript expertise, properties allow Objective-C statements to get and set instance variable values through the same dot syntax (*objectName.propertyName*)

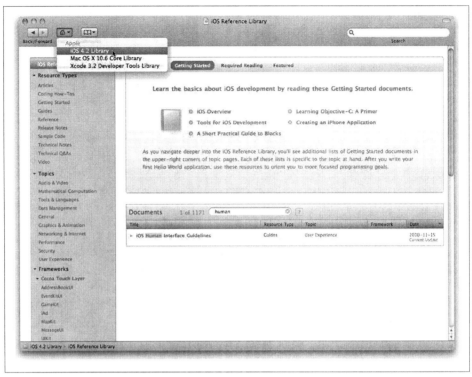

Figure 8-7. Locating the Human Interface Guidelines documents for iPhone and iPad

that is so automatic to you by now. On the one hand, the syntax might feel comfortable to you, but on the other hand, it adds to what sometimes feels like "syntax soup" in writing iOS SDK app code (old C constructs, original Objective-C syntax, and Java-Script-like Objective-C expressions).

Creating properties is a two-step process. I'll treat each step separately.

Specifying Properties in the Header File

Because properties are there to help build getter and setter methods behind the scenes, you must still declare your instance variables in the @interface section of the header file as before. Nothing changes there.

Property declarations go below the curly brace section of the header, where your instance methods (if any) also go. Even though properties feel like they're instance variables, they are in truth specifications for getter and setter methods—thus they are defined where other object methods are declared. It is best practice to declare properties before methods so that if you ever find the need to override a property's setter method, you can still keep both the property declaration and add the customized setter declaration.

Each instance variable you wish to declare as a property requires the `@property` compiler directive, followed by one or two attributes for some variable types, and a repetition of the instance variable declaration from the ivar section of the header file. Recall the `DGCar` and `DGCarAlternate` classes from previous chapters. Only the `DGCarAlternate` class had getter and setter methods written for it, but it's time to bring `DGCar` into the 21st century so it has getter and setter methods for its instance variables. Example 8-6 shows the revised *DGCar.h* file with additions in bold.

Example 8-6. DGCar.h with @property Directives

```
#import <Foundation/Foundation.h>


@interface DGCar : NSObject {

    NSString *make;
    NSString *model;
    NSString *year;

}

@property (nonatomic, retain) NSString *make;
@property (nonatomic, retain) NSString *model;
@property (nonatomic, retain) NSString *year;

- (DGCar *)initWithCarMake:(NSString *)inputMake
                    model:(NSString *)inputModel
                     year:(NSString *)inputYear;
- (NSString *)getFormattedListing;

@end
```

Inside the parentheses are some additional directives that tell the compiler about interior details of the setter methods it will write for you. The `nonatomic` attribute indicates that the setter does not have to worry about the possibility of multiple execution threads trying to modify the value of the ivar at the same time. Threading is beyond the scope of this book, but will likely become part of your app development repertoire as your apps grow in complexity. Suffice it to say that `DGCar` is not expected to run in a threaded environment, so the `nonatomic` attribute is appropriate.

Recall the discussion in Chapter 6 about a setter method being responsible for memory management; the `retain` attribute shown in Example 8-6 tells the compiler to write a setter method that manages retain counts for the ivar object the way the original setter did it manually. It's a good reminder that because the ivar has been retained, it must eventually be released (in the implementation file).

At the tail end of the property declaration is the repetition of the instance variable declaration. If the variable is a pointer, the pointer notation must also be repeated, as shown.

Synthesizing Properties in the Implementation File

To complete the job of equipping your class with fully functional properties, you must tell the compiler to generate the getter and setter methods for the desired properties. That's what the @synthesize compiler directive does. It must go after the @implementation directive, and preferably as the first statement(s). You simply supply the name of the properties declared in the header file. You can use one directive per property, as in:

```
@synthesize make;
@synthesize model;
@synthesize year;
```

Or you can combine multiple property names in a comma-separated list:

```
@synthesize make, model, year;
```

Even if the properties are defined as pointers, the pointer stars are not included in these directives.

To keep memory management under control, you have to be mindful of properties that are retained objects (based on the specifications in the header). Each of them should be released in a dealloc method of the class. Therefore, for the DGCar class, you should add the following method to the implementation file just above the @end directive:

```
- (void)dealloc {
    [make release];
    [model release];
    [year release];
    [super dealloc];
}
```

This method is invoked automatically any time an instance of DGCar is released by whoever owns it.

Using Properties

Your code statements will either be assigning a value to a property or be reading its current value. To reference a property, use the following syntax model:

```
objectInstance.propertyName
```

Very often, you will be referencing a property in the very class in which it is defined. That's the case in DGCar, where an initialization method receives values for three instance variables. These values should be assigned to the ivars through properties to make sure the retain counts are handled properly behind the scenes, but in this case the *objectInstance* part of the reference is the same class, or self. The following revision of the initialization method for DGCar passes the argument values to the properties (changes in bold):

```
- (DGCar *)initWithCarMake:(NSString *)inputMake
                    model:(NSString *)inputModel
```

```
                     year:(NSString *)inputYear {
    if (self = [super init]) {
        self.make = inputMake;
        self.model = inputModel;
        self.year = inputYear;
    }

    return self;
}
```

Using the properties within the same class in which they're defined offers two possibilities. Because the synthesized properties are assigning values to the instance variables, you can use those instance variables directly, without going through the self object instance. In other words, you can create the instance method that assembles values into a string in one of two ways. You can go via the getter method of the synthesized property:

```
result = [NSString stringWithFormat:@"[%@] %@ %@",
    self.year, self.make, self.model];
```

Or you can reference the ivars directly, just as you did in the original version:

```
result = [NSString stringWithFormat:@"[%@] %@ %@",
    year, make, model];
```

I prefer to use the self reference when assigning a value to one of these ivars to make sure memory management is handled safely through the synthesized setter method.

When you are creating an instance of an imported class, you must use the object reference for both getting and setting values. Example 8-7 shows a modified version of the runMyCode: method that employs the DGCar and DGCarAlternate classes. One instance has its ivar values assigned through properties. Then two statements read individual ivar values, one from each object. Notice that the object instance is part of all references.

Example 8-7. The runMyCode: method modified for properties

```
- (IBAction)runMyCode:(id)sender {

    DGCar *myCar1 = [[DGCar alloc] initWithCarMake:@"Chevrolet"
                                      model:@"Malibu" year:@"2007"];
    DGCarAlternate *myCar2 = [[DGCarAlternate alloc] init];

    // Set properties
    myCar2.make = @"Ford";
    myCar2.model = @"Taurus";
    myCar2.year = @"2010";

    // Read individual properties
    NSLog(@"My previous car was a %@", myCar1.model);
    NSLog(@"My current car was made by %@", myCar2.make);

    [myCar1 release];
    [myCar2 release];
```

}

You'll recall that DGCarAlternate is a subclass of DGCar. The subclass inherits the properties of its superclass without any further intervention on your part—you do not have to redeclare or synthesize the properties in the subclass code.

Properties in Framework Classes

Some SDK framework classes are loaded with properties, while others have none or very few because the class is action-oriented with no instance variable values. Use the SDK class reference documents to find which class members are properties. Figure 8-8 shows the beginning of the task summary for the MKMapView class (used to display maps inside apps). Notice that many members are shown to be properties. Any member reporting itself as a property can be accessed via dot syntax.

Figure 8-8. MKMapView Class Reference excerpt showing many property members

You must still drill down into the property description to learn about its data type and other attributes that may be set for it. Examine three property listings from the MKMap View class and see what the listings tell you about how to use them:

```
@property (nonatomic, readonly) NSArray *annotations
```

The annotations property is read-only and is returned as a pointer to an NSArray (an important class described later in this chapter). This is a straightforward application of a framework class property:

```
@property (nonatomic) CLLocationCoordinate2D centerCoordinate
```

The centerCoordinate property can be assigned and read. A value assigned to the property must be the CLLocationCoordinate2D type (details of this struct are in the CLLocation class reference):

```
@property (nonatomic, getter=isZoomEnabled) BOOL zoomEnabled
```

Boolean properties, such as zoomEnabled, typically include an attribute that names an alternative getter property name. This means that when you read the property, you can use either *objectReference*.zoomEnabled or *objectReference*.isZoomEnabled. The "is" version is in keeping with an Objective-C convention that makes an expression with a Boolean value more human readable.

Properties and Their Accessor Methods

Properties really do generate getter and setter methods for instance variables, even though you can't see the method code. Therefore, if you are more comfortable in some situations using Objective-C messages rather than dot syntax, you can do so. Simply refer to the getter method with the ivar name and the setter method with the standard setter method name, which consists of lowercase "set" followed by an initial capital property name. For example, the MKMapView class zoomEnabled accessor methods can be referenced in either of two ways:

```
// Property syntax
if (myMapView.isZoomEnabled) { ... }
myMapView.zoomEnabled = YES;

// Getter and setter method syntax
if ([myMapView isZoomEnabled]) { ... }
[myMapView setZoomEnabled:YES];
```

This choice extends to properties you create in your own custom classes and for those in the Cocoa Touch framework classes. However, if the object in question is of the id dynamic type, you will have to send messages to the accessor methods rather than use dot syntax. This is because the compiler won't be able to resolve the dot syntax property against an indeterminate data type. When you use the message syntax with a dynamic data type, the compiler leaves the resolution to runtime.

About NSString

The NSString class provides a more convenient way of working with strings than dealing with traditional C strings. That's not to say that you are completely free and clear of C strings (NSStrings are stored as C strings beneath the covers), but for day-to-day string handling, you will likely stay within the NSString realm.

One more potential complexity is character encoding, especially if your app retrieves explicitly encoded text from a server. The NSString class has many methods that convert and accommodate a wide range of character encodings. If these issues are important to your coding, you should read the "String Programming Guide for Cocoa" in the SDK documentation once you have a good working knowledge of the basics revealed in this chapter.

Regular expression support is available only beginning with iOS 4. Chapter 9 demonstrates how to use regular expressions with NSString objects. If your app is designed to include earlier iOS versions and you want to use regular expressions, you'll be out of luck (although some third-party libraries exist).

As is the case with all basic data classes in Cocoa Touch, once you create an object, you usually cannot modify its content. That is to say, you cannot insert or delete segments of the string. All NSString methods that sound on the surface to be modifying the current object (e.g., the uppercaseString method) actually perform the modifications and return a new NSString object. You can, of course, assign the new object to the old variable. If you'd rather keep the same object going and modify some of its content, use the NSMutableString class instead. I cover this class at the end of this section.

Creating an NSString

The simplest way to create an NSString object from a fixed series of characters is to use the Objective-C string literal:

```
NSString *myString = @"Your string goes here.";
```

You can now use the variable as a receiver for any message known to the NSString class.

NSString accommodates Unicode characters. For example, the following statement assigns the Hebrew word "shalom" (peace) to an NSString variable:

```
NSString *peaceString = @"\u05e9\u05dc\u05d5\u05dd"; // שלום
```

Although the Unicode characters are entered from left-to-right (i.e., character \u05e9 is the Hebrew letter shin—ש—for the "sha" part of the word), if you display the value of the string (or assign it as text to a UI element with a font family that supports Hebrew characters), characters are displayed right-to-left (with the shin starting the word on the right).

The NSString class supplies over two dozen methods that either create or initialize an NSString instance. The majority of these methods are instance methods (to be used in concert with an alloc method call) specializing in various character encodings and source material (e.g., C strings). You will be responsible for releasing objects created in this fashion. Or you can use one of the many class methods that create autoreleased instances. For example, if you wish to declare an NSString but not commit any specific content to it, you can use a method that creates an empty string:

```
NSString *myString = [NSString string];
```

If you have an existing NSString object and wish to create a copy of its current state into another NSString, use the following:

```
NSString *myString = [NSString stringWithString:existingStringVar];
```

The copying performed by this method disconnects the two instances so that if the *existingStringVar* content is reassigned a new value, the myString value remains what it was at the time it was created.

Many times you need to create an NSString by combining multiple NSString variables or mixing NSString variables and/or values of other basic data types within fixed text. That's where the notion of formats comes into play. Just as you have seen many times throughout this book where you assembled strings for the NSLog() function, you can create placeholders (*format specifiers*) inside an Objective-C string, after which come the variables whose values are to be inserted into the placeholders. The NSString class offers multiple creation and initialization methods that accommodate format specifiers, but the one you will probably use most is the **stringWithFormat:** class method (or its **initWithFormat:** instance method counterpart). In the following example you should try in Workbench, an existing NSString and two int values are inserted into fixed text to generate a new NSString object consisting of a complete sentence.

```
- (IBAction)runMyCode:(id)sender {

    // Variables established earlier
    int trackCount = 1023;
    int beatlesTracks = 43;
    NSString *artist = @"The Beatles";

    // Create new NSString
    NSString *excerpt =
        [NSString stringWithFormat:
            @"Of my %d total tracks, %d were recorded by %@",
            trackCount, beatlesTracks, artist];

    // Output to console
    NSLog(@"%@", excerpt);

}
```

Results from the above code appear as follows:

```
Of my 1023 total tracks, 43 were recorded by The Beatles
```

To use the **stringWithFormat:** method effectively, you need to know at least a basic set of format specifiers for a variety of data types that are returned by Cocoa Touch methods. If you fail to provide a data specifier that matches the type of the variable, you will receive unexpected, if not misleading, results. Therefore, be sure you know the precise data type for the values you wish to plug in to a format string and use the correct specifier. Admittedly, you will sometimes have to make an educated guess when a data type doesn't have an exact matching format specifier. For example, if a value is returned as a CGFloat type, you would obviously try the specifiers that address floating-point values. Table 8-1 shows the most common specifiers and their corresponding data types.

Table 8-1. Selected format specifiers and their data types

Specifier(s)	Data type
%@	Any Objective-C object
%d, %D, %i	`int` (signed 32-bit integer)
%u, %U	`unsigned int` (unsigned 32-bit integer)
%hi	`short` (signed 16-bit integer)
%hu	`unsigned short` (unsigned 16-bit integer)
%f	`double` (64-bit floating-point number)
%F	`double` (64-bit floating-point number as decimal)
%c	`unsigned char` (8-bit ASCII character or Unicode hexadecimal)
%C	`unichar` (16-bit ASCII character or Unicode hexadecimal)
%s	Null-terminated array of 8-bit unsigned characters (`char[]`)
%S	Null-terminated array of 16-bit Unicode characters (`char[]`)

As you have seen in many previous examples, the %@ format specifier obtains the value of an Objective-C object's `description` property. For an `NSString` object, that value is the string of characters stored in the object.

 It's a good idea to override `NSObject`'s `description` method in your custom classes so that it returns a meaningful string—perhaps even some ivar values—to help you identify the object while debugging your code.

For more complex C values, such as `structs`, you will have to drill down into the struct to obtain specific values. For example, a `CGRect` value has two components (`CGPoint` and `CGSize` types), each of which has two `CGFloat` components. There is no specifier that grabs all values of the `CGRect` in one swoop, so you'll have to dig out the values individually:

```
CGRect spriteFrame = sprite.view.bounds;

// Generate string with view width/height
NSString *dimensions =
    [NSString stringWithFormat:
        @"The element is %f pixels wide by %f pixels tall",
        spriteFrame.size.width, spriteFrame.size.height];
// Output to console
NSLog(@"%@", dimensions);
```

Additionally, you may need to pay close attention to the format of the value inserted via a format specifier. In the above example, the values are `CGFloat` types, which return values with six decimal places—all zeros in this case. But you are free to substitute any valid expression for the variables in these places. If you want to display only integer values for the results above, you can change the format specifier to an integer and cast the values to integers:

```
NSString *dimensions =
    [NSString stringWithFormat:
        @"The element is %d pixels wide by %d pixels tall",
        (int)spriteFrame.size.width, (int)spriteFrame.size.height];
```

Any expression works in these places, including messages to Objective-C objects whose methods return values. In the following example, the length of text being typed into a text field is subtracted from the Twitter maximum of 140 characters to create a string advising how many character spaces remain:

```
NSString *messageInput; // Obtained from a text field

// Generate string showing characters remaining
NSString *spaceRemaining =
    [NSString stringWithFormat:@"%d characters remaining.",
    (140 - [messageInput length])];
// Output to console
NSLog(@"%@", spaceRemaining);
```

When you look through the long list of NSString object creation methods, you might be tempted by the series of methods that download a file from a URL and create an NSString object out of the data that arrives from that download (such as stringWith ContentsOfURL:encoding:error:). Don't go there! Cocoa Touch provides a much more robust way of retrieving data from an external server on the network—one that operates in its own thread, has a delegate system affiliated with it and reports download errors in a manageable way. I'm speaking of the NSURLConnection class, which I'll describe in Chapter 9. If you try to use the NSString methods that download data, these methods act synchronously, meaning all subsequent code execution and user interface activity is frozen until the download completes (which may be never if there is a problem). It is, however, safe to create an NSString object loaded from a previously saved file on the device.

JavaScript String Method Equivalents in Objective-C

Until you get comfortable with the vast assortment of NSString methods, this section reveals the NSString methods you will use to perform the same jobs you currently use with the JavaScript String object methods. Table 8-2 presents methods for operations the two objects have in common.

Table 8-2. JavaScript string and Cocoa Touch NSString methods

JavaScript string	Obj-C NSString
charAt(*index*)	(see text)
charCodeAt(*index*)	- (unichar)characterAtIndex:(NSUInteger)*index*

JavaScript string	Obj-C NSString
concat(*string*)	- (NSString *)stringByAppendingString:(NSString *)*aString*
indexOf(*string*)	- (NSRange)rangeOfString:(NSString *)*aString*
lastIndexOf(*string*)	- (NSRange)rangeOfString:(NSString *)*aString*
	options:NSBackwardsSearch
localeCompare(*string*)	- (NSComparisonResult)localizedCompare:(NSString *)*aString*
split(*delimiter*)	- (NSArray *)componentsSeparatedByString:(NSString *)*separator*
substring(*startIndex*)	- (NSString *)substringWithRange:(NSRange)*aRange*
toLowerCase()	- (NSString *)lowercaseString
toUpperCase()	- (NSString *)uppercaseString

Getting single characters and character codes

JavaScript offers separate methods to obtain either the character or the character code at a desired offset from the beginning of the string. In Cocoa Touch, you have one method (characterAtIndex:) that obtains a Unicode character value. By choosing different format specifiers in an NSString initialization method, you can extract either the character code (%d) or the actual character (%C) from the same value.

Appending to a string

Although not part of the ECMA standard, the concat() method is supported by all browsers, so you may have used it in place of the addition (+) operator. For Cocoa Touch, the stringByAppendingString: method returns a new NSString instance combining the receiver with the string passed as an argument. The original object (the receiver) is left untouched.

Finding the offset of a matching substring

JavaScript's indexOf() method returns just an integer of the offset within the main string where a search string is found (or -1 if it's not found). The Cocoa Touch equivalent, however, returns an NSRange struct, which has two integer elements, named location and length. The location value is a zero-based index of the offset from the start of the receiver NSString. But if the search string is not found, the NSRange value returned from the method is {NSNotFound, 0}. NSNotFound is a constant, for which you can test in the usual manner. Try the following code in the runMyCode: method of Workbench to see how it performs:

```
NSString *myString = @"Four score and seven years ago...";
NSString *searchString = @"and";

NSRange matchRange = [myString rangeOfString:searchString];

if (matchRange.location == NSNotFound) {
    NSLog(@"\"%@\" not found.", searchString);
```

```
    } else {
        NSLog(@"\"%@\" found at position:%d", searchString, matchRange.location);
    }
```

Notice that an NSRange value is not a pointer, so don't define it with the pointer star.

Another variation of the rangeOfString: method lets you define additional options for how the search should be carried out. One such option, NSBackwardSearch, causes the method to work like the JavaScript lastIndexOf() method does, starting the search from the end of the receiver. As with the lastIndexOf() method, the offset value returned for a successful search is measured from the beginning of the string.

Options of this kind are applied in the form of *bit masks*, where you can specify one or more constants whose values are designed to form unique numeric values when combined with the bitwise OR operator (|). For example, if you want to apply both the backward search and case-insensitive search at the same time, create a statement like the following:

```
NSRange matchRange = [myString rangeOfString:searchString
                      options:NSBackwardsSearch | NSCaseInsensitiveSearch];
```

Replacing substrings

Table 8-2 does not list the JavaScript replace() method, because the method accepts a regular expression for the search string portion, and NSString does not offer a completely comparable method. Regular expression support is new in iOS 4, but replacing substrings with the aid of regular expressions requires approaching the task through a method of the NSRegularExpression class, not NSString (see Chapter 9 for an example). NSString does offer substring replacement, but only for a fixed search string via the stringByReplacingOccurrencesOfString:withString: method of NSString. The lengthy name of this method leaves no doubt as to what its purpose is and what the role of each argument is. This method returns a copy of the receiver string, but modified to replace all occurrences of a search string with a replacement string specified as the second argument. If there is no match found for the search string, the method returns a copy of the original string without changes. Although you cannot specify a regular expression pattern to search, the method does behave as if you specified the global attribute to replace all occurrences.

Dividing a string into an array

To achieve the same result as the JavaScript split() method, use the NSString compo nentsSeparatedByString: method. The method returns an NSArray object (described later in this chapter). For example, if an NSString contains a comma-delimited string, you can divide that string into an NSArray with the following statement:

```
NSArray *newArray = [commaDelimitedString componentsSeparatedByString:@","];
```

The separating string (which can be a string of any length and not a regular expression) is not included in the array elements.

Extracting a substring

As you might expect, the Cocoa Touch method that extracts a substring specifies its parameters by way of an NSRange value. The JavaScript substring() method passes its values as two integers for the offset from the front of the main string and the length of the substring. An NSRange value supplies the same pair of values within the single struct. Don't forget that you can use the NSMakeRange() function to generate an NSRange value right in the argument to the substringWithRange: method call:

```
NSString *myString = @"Four score and seven years ago...";

NSString *extract = [myString substringWithRange:NSMakeRange(5, 5)];

NSLog(@"%@", extract); // "score"
```

Changing case

Both JavaScript and Cocoa Touch provide one-stop methods that change the case of a string to all uppercase or all lowercase. In both environments, the methods return modified copies of the original strings, while leaving the originals intact. Cocoa Touch even offers a capitalizedString method, which capitalizes the first letter of every word following white space.

Escaping and unescaping URL strings

Although not part of the JavaScript String object, the encodeURI() and decodeURI() global functions (modern replacements for the escape() and unescape() functions) handle vital string conversions for dealing with URLs (or URIs). For Cocoa Touch, these conversions are handled by NSString methods, stringByAddingPercentEscapesU singEncoding: and stringByReplacingPercentEscapesUsingEncoding:. The lone argument for these methods is an enumerated constant for the type of text encoding. Table 8-3 lists common text encoding constants.

Table 8-3. Selected NSStringEncoding values

Value	Constant
1	NSASCIIStringEncoding
4	NSUTF8StringEncoding
5	NSISOLatin1StringEncoding
10	NSUnicodeStringEncoding

The following example encodes a URL:

```
NSString *myURLString = @"http://www.dannyg.com/img/big logo.jpg";
NSString *escapedURLString = [myURLString
    stringByAddingPercentEscapesUsingEncoding:NSUTF8StringEncoding];
// "http://www.dannyg.com/img/big%20logo.jpg"
```

Be sure to look through Chapter 9 for additional string-based operations in Objective-C.

NSMutableString

Although you can grab excerpts from strings and append one string to another for NSString, the results of those methods all yield new autoreleased NSString objects. This can leave behind a trail of autoreleased objects that could eat up memory if used in a high-volume repeat loop. If your code requires a lot of string manipulation—especially inserting, deleting, replacing, and appending within a single string—you can use the NSMutableString class to generate the main string object and restrict activity to that one object.

NSMutableString is a subclass of NSString, which means all methods of the superclass are available for your mutable object. The inherited NSString methods, however, don't change their stripes just because you're using a mutable version. For example, the uppercaseString method still returns a new object with an uppercased copy of the original.

But what you do have at your disposal are a series of methods dedicated to modifying a mutable string:

```
- (void)appendFormat:(NSString *)format
- (void)appendString:(NSString *)aString
- (void)deleteCharactersInRange:(NSRange)aRange
- (void)insertString:(NSString *)aString
            atIndex:(NSUInteger)anIndex
- (void)replaceCharactersInRange:(NSRange)aRange
                      withString:(NSString *)aString
- (NSUInteger)replaceOccurrencesOfString:(NSString *)target
                              withString:(NSString *)replacement
                                 options:(NSStringCompareOptions)opts
                                   range:(NSRange)searchRange
- (void)setString:(NSString *)aString
```

Notice that none of these methods returns a string object. Most return void, while the major string replacement method reports the number of replacements made.

If you want to use this class, make sure you create an instance with one of the two methods designed for the task:

```
NSMutableString *myEditableString = [[NSMutableString alloc] initWithCapacity:200];
NSMutableString *myEditableString = [NSMutableString stringWithCapacity:200];
```

Don't be too concerned about the requirement to specify a size (number of characters). The value allocates an initial block of memory for the object, but if the length of the mutable string grows beyond that size, the object automatically allocates additional memory as needed. It is more efficient, however, to preallocate the memory you expect—as long as you don't go crazy and reserve a bunch of precious memory you'll never use. You can always pass an NSMutableString object as a method argument that requires an NSString type, but the method will cast the object to the more restrictive NSString type for its operations. If you are designing custom methods that need to preserve mutability, specify the arguments as NSMutableString data types.

All of the Cocoa Touch mutable classes (including those for arrays and dictionaries) are powerful constructions that save you lots of slashing and pasting together object pieces to make changes. At the same time, however, they use more resources than their immutable parents. Use them only when needed.

About NSArray

Like JavaScript arrays, a Cocoa Touch array is an ordered collection of data, with each element of the array referenced through a zero-based index number. You can use that index to iterate through both styles in for repeat loops. Although both objects have a handful of methods that perform similar tasks with arrays, you have more restrictions and more possibilities with the NSArray than you do with JavaScript arrays.

The most important departure is that when you create an NSArray, you have one shot to include elements in the instance of the array. That instance remains fixed for its life with respect to its content and order. Methods allow you to create new NSArray instances that append additional elements to the original, extract copies of elements from the array, and obtain a copy of the array sorted according to criteria you devise. To create an array that has the same type of self-modifying behavior as the JavaScript array, you can use the NSMutableArray class.

Arrays are often vital components of iOS apps because they typically become the data sources for table views. You can write an NSArray to a file (or deliver a file in your app bundle) and, in a subsequent session, load that file to recreate the NSArray object for your code to use. The sorted order of an array determines the sorted order of cells in the table view.

The NSArray class is far more adaptable than a C array, whose elements must all be of the same data type. That restriction is gone from NSArray, but its elements must all be Objective-C objects. In other words, you cannot create an NSArray to store a bunch of int values directly; but an NSArray is capable of storing NSNumber objects (which can represent many different types of numbers). You can therefore mix NSNumber, NSString, NSDate, NSArray, and other full-fledged objects (including your own custom objects subclasses of NSObject) in the same NSArray instance.

Wrapping Values in NSValue Objects

If you need to store nonobject values in NSArray, NSDictionary, or other Cocoa Touch collections, the NSValue class comes to the rescue. This class is capable of wrapping the data—including C structs and scalar data types such as int, float, and double values—into a generic object that collections can store internally, write to a file, and load from a file for reuse later.

As an example, the following code (which you can run in the Workbench runMyCode: method to try for yourself) obtains the frame of the current view, which is a CGRect type:

```
CGRect myRect = self.view.frame;
NSValue *myValue = [NSValue valueWithBytes:&myRect
                    objCType:@encode(CGRect)];
NSArray *myArray = [NSArray arrayWithObject:myValue];

NSLog(@"%@", myArray);
```

If you inspect the CGRect details in the SDK documentation, you see that it is a C struct with a type definition of CGRect. To get that data into an NSValue, use the value WithBytes:objCType: class method, which is defined as follows:

```
+ (NSValue *)valueWithBytes:(const void *)value
              objCType:(const char *)type
```

The value must be passed as a pointer, but because the myRect variable is not a pointer, you must reference the variable with the & operator (which supplies the pointer to the variable). The second argument uses the @encode compiler directive to produce a compiler-friendly string for the name of the type of the data. For C structs, you can use the typedef value (not quoted). With the value preserved in the NSValue instance, it can now be assigned to an array, dictionary, or other collection object.

To retrieve the value later, use the NSValue's getValue: method, which uses a construction called a *buffer*. Here's the specification for the getValue: method:

```
- (void)getValue:(void *)buffer
```

Notice that the method does not return a value. Instead, the value is assigned to the pointer of a variable that you have predeclared of the data type of the value. The following code extends the example above by creating a buffer (named retrievedRect) and having the getValue: method assign the value to the buffer (via the same & pointer reference we used to turn a variable into a pointer earlier). The variable can then act as a regular CGRect, from which a value is extracted and displayed in the console:

```
CGRect myRect = self.view.frame;
NSValue *myValue = [NSValue valueWithBytes:&myRect
                    objCType:@encode(CGRect)];
NSArray *myArray = [NSArray arrayWithObject:myValue];

// Create buffer variable
CGRect retrievedRect;
// Read array member and put its value into buffer
[[myArray objectAtIndex:0] getValue:&retrievedRect];

NSLog(@"%f", retrievedRect.size.height);
```

Although the NSNumber class is a subclass of NSValue, it is more convenient to store NSNumber objects directly, as in the following example:

```
NSNumber *myValue = [NSNumber numberWithDouble:3.14159];
NSArray *myArray = [NSArray arrayWithObject:myValue];
```

Upon retrieval, you can obtain the NSNumber object and extract the desired value type:

```
NSLog(@"%F", [[myArray objectAtIndex:0] doubleValue]);
```

When you reference an NSArray object to fill a %@ format specifier (as you will do often with NSLog() to examine array contents during development), the contents of an array appear as a comma-delimited list inside parentheses. The commas are not part of the array, but merely delimit the values for the list. *

Creating an NSArray

As with many Cocoa Touch versions of common value classes, you have a choice of using instance initialization methods (used in concert with the alloc method) or class methods that create autoreleased instances. For the sake of simplicity, the descriptions here demonstrate the class methods.

The two most common methods let you specify the object or objects that are to become elements of the new instance. One method is for a single-element array. If you're wondering why you'd need to create a single-element array, it's because some other framework classes have methods whose parameters require an array, even if you need to pass only a single value. The format for this one-element array creation is as follows:

```
+ (id)arrayWithObject:(id)anObject
```

Although the method returns an id data type, the returned object conforms to the NSArray class. The single argument is any Objective-C object, passed as either a variable or an explicit object message that returns an instance of that object. Here are some examples:

```
NSArray *myArray = [NSArray arrayWithObject:@"Custom string"];

NSArray *myArray = [NSArray arrayWithObject:[NSDate date]];

NSArray *myArray = [NSArray arrayWithObject:[NSNumber numberWithDouble:3.14159]];
```

More commonly, however, you will assign multiple items to an array, which you must do in one statement (unless you go with an NSMutableArray). The creation method looks almost identical, but uses the plural construction:

```
+ (id)arrayWithObjects:(id)object1[, (id)object2[, ...]], nil
```

Multiple items are in a comma-delimited list, with the final item being nil. The nil item does not become an element of the array, but simply tells the OS to stop accumulating items for the array. This also means, however, that you cannot assign nil as a member of the array. If you need a null value as an element, use NSNull. The following example creates an array holding three UIColor objects for flag colors:

```
NSArray *myFlagColors = [NSArray arrayWithObjects:[UIColor redColor],
                                                  [UIColor whiteColor],
                                                  [UIColor blueColor],
                                                  nil];
```

If you already have an array that you'd like to copy into a new NSArray instance, use the creation method tailored for that purpose:

```
NSArray *newArray = [NSArray arrayWithArray:existingArray];
```

Retrieving Array Elements

In typical usage, your code loops through an array to retrieve its elements in sequential order. Array elements are accessed most often by their zero-based index number, just as they are in JavaScript. But, this being Objective-C, the syntax is a bit more verbose, requiring use of the objectAtIndex: method. In the following example, a repeat loop accesses each element of an array of string values and displays the element content in the console window:

```
NSArray *thePlanets = [NSArray arrayWithObjects:@"Mercury",
                       @"Venus", @"Earth", @"Mars", @"Jupiter",
                       @"Saturn", @"Uranus", @"Neptune", nil];

for (int i = 0; i < [thePlanets count]; i++) {
    NSLog(@"Planet at index %d = %@",
          i, [thePlanets objectAtIndex:i]);
}
```

Notice that the number of elements in an NSArray is obtained via the count method (unlike the JavaScript length property). The NSArray class has many more methods available for obtaining multiple items from an array at a time (either through a list of disparate index numbers or specified by an NSRange of consecutive elements).

JavaScript Array Method Equivalents in Objective-C

Because of the immutability of Cocoa Touch arrays, several popular JavaScript array methods are missing from NSArray. For example, push() and pop() facilities are absent (even the NSMutableArray lacks these stack-like operations). Table 8-4 shows a list of comparable methods in both environments to help you acclimate to the NSArray object for operations you've used in the past.

Table 8-4. JavaScript Array and Cocoa Touch NSArray Methods

JavaScript Array	Obj-C NSArray
length	- (NSUInteger)count
concat(item1[, item2...])	- (NSArray *)arrayByAddingObject:(id)anObject

JavaScript Array	Obj-C NSArray
	- (NSArray *)arrayByAddingObjectsFromArray:(NSArray *)*otherArray*
join(*delimiter*)	- (NSString *)componentsJoinedByString:(NSString *)*separator*
sort()	- (NSArray *)sortedArrayUsingFunction:(NSInteger (*)(id, id, void *))*comparator* context:(void *)*context*
toString()	- (NSString *)description

Appending items to an array

NSArray has two methods that let you tack on either a single object or another array to the end of the current array, but only in the process of creating a new NSArray instance with the combined elements. This behavior tracks the JavaScript concat() method, but makes it a little more cumbersome to add multiple items, which you must first put inside another array before passing them to the arrayByAddingObjectsFromArray: method.

Combining array elements into a delimited string

If you have elements in an NSArray that you'd like to transfer to an NSString, the componentsJoinedByString: method works just like the JavaScript join() method. For example, the following code outputs a return-delimited string with array values:

```
NSArray *thePlanets = [NSArray arrayWithObjects:@"Mercury",
                @"Venus", @"Earth", @"Mars", @"Jupiter",
                @"Saturn", @"Uranus", @"Neptune", nil];

NSString *planetList = [thePlanets componentsJoinedByString:@"\n"];

NSLog(@"The Planets:\n%@", planetList);
```

Sorting arrays

An NSArray offers many ways of producing sorted copies of itself. The one shown in Table 8-4 is similar to the way JavaScript sorts arrays via an external sorting function that compares individual values. The details of how this is done are covered in Chapter 9.

NSMutableArray

As with the NSMutableString, you have two ways to create an NSMutableArray:

```
// Managed Memory style
NSMutableArray *myEditableArray = [[NSMutableArray alloc] initWithCapacity:100];

// Autoreleased style
NSMutableArray *myEditableArray = [NSMutableArray stringWithCapacity:100];
```

The initial capacity is only an initial memory allocation. If you add items to the array beyond the initial count, the object adjusts its memory allocation accordingly (and automatically).

The list of methods for changing the content of an NSMutableArray is too long to be quoted here, but you should be aware of the types of modifications available to you. You can add one or more objects to an array, either at the end of the array or at a designated spot within the existing order. There are no fewer than 10 methods for deleting one or more items from an array, including removeAllObjects, which takes the count down to zero while maintaining the object as a valid object. Additional modifications include replacing one or more items either at specific index points or within a contiguous range of elements. Finally, you can sort elements of an NSMutableArray within the very same object. A full list of methods is available in the NSMutableArray class reference document in the iOS SDK.

About NSDictionary

In the Cocoa Touch world, a dictionary is an object that holds a collection of values, each of which is associated with a unique *key* (sort of like a label). A combination of the key and its value is known as a *key-value pair* and makes up an *entry* in the dictionary. Keys within a single dictionary need to be unique, but you are free to reuse key names in different dictionary objects in the same scope. Cocoa Touch provides an NSDictionary class for a dictionary whose contents and size remain fixed once it is created and an NSMutableDictionary class (a subclass of NSDictionary) for a dictionary whose individual entries can change over time. If you're looking for an analogue in the JavaScript world, the associative array comes closest in conception in that you can access a value by way of the value's name. But NSDictionary is a far more powerful entity than what JavaScript offers.

Each value stored in an NSDictionary must be an Objective-C object—the same requirement as for NSArray. For example, numeric values are best represented by the NSNumber class, and you must wrap scalar values inside the NSValue class. An object may also be another dictionary, allowing for nested dictionaries if your data requires such a structure. Although you can use any Objective-C object as a key, an NSString is the most common way to represent a key.

Creating an NSDictionary

One point to always keep in mind when creating an NSDictionary is that you have to supply data in pairs—one key and one object per entry. The class provides several creation methods (both instance methods to be used in concert with alloc and class methods that generate autoreleased objects) to assign entries, depending on how many entries you need to create and how you have fashioned the data ahead of time. Although there is a special method for creating a single-entry dictionary, I'll focus on creating dictionaries with multiple entries, for which two class methods are the most common.

The first method assumes that you will manually assign keys and values in carefully orchestrated pairs. The format for this method is:

```
+ (id)dictionaryWithObjectsAndKeys:
        (id)object1, (id)key1[, (id)object2, (id)key2[, ...]], nil
```

Notice that the wording of the method name gives you clues as to the expected order of values and keys: for each entry the object value comes first, followed by the key. After the final key comes nil to tell the method to stop making entries for the dictionary (the same usage as when creating an NSArray object). If you need a nil value for an entry, use the NSNull object (created via the [NSNull null] message). The following example creates a three-entry NSDictionary holding information about the State of Illinois:

```
NSDictionary *illinois = [NSDictionary dictionaryWithObjectsAndKeys:
                @"Illinois", @"name",
                @"Springfield", @"capital",
                [NSNumber numberWithInt:1818], @"enteredUnion", nil];
```

Here, "name" is a key whose value is "Illinois", and so on. The example is formatted to reinforce the pairs of objects and keys, but there is no requirement that you format this method's arguments the same way. The example uses a combination of string literals and NSNumber object creation for the values to be stored; all keys are string literals.

At times it is more convenient to gather all values and all keys into two parallel arrays. You can then supply the two arrays as arguments to a class method designed for this purpose:

```
+ (id)dictionaryWithObjects:(NSArray *)objects forKeys:(NSArray *)keys
```

Again, the verbosity of the Objective-C language reminds you which array goes where. In the following example, the Illinois information is first gathered into arrays, which are then fed to the dictionary creation method:

```
NSArray *illinoisData = [NSArray arrayWithObjects:@"Illinois", @"Springfield",
                [NSNumber numberWithInt:1818], nil];
NSArray *illinoisKeys = [NSArray arrayWithObjects:@"name", @"capital",
                @"enteredUnion", nil];
// Declare illinois dictionary
NSDictionary *illinois;
if ([illinoisData count] == [illinoisKeys count]) {
    illinois = [NSDictionary dictionaryWithObjects:illinoisData
                                            forKeys:illinoisKeys];
}
```

Bad things happen if the two arrays don't have the same number of elements. Therefore, it is your responsibility to make sure the arrays are generated with equal numbers of items.

It's important to remember that dictionary entries are not necessarily stored in the same order in which their values and keys appear in creation method arguments. The purpose of the key is to let you jump into the collection and grab that key's associated value, regardless of where it is in the order of entries.

Retrieving Dictionary Entries

How you go about retrieving information from a dictionary depends largely on how much about the dictionary your code knows when it's time to get data. In most cases, the dictionary will hold on to a very regular set of values that your code expects to find. Other times, the dictionary may be a "black box" with an unknown or variable set of keys.

When your code knows the key of the value you wish to retrieve, use the `objectFor Key:` method:

```
- (id)objectForKey:(id)aKey
```

The following example (which you can try in Workbench) retrieves two values from a dictionary to fill `NSLog()` format specifiers:

```
- (IBAction)runMyCode:(id)sender {

    NSArray *illinoisData = [NSArray arrayWithObjects:@"Illinois", @"Springfield",
                                [NSNumber numberWithInt:1818], nil];
    NSArray *illinoisKeys = [NSArray arrayWithObjects:@"name", @"capital",
                                @"enteredUnion", nil];
    // Declare illinois dictionary
    NSDictionary *illinois;
    if ([illinoisData count] == [illinoisKeys count]) {
        illinois = [NSDictionary dictionaryWithObjects:illinoisData
                                        forKeys:illinoisKeys];
    }

    NSLog(@"The State of %@ entered the Union in %@.",
        [illinois objectForKey:@"name"],
        [illinois objectForKey:@"enteredUnion"]);

}
```

Even if a dictionary is a "black box," the `NSDictionary` class has methods that let you inspect it to retrieve all of its keys or all of its values in bulk (as arrays):

```
- (NSArray *)allKeys // Returns array of all keys
```

```
- (NSArray *)allValues // Returns array of all object values
```

Another way to work on a collection of keys or values is to iterate through all entries with the help of an `NSEnumerator` object (which lets you construct a `while` loop that works like the JavaScript `for-in` loop). The following code iterates through all values of the previous `illinois` dictionary in search of items of the `NSNumber` class, and then reports both the key and value name to the console:

```
NSEnumerator *myEnumerator = [illinois keyEnumerator];
id key;

while ((key = [myEnumerator nextObject])) {
    if ([[illinois objectForKey:key] isKindOfClass:[NSNumber class]]) {
        NSLog(@"Key \"%@\" is an NSNumber of value %@",
            key, [illinois objectForKey:key]);
    }
}
```

This is a situation in which the id data type declaration for the key variable is most appropriate. Although keys are usually NSString types, that is not a requirement. By specifying an id type, the variable can handle whatever the nextObject method of myEnumerator throws at it.

NSMutableDictionary

If your code cannot assemble all entries of an NSDictionary in one statement, use an NSMutableDictionary and add key-value pairs as needed. Begin by creating an NSMutableDictionary instance with an expected number of entries:

```
NSMutableDictionary *myMutableDictionary =
    [NSMutableDictionary dictionaryWithCapacity:10];
```

As with other mutable classes you've met so far in this chapter, the initial capacity is merely a guide for internal memory allocation. Adding entries beyond that capacity is allowed.

To add an entry to an existing NSMutableDictionary, use the setObject:forKey: method:

```
- (void)setObject:(id)object forKey:(id)key
```

If the key already exists, the previously stored object value is sent a release message and is replaced by the new object value.

You can also add an existing dictionary's entries to an NSMutableDictionary:

```
- (void)addEntriesFromDictionary:(NSDictionary *)otherDictionary
```

The following example (for testing in Workbench) combines these two methods to demonstrate how an NSMutableDictionary can combine a static dictionary with an extra entry:

```
- (IBAction)runMyCode:(id)sender {

    NSArray *stateKeys = [NSArray arrayWithObjects:@"name", @"capital",
                        @"enteredUnion", nil];
    NSArray *illinoisData = [NSArray arrayWithObjects:@"Illinois", @"Springfield",
                        [NSNumber numberWithInt:1818], nil];
    NSDictionary *illinois = [NSDictionary dictionaryWithObjects:illinoisData
                                                forKeys:stateKeys];

    NSMutableDictionary *mutableIllinois =
        [NSMutableDictionary dictionaryWithCapacity:4];
```

```
    [mutableIllinois addEntriesFromDictionary:illinois];
    [mutableIllinois setObject:@"Cardinal" forKey:@"bird"];

    NSLog(@"%@", mutableIllinois);

}
```

Console output looks as follows:

```
{
    bird = Cardinal;
    capital = Springfield;
    enteredUnion = 1818;
    name = Illinois;
}
```

Notice that when NSLog() outputs an NSArray, the comma-delimited values are displayed inside parentheses, but for NSDictionary, the semicolon-delimited values are displayed inside curly braces. These are merely the ways the frameworks define how the description method of each class formats its value. You can override the description method of any object if you prefer a different format.

You can also remove entries in NSMutableDictionary objects. Three different methods let you remove all entries, a single entry (by key), or all entries matching keys supplied in an array. These changes are made to the receiver of the messages (all methods return void). The methods are defined as follows:

- (void)removeAllObjects
- (void)removeObjectForKey:(id)*key*
- (void)removeObjectsForKeys:(NSArray *)*keyArray*

Arrays and Dictionaries in Action

The sooner you reach comfort levels with the NSArray and NSDictionary classes (and their mutable subclasses) the sooner you'll be able to apply these data structures to many critical iOS app uses. Although you will see several specific applications in Chapter 9, let me whet your appetite.

When you inspected TheElements sample application, you saw that all data for the atomic elements displayed throughout the app arrived in the form of a *.plist* file. Open that project in Xcode and click on the *Elements.plist* file (inside the Resources group). Figure 8-9 shows the beginning of the file in the editor window.

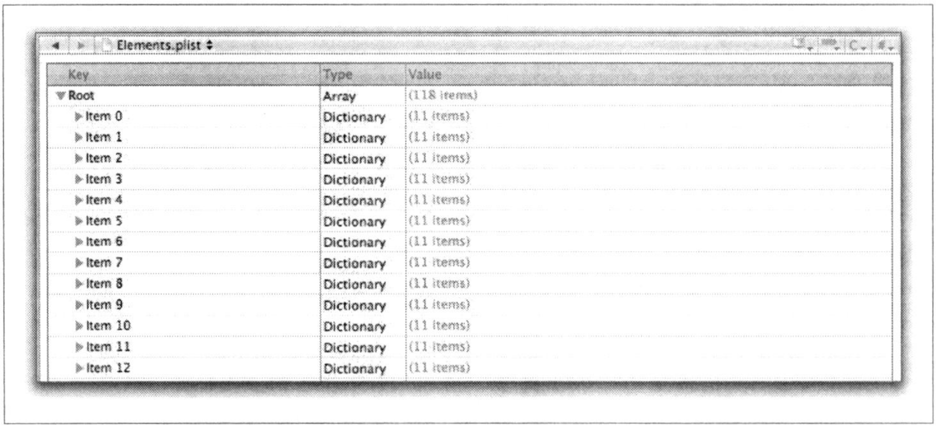

Figure 8-9. Start of Elements.plist file content

The property list is formatted at its root as an array of 118 members. This is an NSArray type, which means that you can create an NSArray object in code by loading this file directly into it (via the arrayWithContentsOfFile: class method). That's all you need to do to create the app's giant array from data delivered with the app. Other apps might download frequently updated data stored as a *.plist* file on a server—yet another way to get data into a live app (but via the asynchronous NSURLConnection class, rather than NSArray's synchronous arrayWithContentsOfURL: class method).

Now, notice that each of the 118 members of the root array is a dictionary. Expand the first item (Item 0) to see what the dictionary looks like (Figure 8-10).

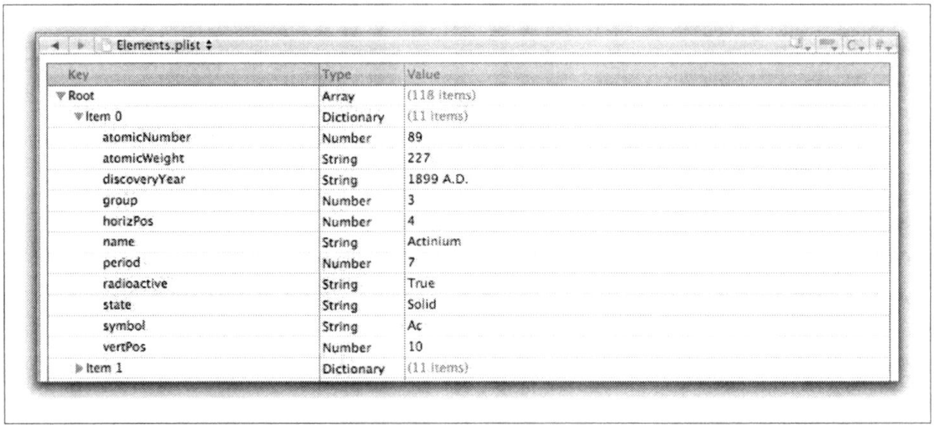

Figure 8-10. The dictionary for one element

The leftmost column reveals the keys for the key-value entries in the dictionary. Some values are string objects (NSString), while others are numbers (NSNumber). Entries could also be nested arrays or dictionaries if the data requirements of the app led in that direction. Property list entries can also be arbitrary data (of the NSData type), but if you intend to associate an image with a property list item, it's best to do so as a string holding the name of the file in the app bundle or external URL.

Because of the design of TheElements app, it turns out to be more efficient to use the property list dictionaries to build model objects (of class AtomicElement), because those objects are reused in each of the four sorted table views and then in the detail views. For simpler cases, the NSArray read from the *.plist* file could be all that's needed to generate content for a table view and associated detail views.

I don't know how the author of TheElements created the property list file. It's possible that he or she entered it manually via Xcode or the separate Property List Editor program, although that would be a tedious task. But if the source material was available in another source, such as a text file of some type, the author could have written a helper app (something like Workbench) that opened that file, parsed it to create dictionary entries for each element, and assembled the dictionaries into a large array subsequently saved as a *.plist* file. Then the author could have copied that file from the simulator app's directory into the project, ready to go.

Recap

In this chapter you have probed deeper into Objective-C classes and received an over-view of the most common Cocoa Touch classes that will handle your code's data. When you first encounter the class reference documents for classes such as NSString, NSArray, and NSDictionary, their idiosyncratic complexity may overwhelm you. It's more important at this stage of your learning to gain a solid grounding on the basics presented here, which should get you to the equivalent point of your knowledge of the JavaScript analogues. In time, you'll discover operations you can perform with these basic data objects in iOS that you only dreamt of in the JavaScript world. Despite the learning curve, you will eventually feel liberated.

To assist further in making the transition from JavaScript to Objective-C and iOS frameworks classes, the next chapter offers what amounts to recipes in the new environment for tasks you likely perform in JavaScript. Sometimes the analogues are clear, but not always. Where necessary, I will try to guide you to the new ways you have to approach tasks for your iOS apps.

CHAPTER 9

Common JavaScript Tasks in Cocoa Touch

We've covered a lot of the basics up to this point. But there are still lots of things you know how to do in JavaScript that could throw you if you intend to implement them in an iOS app. This chapter identifies many of those tasks and shows you how to accomplish them with Cocoa Touch classes and Objective-C techniques. Some tasks are pretty mundane—formatting numbers or calculating dates. But eventually the chapter becomes a bit more fun as you interact more with display elements in the iOS Simulator.

Even if you don't have a burning need to know how to accomplish one of these tasks in iOS, it will be worth reading through every section. Along the way you'll learn something new about Xcode, the frameworks, or Objective-C that will be of value in your day-to-day coding. I also don't expect you to remember everything shown in this chapter, so feel free to come back to it as a reference when the needs arise in the future.

Formatting Numbers for Display

You have seen that working with numbers in the Objective-C environment requires careful observation of data typing. Number values and objects (such as the `NSNumber`) concern themselves with the values they represent, rather than how the numbers are to be formatted for display as currency, percentages, or nicely aligned columns with necessary zero padding. Just as can happen in JavaScript, blindly converting a number to a string for display can cause unexpected results, such as too many or too few digits to the right of the decimal. JavaScript provides the `toFixed()` and `toPrecision()` methods of number objects (and values) as helpers, but Objective-C requires passing numbers through an abstract class, `NSNumberFormatter`, to assist with turning numeric data types into properly formatted strings.

The typical sequence requires creating an instance of `NSNumberFormatter`, then setting the formatting attributes of the object with the help of preformatted styles supplied by

Cocoa Touch. Once you have set the attributes, you send the `stringFromNumber:` message to that number formatter object, passing a numeric value as an argument. The method returns an `NSString` type with the formats applied to the number.

Preformatted Number Styles

Taking advantage of the preformatted styles of `NSNumberFormatter` is a multistep process. It begins by instantiating an `NSNumberFormatter` object and assigning one of the styles. In the following example, the `NSNumberFormatterDecimalStyle` constant is applied as an argument:

```
NSNumberFormatter *outputFormatter = [[NSNumberFormatter alloc] init];
[outputFormatter setNumberStyle:NSNumberFormatterDecimalStyle];
```

Table 9-1 lists your choices for number styles, along with examples of how to apply the style to a double value of 3.14159 with no additional formatting behaviors applied and with U.S. English International settings.

Table 9-1. NSNumberFormatter object preformatted styles

Style constant	Output for 3.14159
NSNumberFormatterNoStyle	3
NSNumberFormatterDecimalStyle	3.142
NSNumberFormatterCurrencyStyle	$3.14
NSNumberFormatterPercentStyle	314%
NSNumberFormatterScientificStyle	3.14159E0
NSNumberFormatterSpellOutStyle	three point one four one five nine

A number style sets only a basic category of representation, leaving many additional factors to be specified, especially zero padding to the left of the decimal and the number of digits to set aside for the fraction to the right. That's where a series of attribute settings come into play as separate methods of the `NSNumberFormatter` object. The list of all possible settings is huge (documented in the "NSNumberFormatter Class Reference" document in the SDK documentation), but I'll highlight several that probably remind you of the kinds of formatting you have used in JavaScript programming and web page display.

Watch out for the `NSNumberFormatterPercentStyle`. It assumes that source values are already factored for use as percentages. For example, a source value of 0.5 is displayed as 50%.

Table 9-2 shows several `NSNumberFormatter` methods that impact the display of group separators, integers to the left of the decimal, and fraction digits to the right of the decimal.

Table 9-2. Selected NSNumberFormatter formatting attribute methods

Method	Formatting effect
setMinimumIntegerDigits:	Left of decimal
setMaximumIntegerDigits:	Left of decimal
setMinimumFractionDigits:	Right of decimal
setMaximumFractionDigits:	Right of decimal
setUsesGroupingSeparator:	Thousands, millions, etc.
setRoundingMode:	How to round for display

The two methods for integer digits control how the resulting string displays numbers to the left of the decimal point. You have to be careful not to set the maximum so low that it truncates potentially larger numbers. Set the minimum integer value if you want your smaller values to be padded with zeros to the left.

You'll probably spend more formatting time on the numbers to the right of the decimal. The standard current style may do the job for you (but be mindful about currency symbols for users in different countries and test with alternate international settings). Setting low minimum fraction digits may cause numbers containing more digits to round their values. High minimum values cause numbers to the right of the decimal to be padded to reach the minimum number of digits.

The `setUsesGroupingSeparator:` method accepts a Boolean value to control whether separator characters appear where the current localized numbering system expects them. For U.S. English, that means commas every three characters to the left of the decimal. Other methods let you hardwire the separator symbol across all international systems.

To help you experiment with number formats, Example 9-1 provides a Workbench laboratory for the `runMyCode:` method. It assigns three different `NSNumber` values with which to play, along with some initial number format styles and attributes. Change some of the values and observe the results in the console when you click the button in the Workbench app.

Example 9-1. Number format laboratory for Workbench

```
- (IBAction)runMyCode:(id)sender {

    // Result for console
    NSString *result = [NSString string];

    // Three types of test values
    NSNumber *myDouble = [NSNumber numberWithDouble:3.14159];
    NSNumber *myGiantInteger = [NSNumber numberWithInt:74500899];
    // Arithmetic with NSNumber objects
    NSNumber *myComboNumber = [NSNumber numberWithDouble:
                            [myDouble doubleValue] + [myGiantInteger intValue]];
```

```
    // Create number formatter
    NSNumberFormatter *outputFormatter = [[NSNumberFormatter alloc] init];

    // Number style
    [outputFormatter setNumberStyle:NSNumberFormatterDecimalStyle];
    // Specific format settings to experiment with
    [outputFormatter setUsesGroupingSeparator:YES];
    [outputFormatter setMinimumIntegerDigits:3];
    [outputFormatter setMaximumIntegerDigits:10];
    [outputFormatter setMinimumFractionDigits:7];

    // Show result (NSString) through formatter's "eyes"
    // Try different numbers defined above:
    //     (myDouble, myGiantInteger, myComboNumber)
    result = [outputFormatter stringFromNumber:myComboNumber];

    NSLog(@"result = %@", result);

    [outputFormatter release];

}
```

As a bonus, Example 9-1 demonstrates how to perform simple arithmetic with NSNumber objects to yield an NSNumber object result. The math is done on values extracted from NSNumber objects and the resulting value is fed back into an NSNumber-generating method.

Rounding Numbers for Display

You have many number-rounding choices for your formatted numbers, selectable by passing one of seven constants to the setRoundingMode: method. Table 9-3 summarizes the available rounding modes. Notice that there are sometimes more than one constant for the same rounding action.

Table 9-3. Rounding mode constants for NSNumberFormatter objects

Constant value	Rounding action
NSNumberFormatterRoundCeiling	Round up to next larger number.
NSNumberFormatterRoundUp	Round up to next larger number.
NSNumberFormatterRoundFloor	Round down to next smaller number.
NSNumberFormatterRoundDown	Round down to next smaller number.
NSNumberFormatterRoundHalfEven	Round the last digit (when followed by a 5) toward an even digit.
NSNumberFormatterRoundHalfDown	Round down the last digit (when followed by a 5).
NSNumberFormatterRoundHalfUp	Round up the last digit (when followed by a 5).

If you specify no rounding mode, the default action is `NSNumberFormatterRoundHalf Even`, which adheres to the same IEEE standard JavaScript uses for its rounding actions.

Creating a Date Object

Working with the JavaScript `Date` object is the bane of many programmers, mostly due to the need for web pages to operate for a global audience where formats and time zones confound even the best of plans. If you thought that the JavaScript `Date` object was a headache, I don't have good news for you on the Cocoa Touch side of things. To perform even simple tasks often requires navigating through multiple classes dealing with dates, calendars, and date components—and that's not even getting into the formatted display of date and time data. That's one reason why the discussion involving dates is spread across a few sections in this chapter.

Despite this potentially fearsome complexity, one factor that is actually much simpler to deal with in an iOS app is obtaining a valid date and time input from the user. The whole issue of validating text field entries in web forms thankfully becomes a nonissue with the aid of the `UIDatePicker` control, shown in Figure 9-1.

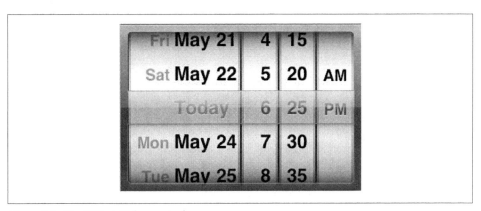

Figure 9-1. The UIDatePicker control

Adding a UIDatePicker to Workbench

If you want to try out some of the examples dealing with dates, I recommend you add (at least temporarily) a `UIDatePicker` control to the Workbench app, as well as a method that executes when a user chooses a date. Begin by adding a little bit of code to the `WorkbenchViewController` class files. First, add the following method declaration to *WorkbenchViewController.h* below the `runMyCode:` declaration:

```
- (IBAction)dateHasBeenPicked:(id)sender;
```

Next, add the method definition to the *WorkbenchViewController.m* file below the `runMyCode:` method:

```
- (IBAction)dateHasBeenPicked:(id)sender {
    NSDate *chosenDate = [sender date];

    NSLog(@"result = %@", chosenDate );

}
```

Save both files.

Double-click the *WorkbenchViewController.xib* file to open the nib file in Interface Builder. In the Library palette, narrow the display to Data Views. Then scroll down to see the Date Picker item. Drag the date picker to the bottom of the View window, as shown in Figure 9-2.

Figure 9-2. Positioning the date picker template in the view

With the date picker still selected, turn your attention to the Inspector palette and the Attributes pane, shown in Figure 9-3.

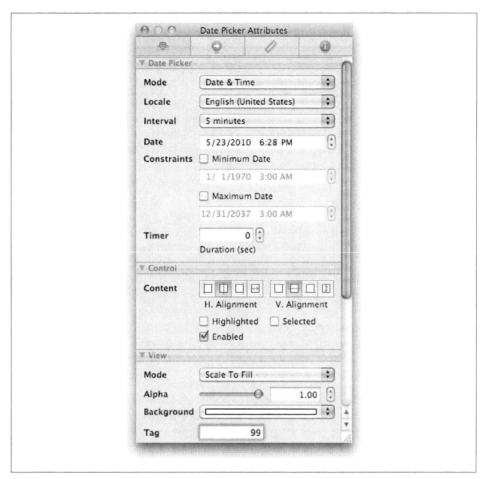

Figure 9-3. Attributes inspector of the date picker

You can look through the choices available to you. Keep the mode at the default Date & Time setting. Further down the Attributes inspector you'll find a field labeled Tag. Enter the number **99** into that field, as shown. You'll use this ID (a number I chose arbitrarily) to reference the date picker from other methods in the Workbench ViewController class.

Finally, connect the date picker to the dateHasBeenPicked: method. Change to the Connections view in the inspector palette. Drag from the empty dot on the right of the Value Changed event name to the File's Owner item in the document window. A pop-up list appears with the two IBAction methods in the class. Select dateHasBeen Picked:. The Connections inspector should look like Figure 9-4.

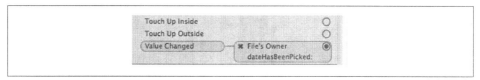

Figure 9-4. After connecting the Value Changed event to the File's Owner

Save the Interface Builder file and return to the Xcode project window. Build and run the app in the simulator. If you change any of the wheels in the date picker, the console window should show the selected date and time.

Understanding NSDate

One similarity between JavaScript and Cocoa Touch is that a date is encapsulated as an instance of a master date object. In JavaScript, the master object is, indeed, the Date object; in Cocoa Touch, it's the NSDate class. The main difference is that a JavaScript date object instance has a full range of methods that grant you read-write access to individual components of a date—month, date, year, hour, minute, and so on. While an instance of an NSDate object stores the specifications for a snapshot of time, getting and setting its component values requires quite a bit more work and help from other classes. Despite sometimes circuitous routes, your NSDate instance remains the core of the information about a date. Changes you make to date components need to find their way back to an NSDate object instance in the end. You'll see more of that in a bit.

For now, look at the dateHasBeenPicked: method you added to WorkbenchViewControl ler. It relies on a reference to the UIDatePicker being passed as an argument (sender). Checking the UIDatePicker class reference documentation, you'll find that one of the properties of this user interface control is date, an instance of NSDate. Although it is a property, the argument is defined as an id data type. You can cast the value to a UIDatePicker type to use the dot syntax of an Objective-C property without compiler complaint or you can send the date message to reach the implied getter method. The latter is the approach displayed in the example.

The NSLog() function outputs the value returned by an NSDate object's description property, as in the following:

```
2010-05-25 18:25:45 -0700
```

That's a pretty bare-bones representation of May 25, 2010 at 6:25:45 PM Pacific Daylight Time. The time zone is determined automatically by reading the device's time zone in Settings. Parsing that string to obtain components is most definitely *not* the way to interact with the object. But you can save instances of NSDate as objects in arrays and dictionaries so you can write them to a file if necessary.

You can also use code to create a brand-new date object. The most common way is to invoke the class method designed for that purpose:

```
NSDate *myDate = [NSDate date];
```

You'll take comfort in knowing that this statement works just as the JavaScript new Date() constructor statement works: they both produce a date object instance whose date and time represent a snapshot of the system clock at the instant they ran.

Creating a Date Object for a Specific Date

The sequence for creating an NSDate object for a specific date requires two extra classes: NSDateComponents and NSCalendar. Much of the need to have these very abstract classes in the Cocoa Touch frameworks comes from the desire to make the system work in all parts of the world, including those where alternative calendar systems are observed.

You begin by creating an instance of NSDateComponents. That object has a series of instance variables representing components that a date is capable of holding—such as month, year, hour, and so on. You access these ivars only via getter and setter methods (i.e., they are not referenced as properties). Table 9-4 shows the parallel methods for getting and setting individual components. All values in and out are NSInteger data types.

Table 9-4. NSDateComponents accessor methods

Getter	Setter
- era	- setEra:
- year	- setYear:
- month	- setMonth:
- day	- setDay:
- hour	- setHour:
- minute	- setMinute:
- second	- setSecond:
- week	- setWeek:
- weekday	- setWeekday:
- weekdayOrdinal	- setWeekdayOrdinal:

 Cocoa Touch values for month and weekday are one-based, unlike JavaScript's zero-based ranges. Months in Cocoa Touch are values 1 (January) through 12 (December); weekdays are 1 (Sunday) through 7 (Saturday).

When you generate a new NSDateComponents object, all values are set initially to the NSUndefinedDateComponent constant. Therefore, only those components that you explicitly set contain useful values. And yet, if you supply values for the day, month, and year that eventually find their way into an NSDate object, the time portion of the date object defaults to 12:00:00 AM. Conversely, if you set only time components, the eventual `NSDate` object date components default to 1/1/0001.

To set the components for a date, you'll need to send at least three messages for the day, month, and year. Values for day and month are one-based. The following sequence assigns December 25, 2010 components:

```
NSDateComponents *components = [[NSDateComponents alloc] init];

[components setMonth:12];   // December
[components setDay:25];     // 25th day
[components setYear:2010];  // Year 2010
```

Once you have set the values for the date components, you must then apply those components to an `NSCalendar` instance, which has been initialized to the desired calendar system. Unless you know that you need to accommodate the Buddhist, Chinese, Hebrew, Islamic, or Japanese calendars, you will operate exclusively with the Gregorian calendar system. To initialize a Gregorian calendar object, use the following statement:

```
NSCalendar *gregorian = [[NSCalendar alloc]
                         initWithCalendarIdentifier:NSGregorianCalendar];
```

This calendar object generates the `NSDate` object instance when you supply the previously created components object:

```
NSDate *xmas2010 = [gregorian dateFromComponents:components];
```

 When you use `alloc` to create objects, don't forget to release them when you are finished with them!

To let you experiment with this way of creating dates, Example 9-2 provides a replacement for the Workbench `runMyCode:` method. It assumes that you have added the `UIDatePicker` control to the app as described earlier in this chapter, including adding the tag number identifier to the picker in Interface Builder. With this method, you will set the wheels of the date picker to the code-generated date whose components you set whenever you click the Workbench button. As shown, it reveals Christmas Day, because the date picker control accepts an `NSDate` object to adjust its wheels in the display.

Example 9-2. Setting the UIDatePicker to a specific date

```
- (IBAction)runMyCode:(id)sender {

    // Keep date picker reference handy
    id myDatePicker = [self.view viewWithTag:99];

    NSDateComponents *components = [[NSDateComponents alloc] init];

    [components setMonth:12];
```

```
[components setDay:25];
[components setYear:2010];
NSCalendar *gregorian = [[NSCalendar alloc]
                            initWithCalendarIdentifier:NSGregorianCalendar];
NSDate *date = [gregorian dateFromComponents:components];
[myDatePicker setDate:date];

[components release];
[gregorian release];
```

}

Using a tag to reference the date picker is convenient for demonstration. In a production environment, however, the UIDatePicker object added to the user interface in Interface Builder would normally be assigned as a property (an IBOutlet) of the view controller class, allowing direct referencing in code as if it were an ivar of the class.

Extracting Components from an NSDate Object

Now consider the opposite journey: You have a date object (perhaps obtained from a UIDatePicker) from which you want to read one or more components for display or calculation. Your route takes you through NSCalendar once again, this time back to the NSDateComponents class. Just as NSCalendar provides the gateway from components to a date object, the same class serves the reverse purpose, acting as the go-between. Referencing the components, however, takes a different form.

Let's start with an example, then fill in the explanations. The following sequence obtains a date from a UIDatePicker and extracts an index for the day of the week on which the selected date falls:

```
NSDate *chosenDate = [sender date];

NSCalendar *gregorian = [[NSCalendar alloc]
                            initWithCalendarIdentifier:NSGregorianCalendar];

NSDateComponents *weekdayComponents =
                    [gregorian components:(NSWeekdayCalendarUnit)
                                fromDate:chosenDate];
[gregorian release];

NSLog(@"%@ falls on a %d", chosenDate, [weekdayComponents weekday]);
```

The code begins by obtaining the date object, then creates an NSCalendar object of the Gregorian persuasion. At the core of the operation is the NSCalendar's components:from Date: method, which returns an NSDateComponents object. Values for the first argument come from a list of constants that generate a bit mask of all the desired components you want to be able to read for the date object. In the example above, only one component—NSWeekdayCalendarUnit—is specified, because the code is interested only in discovering the day of the week for the date. But if you want more components preserved in the `NSDateComponents` object, you must add more constants with the bitwise OR operator (|). For example, if you want the day of the week, month, and date from a date object, specify three constants in any order as follows:

```
NSDateComponents *dateComponents =
  [gregorian components:(NSWeekdayCalendarUnit |
                         NSMonthCalendarUnit | NSDayCalendarUnit)
              fromDate:chosenDate];
```

Once the `NSDateComponents` object is created, you can then use any of the getter methods listed here to obtain values, but only of components you specified when the date components object was created. Any other component returns a value that is equal to the `NSUndefinedDateComponent` constant. In the example above, the weekday integer is returned (Sunday = 1...Saturday = 7). You can apply any of the following constant values to the components bit mask for the `components:fromDate:` method:

NSEraCalendarUnit
NSYearCalendarUnit
NSMonthCalendarUnit
NSDayCalendarUnit
NSHourCalendarUnit
NSMinuteCalendarUnit
NSSecondCalendarUnit
NSWeekCalendarUnit
NSWeekdayCalendarUnit
NSWeekdayOrdinalCalendarUnit

Having to refer to date components in so many different ways—component bit masks, setter methods, getter methods—might make your head spin at first. But once you get the basic functionality down in your code, you'll have models that remind you of the correct reference type in various situations as you tweak the components you want to use.

Creating NSDate Objects from Strings

The technique shown earlier in this chapter to create an `NSDate` object out of components in code does not fit all situations. For instance, you may retrieve data from a server that arrives as JavaScript Object Notation (which you parse using a third-party JSON library) or as a comma-delimited string of text. You need to convert those strings into `NSDate` objects suitable for array or dictionary collections. To paraphrase a one-time Apple iPhone advertising slogan, "There's a class for that!": the `NSDateFormatter` class.

JavaScript offers the option to specify a date string as an argument to the new Date() constructor function, provided the string is formatted in a limited range of the correct ways, as in new Date("October 28, 2010 15:30:00"). But what if the source material is in an entirely different format? The NSDateFormatter class has the answer to that query.

The NSDateFormatter in Cocoa Touch offers some shortcuts, but they rely on the data strings being in one of several fixed formats. The real world is rarely that easy. Therefore, mastery of the NSDateFormatter class takes a fair amount of study not only of the Cocoa Touch class itself, but also of a complementary Unicode standards document that explains date and time format coding in excruciating detail (*http://unicode.org/reports/tr35/tr35-6.html#Date_Format_Patterns*). The coding is almost a language unto itself, some of which is obvious, but mostly not. I will supply an introduction to the concepts and several examples to give you an idea about usage.

An NSDateFormatter object is a pretty powerful entity in that you can use it both for converting a string into an NSDate object and for extracting dates as strings in highly customizable formats for display on screen. For converting a string to an NSDate object, the format acts as a template that guides the object creation process to interpret specific character sequences as date components. Consider the following possible North American English representations of the same date:

- 3/4/11
- 03-04-2011
- 4 March 2011
- Mar. 4, 2011

I specifically cite North American English because in many parts of the English-speaking world, the first two dates refer to April 3, rather than March 4. These are only a handful of possible ways to represent a date. Add the day of the week, time, and time zone to the statement, and the possibilities are almost endless.

Fortunately, when you need to work with a date format that arrives from a computerized source, the format will likely be the same for all similar values. It's your job to design a template that matches the formatting of the incoming string to identify each of the component parts of the date (and/or time). In the Unicode formatting document is a lengthy table that describes the placeholders for date and time components and how their representation affects the format. For example, the uppercase "M" signifies the month, but the number of Ms in the position affects how the format expects the month to be portrayed. One or two "M" characters means the month is represented numerically; three "M" characters means it's the short spelled-out version (e.g., "Mar"); four "M" characters means it's the fully spelled-out version (e.g., "March"). Table 9-5 presents an abbreviated version of the Unicode table showing the placeholders and formats you are most likely to encounter.

Table 9-5. Selected Unicode format specifiers

Symbol	Meaning	Example	Description
yy	year	11	Two-digit year
yyyy	year	2011	Four-digit year
M or MM	month	03	Two-digit month (zero-padded)
MMM	month	Mar	Short month name
MMMM	month	March	Long month name
d or dd	day	3	Day of the month
E, EE, or EEE	weekday	Fri	Short day name
EEEE	weekday	Friday	Long day name
EEEEE	weekday	F	Single-letter day
a	period	AM	AM or PM
h or hh	hour	3	12-hour time
H or HH	hour	15	24-hour time
m or mm	minute	05	Two-digit minute (zero-padded)
s or ss	second	09	Two-digit second (zero-padded)
z, zz, or zzz	time zone	PST	Short time zone
zzzz	time zone	Pacific Standard Time	Long time zone
Z, ZZ, or ZZZ	time zone	-0800	GMT offset format
ZZZZ	time zone	GMT -0800	GMT offset format (with GMT)

In addition to the placeholder characters, you can specify other characters, such as delimiters and even longer strings. Here are the specifiers for the four examples shown earlier:

```
MM/dd/yy
MM-dd-yyyy
dd MMMM yyyy
MMM. dd, yyyy
```

Format specifiers are Objective-C strings, passed as arguments to the setDateFormat: method. After you create the date formatter, its dateFromString: method generates a new NSDate object. The following is the complete sequence that turns a date string into an NSDate object using a formatter matched to the date string:

```
// Simulated date string from an external source
NSString *incomingDateString = @"Mar. 4, 2011";

// Create date formatter
NSDateFormatter *incomingFormatter = [[NSDateFormatter alloc] init];
// Assign format
[incomingFormatter setDateFormat:@"MMM. dd, yyyy"];

// Create date object with formatter
```

```
NSDate *incomingDateAsDate =
    [incomingFormatter dateFromString:incomingDateString];
[incomingFormatter release];

NSLog(@"%@", incomingDateAsDate);
```

Converting an NSDate to a String

If you have an NSDate object and want to output the results to a nicely formatted string, the NSDateFormatter class is your friend. The class comes with a number of predefined format styles that might fill your requirements without requiring you to build complex format strings. And, just as the NSDateFormatter class has a method to generate an NSDate object from an NSString, so, too, does it have one to generate an NSString out of an NSDate object by applying formatting instructions.

The normal sequence of statements—assuming you have an NSDate object to convert—is to create the NSDateFormatter instance, assign date and/or time formats (either from the predefined styles or a customized format), then invoke stringFrom Date:. If you use the predefined styles, you need to set date and time formats separately (via the setDateStyle: and setTimeStyle: methods). If you set only one format, the output contains only that part of the NSDate object. Table 9-6 shows the predefined format constants and an example of the output for each one (on a U.S. English-language system).

Table 9-6. NSDateFormatter style constants

Format constant	Date example	Time example
NSDateFormatterNoStyle		
NSDateFormatterShortStyle	3/4/11	3:15 PM
NSDateFormatterMediumStyle	Mar 4, 2011	3:15:00 PM
NSDateFormatterLongStyle	March 4, 2011	3:15:00 PM PST
NSDateFormatterFullStyle	Friday, March 4, 2011	3:15:00 PM PT

You can experiment with this conversion using the UIDatePicker added to Workbench earlier in this chapter and the dateHasBeenPicked: method that runs whenever a user activates the date picker's wheels. Example 9-3 shows the entire method.

Example 9-3. Converting a UIDatePicker value to a string

```
- (IBAction)dateHasBeenPicked:(id)sender {

    // Get selected date from date picker
    NSDate *chosenDate = [sender date];

    // Create date formatter object
    NSDateFormatter *outgoingFormatter = [[NSDateFormatter alloc] init];

    // Assign styles for both date and time
```

```
[outgoingFormatter setDateStyle:NSDateFormatterFullStyle];
[outgoingFormatter setTimeStyle:NSDateFormatterFullStyle];

// Generate string for the selected date
NSString *myDateString = [outgoingFormatter stringFromDate:chosenDate];
NSLog(@"You chose: %@", myDateString);
```
}

Each time you touch the date picker's wheels, the formatted date appears in the console.

If you would rather fashion your own format, use the `setDateFormat:` method of the date formatter object. That method's argument is a string containing the Unicode format string described earlier using symbols from Table 9-5. Try the following statement in the `dateHasBeenPicked:` method above, using the one statement to replace the two that set the date and time styles:

```
[outgoingFormatter setDateFormat:@"(EEE) MMM. dd, yyyy 'at' hh:mm a"];
```

The result for this format is as follows:

```
(Fri) Mar. 04, 2011 at 03:15 PM
```

Notice that the format contains a string in single quotes to contain characters that would otherwise be interpreted as format placeholders.

If you want to test how your strings look in other languages on a device, you can go to the Settings app, tap the General item, then International. First, make note of which items (by position) let you change the Language and Region Format (so you can change them back once the menu labels are in other languages). Then choose both languages and formats in target countries around the world. Build and run the app again to see how the `UIDatePicker` displays values and how the formats appear in the console window. Despite the comparatively more complex way Cocoa Touch converts a date object to a string, you are less reliant on the wide differences between web browser treatments of JavaScript `Date` object formats. You also have everything you need right inside your development device(s) to check out how things will look and behave for international users.

Getting Month and Day Names

If your date calculations and formatting require that you have a list of strings for the names of months and days in the device's current language, you can use the `NSDateFor matter` class to obtain those strings. Two methods, `monthSymbols` and `weekdaySymbols` (plus many variations for long and short versions of the names), return arrays of those symbols (January, February, etc., and Sunday, Monday, etc.). The arrays, of course, use zero-based indices, while the component values for months and days are one-based, so you'll have to adjust for that offset.

Let's say you want to display shortened labels for days of the week across the top of a calendar display. To obtain those strings, use the following:

```
NSDateFormatter *myFormatter = [[NSDateFormatter alloc] init];
NSArray *weekdaySymbolsArray = [myFormatter shortWeekdaySymbols];
[myFormatter release];
```

The array now contains the day names starting with Sunday in the language and localized date system as chosen in the International settings of the device.

Calculating Dates

As you've seen earlier in this chapter, the number of moving parts required to work with Cocoa Touch dates is far greater than the one moving part of the JavaScript Date object. When it comes to dealing with date calculations, you must once again forget what you know about JavaScript and prepare to get into calendars and components. In this section, I'll describe two typical date calculation tasks: determining the date for 10 days from today and determining the number of days between two dates. Although the two tasks use the same classes to achieve their results, the processes are quite different.

10 Days in the Future

The act of adding or subtracting minutes, days, months, or any other units from a date means that you are modifying one or more components of the date. You must carry out such modifications within the context of a particular calendaring system. Even if all of your date manipulation occurs in the Gregorian calendar, you must specify a calendar because it is the NSCalendar class that provides the necessary method that calculates a new date object based on modifications to an existing date object. The method, dateByAddingComponents:toDate:options:, assumes you have an NSDateCompo nents object detailing the components being modified and by how much (positive or negative integer values). The method then applies those modifications to the date supplied as the second argument.

You can experiment with this combination in the dateHasBeenPicked: method added to Workbench earlier in this chapter (along with the UIDatePicker control). Example 9-4 reads the date from the date picker, calculates the date for 10 days in the future, and displays the raw date in the console (without any formatting to keep things simple).

Example 9-4. Adding 10 days to a selected date

```
- (IBAction)dateHasBeenPicked:(id)sender {

    NSDate *chosenDate = [sender date];

    NSCalendar *gregorian = [[NSCalendar alloc]
                        initWithCalendarIdentifier:NSGregorianCalendar];

    NSDateComponents *deltaComponents = [[NSDateComponents alloc] init];
```

```
    [deltaComponents setDay:10]; // 10 days in the future

    // Create new date object
    NSDate *futureDate = [gregorian dateByAddingComponents:deltaComponents
                                                    toDate:chosenDate
                                                   options:0];

    [deltaComponents release];
    [gregorian release];

    NSLog(@"Ten days from %@ will be: %@", chosenDate, futureDate);

}
```

After the method obtains the selected date from the date picker, it creates an instance of a Gregorian `NSCalendar` object, which is needed later. Next comes the `NSDateCompo nents` object creation. Component values will be added to the reference date; if you want to modify a component so that it goes back in time, assign a negative integer (e.g., –10 for 10 days before the reference date). Although the code shows adjustment of only one component, you can set as many different components as you like. For example, if you want to create a date for one month and one day in the future, assign both components:

```
        [deltaComponents setMonth:1]; // 1 month in the future
        [deltaComponents setDay:1];   // plus 1 day in the future
```

The `NSCalendar` object created earlier becomes the primary actor when it adds the components to the reference date. Assigning zero to the `options:` argument instructs the method to roll the results ahead to the next unit if necessary. For example, if you calculate 10 days ahead of the 25th of a month, you want the date to roll ahead into the following month.

You can use all of these modification techniques on your choice of date and time components—or both, if necessary. Therefore, if you push the hours ahead beyond the current day, the `NSDate` object returned by the `dateByAddingCompo nents:toDate:options:` method correctly adjusts the rest of the date's components automatically.

Days Between Dates

A different `NSCalendar` method, `components:fromDate:toDate:options:`, takes center stage when you need to calculate the amount of time between two dates. As you can tell from the method name, you'll be dealing with `NSDateComponents` once again.

Assuming you have two `NSDate` objects (derived from whatever source your code dictates), you also need an `NSCalendar` object available. The following example creates that object and obtains the day component of the difference between the two dates. Then the day value is written to the console:

```
// Assume startDate and endDate already exist as NSDate instances

NSCalendar *gregorian = [[NSCalendar alloc]
                         initWithCalendarIdentifier:NSGregorianCalendar];

NSDateComponents *deltaComponents = [gregorian components:NSDayCalendarUnit
                                               fromDate:startDate
                                                 toDate:endDate
                                                options:0];

NSLog(@"delta days = %d", [deltaComponents day] );

[deltaComponents release];
[gregorian release];
```

The first argument of the `components:fromDate:toDate:options:` method is a bit mask of the components you ultimately wish to view. The components are the same constants given in the section "Extracting Components from an NSDate Object" on page 213. Exercise caution if you specify more than one component unit (as bitwise OR'd constants) because the results may be divided among the various components. For example, if the early date is June 1 and the late date is July 15, the results you get depend on the components specified. If you specify only `NSDayCalendarUnit`, the day component reports 44 days. But if you specify the bit mask for both `NSDayCalendarUnit` and `NSMonthCalendarUnit`, the `day` component returns `14`, while the `month` component dutifully reports `1` (which covers the remaining 30 days, the length of the month of June). This same interaction affects other component combinations, including those specifying time components.

Comparing Dates

If you need to uncover how one date compares with another (earlier, later, the same), you have your choice of several `NSDate` object methods that work directly on those objects (without the need to convert to components or other constructions). For example, the `earlierDate:` method returns a new `NSDate` object referencing which of the two date objects in the message comes before the other:

```
NSDate *firstDate = [oneDate earlier:anotherDate];
```

The `laterDate:` method operates in reverse. And the `isEqualToDate:` method returns a Boolean value revealing whether the values of the two date objects are identical:

```
if ([date1 isEqualToDate:date2]) {
    // Statements to execute if two values are identical
    ...
}
```

You should also get to know the `compare:` method (which you can find in many Cocoa Touch classes), because it returns an `NSComparisonResult` value—a value represented by one of three constants shown in Table 9-7.

Table 9-7. NSComparisonResult values for the compare: method

Value	Description
NSOrderedAscending	Receiver is earlier than argument.
NSOrderedSame	Receiver is equal to argument.
NSOrderedDescending	Receiver is later than argument.

Such comparisons are likely to occur in `if` condition tests:

```
if ([date1 compare:date2] == NSOrderedDescending) {
    // Operate on dates given that date1 comes after date2
    ...
}
```

The `compare:` method and `NSComparisonResult` value are quite versatile. You'll find them implemented for many classes throughout Cocoa Touch frameworks (and you'll see them later for array sorting).

If you have been following the date object manipulation sections from beginning to end, you can remove the date picker from the Workbench user interface nib file, along with the `dateHasBeenPicked:` method from the code files. Or you can leave them in place for future experiments on your own.

Downloading Remote Files Asynchronously

The JavaScript language seemed to transform from "toy language" to "serious language" when all mainstream browsers implemented the `XMLHttpRequest` object or similar functionality (it began life as an ActiveX control for Internet Explorer). Suddenly browsers could silently (and under more control than before) communicate with a server and update portions of a web page's content without having to reload or redraw the entire page. Web pages could look more like apps. And thus web apps were truly born. In 2005, Jesse James Garrett described the activity with this object as Asynchronous JavaScript and XML, or Ajax.

Background communication for standalone applications is nothing new, and iOS provides a class that performs the work for which you've been using Ajax on the Web. Some of the concepts are the same, but the iOS version is heavily reliant on the delegate pattern, which makes it easy to grasp (IMHO). Although the `XMLHttpRequest` object automatically accumulates data into a buffer, you have to manage that accumulation in your iOS code. But it's a pretty easy task to take care of and shouldn't cause you any headaches.

You will gain one enormous freedom over Ajax on the Web: there are no same-origin security restrictions on you. If you have a publicly accessible URL, your app can download the data and manipulate it to your heart's content.

It's likely a waste of time to compare fine points between the two systems, because so many web authors use a variety of client-side frameworks to shield themselves from the inner workings of the `XMLHttpRequest` object. In any case, the overall systems have similar feels to them. You generate a request and wait for the object to signal when it has received its data. The iOS version provides even more event-like signals for different parts of the exchange between client and server.

Example Project

To illustrate the techniques in this section, I have created a separate project (*PlistDownload.xcodeproj*) that downloads a demonstration *.plist* file from my server, saves the file to the device, reads information from the file, and deletes the file when the app goes into iOS 4 background mode or quits (so the file can be freshly downloaded the next time you access the app). The file contains information about winners and losers for several World Cup championship matches. After the file is delivered to the device, two buttons retrieve information from the file and display results, as shown in Figure 9-5.

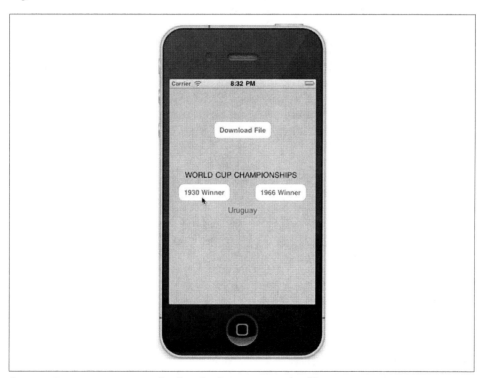

Figure 9-5. Demonstration app for downloading a property list file

All files for the app, including nib files, are included with the project. You are invited to make changes to the project and user interface as you explore the underlying code. For information on downloading sample code, see "How to Contact Us" on page xv in the Preface.

Creating the Request

You control all download activity using an instance of the NSURLConnection class. As mentioned earlier in this book, you will find numerous initialization methods for classes, such as NSArray, NSDictionary, and NSString, that suggest you can create instances of those objects directly by downloading their content from a URL. But those downloading methods are synchronous and therefore potentially block further execution of your app (or user interaction with it) if the connection is slow, the server is down, or for any other reason things don't work like they should. The NSURLConnection object operates asynchronously (by default) and lets users carry on with using your app while the downloading takes place. When the download is finally complete, a delegate method triggers the appropriate action, such as updating the user interface, parsing the incoming data, saving the data to a file, or whatever the app requires.

To set the scene for NSURLConnection, it's helpful to create two properties for the view controller class in which the download operates. One property is for the instance of NSURLConnection and the other is an NSMutableData class object that holds the data arriving from the server. The data holder needs to be mutable because its content builds up over time as the download is in progress. Example 9-5 shows the header file for the PListDownloadViewController class, with the two ivars and properties highlighted in bold. All of the properties are duly synthesized in the implementation file and released in its dealloc method.

Example 9-5. PlistDownloadViewController.h

```
#import <UIKit/UIKit.h>

@interface PlistDownloadViewController : UIViewController {

    NSURLConnection *pListConnection;
    NSMutableData *incomingPlistData;

    // Label for output display
    IBOutlet UILabel *resultsLabel;

}

@property (nonatomic, retain) NSURLConnection *pListConnection;
@property (nonatomic, retain) NSMutableData *incomingPlistData;
@property (nonatomic, retain) UILabel *resultsLabel;

// Methods invoked from buttons
- (IBAction)downloadPlist;
- (IBAction)show1930Winner;
```

```
- (IBAction)show1966Winner;
```

```
@end
```

In the implementation file, the `downloadPlist` method is invoked when a user taps the Download File button, as follows:

```
- (IBAction)downloadPlist {
    [[UIApplication sharedApplication] setNetworkActivityIndicatorVisible:YES];
    NSURL *theUrl = [NSURL URLWithString:@"http://dannyg.com/dl/demo.plist"];

    NSURLRequest *theRequest =
            [NSURLRequest requestWithURL:theUrl
                             cachePolicy:NSURLRequestUseProtocolCachePolicy
                          timeoutInterval:60.0];

    self.pListConnection = [NSURLConnection connectionWithRequest:theRequest
                                                         delegate:self];

}
```

The method begins by activating the network activity indicator in the device status bar through the `UIApplication` object (see Chapter 5). Sending that message displays and spins the indicator until we tell it to stop. Despite what users might think, the indicator is not actually monitoring network traffic or similar activity: your code tells the spinner when to start and when to stop.

Next come two statements that assemble the URL and an `NSURLRequest` object, one of the arguments needed by `NSURLConnection`. Although there are a few ways to initiate the network request, this example uses the class method of `NSURLConnection`, which creates an autoreleased instance of the object and starts the request right away. It also requires a delegate class where progress messages are to be sent. For this app, the current class (`self`) is the delegate and all necessary delegate methods are implemented elsewhere in this file. The returned object instance is assigned to the `pListConnection` property and the network activity begins on a separate thread out of view.

Initializing the NSMutableData Object

At some point, the view controller class needs to allocate and initialize the `NSMutable Data` object that will be gathering incoming data. When a view controller loads its view, the system sends a number of messages in a very strict sequence. One of those messages is `viewDidAppear:`, which is the one the example app uses to initialize the data collector. Example 9-6 shows that process.

Example 9-6. Initializing the NSMutableData object

```
// View has loaded and appeared on screen; perform additional set up
- (void)viewDidAppear:(BOOL)animated {
    [super viewDidAppear:animated];
    // Alloc and initialize receptacle for retrieved plist data
    self.incomingPlistData = [[NSMutableData alloc] initWithCapacity:1000];

}
```

As with other mutable classes, the `initWithCapacity:` method lets you set an initial size that can expand as needed.

Delegate Methods

The `NSURLConnection` class features a collection of 11 delegate methods (four of which deal with authentication, which isn't covered here). The most significant occurrences that cause delegate messages to be sent when retrieving data from a simple URL are:

- Having encountered an error before or during the transfer
- Having received a response from the server
- Having received a batch of data
- Having received all of the data

Let's look at the four corresponding delegate methods.

Handling download errors

You should always implement the `connection:didFailWithError:` method to handle network or server errors gracefully for the user. In fact, Apple insists that apps accessing the Internet notify users in a gentle and helpful manner when the network isn't available for whatever reason. Example 9-7 shows one way to process this method with an aim toward providing meaningful information to the user if there are download problems.

Example 9-7. Error-handling method for NSURLConnection

```
- (void)connection:(NSURLConnection *)connection
    didFailWithError:(NSError *)error {
    // Handle download/connection error here
    // Start with nerdy message to console for debugging
    NSLog(@"Download failed! Error - %@ %@",
        [error localizedDescription],
        [[error userInfo] objectForKey:NSErrorFailingURLStringKey]);

    // Now display problem alert to user.
    UIAlertView *baseAlert;
    NSString *alertTitle = @"Download Problem";
    NSString *alertMessage;
    switch ([error code]) {
        case -1001:
```

```
                alertMessage = @"The server is not responding at this time.";
                break;
        case -1003:
                alertMessage = @"The server is currently unavailable.";
                break;
        case -1009:
                alertMessage =
                @"No internet connection is detected.\nVerify your wireless settings.";
                break;
        default:
                alertMessage = @"Unable to retrieve data.";
                break;
    }
    baseAlert = [[UIAlertView alloc]
                    initWithTitle:alertTitle message:alertMessage
                    delegate:self cancelButtonTitle:nil
                    otherButtonTitles:@"OK", nil];
    [baseAlert show];
    [baseAlert release];

    [[UIApplication sharedApplication] setNetworkActivityIndicatorVisible:NO];
}
```

Details about the error are contained in the NSError object passed as the second argument to the method. This object has several methods that reveal specific codes and descriptions of the error. Although the class can provide native language details, you more than likely will want to customize the message for your application, as is done in Example 9-7. The design choice in the listing is to display the message in a UIAlert view. The method stops the network activity icon in the status bar. If an error occurs, the NSURLConnection object ceases to transfer data, so you should let your users know the app is no longer retrieving data.

Receiving a response

When the connection:didReceiveResponse: method is invoked, it means the request has elicited some type of response from the server. You should use this occasion to empty the mutable data object so it starts out empty when data starts arriving, as shown in Example 9-8.

Example 9-8. Acting upon receiving a server response

```
- (void)connection:(NSURLConnection *)connection
        didReceiveResponse:(NSURLResponse *)response {
    [self.incomingPlistData setLength:0];
}
```

We will revisit this method later to show you how to access response headers from HTTP requests. You may be able to use header information to eliminate downloading a file that has not changed on the server since the last time it was retrieved.

Accumulating incoming data

As the `NSURLConnection` object receives data, it spits out blocks as arguments to multiple invocations of the `connection:didReceiveData:` method. The size of the blocks or how many times they are passed along are of no interest to you. Instead, your job in the method is simply to accumulate the data into the `NSMutableData` property you've defined to hold incoming data. As a mutable class, it offers a method to append data to whatever is currently in the object. Example 9-9 shows how this accumulation works.

Example 9-9. Accumulating incoming data

```
- (void)connection:(NSURLConnection *)connection didReceiveData:(NSData *)data {
    // Accumulate incoming data into mutable data object
    [self.incomingPlistData appendData:data];
}
```

Processing the completed download

You know the download was successful when the `connectionDidFinishLoading:` method is called. At this point, the connection has been closed and your `NSMutable Data` property has the full content ready for you to spin your magic with it. In the sample app, the data is saved to a property list file. Example 9-10 shows the code for this method.

Example 9-10. Processing the download upon successful completion

```
// Success! Now write to local file
- (void)connectionDidFinishLoading:(NSURLConnection *)connection {
    // Write binary data to local file in app's Documents directory
    NSString *plistFilenamePath = [self getDemoFilePath];
    [self.incomingPlistData writeToFile:plistFilenamePath atomically:YES];

    // File is now ready for reading

    [[UIApplication sharedApplication] setNetworkActivityIndicatorVisible:NO];
}
```

The file-writing statements can be handed off to a separate method, especially if additional processing is needed for the received data. The only other requirement is that you turn off the network activity indicator, as shown. Details about working with files are covered in this chapter's section on reading/writing local files.

Downloading Only When Needed

Connectivity through a wireless device—especially when the connection is through a cellular data network—is a precious resource, both in the amount of bytes that wend their way through the air and in the user's time. If a user does not have an unlimited data plan from the cell phone carrier, every downloaded byte may count against the monthly maximum in the user's data plan. Repeated delays can also turn the user against your application, a problem that might not occur to you when you work in the simulator; it will probably behave much better than the actual performance when downloading data on a real device through WiFi or cellular. To do the best for your app's users, you should minimize the amount of data that needs to be downloaded to your app.

Not all data consumed by an app may necessarily be updated every instant. For instance, you might have your app set up to download user tips or other support data that is updated from time to time. It would be a waste to automatically download the whole batch each time the app launches. Fortunately, if your server headers support timestamping, you can preserve the date of each download on the device (as a user preference perhaps) and compare the saved date against the header response of the file just before the actual download begins. If the two dates are the same, cancel the connection and save some bytes. Use a local copy of the file saved after the last download.

To take advantage of timestamping, you need to initiate the NSURLConnection with a request that calls for only the header to be sent back to the client. An efficient way to do this is to declare another property of type NSMutableURLRequest in the header:

```
NSMutableURLRequest *theRequest;
...
@property (nonatomic, retain) NSMutableURLRequest *theRequest;
```

Be sure to synthesize the property in the implementation file and release the property in the dealloc method.

A method of your own creation triggers the download activity. If it includes a Boolean argument indicating whether the method should retrieve only the header, you can branch inside the method to assemble the correct request header type. Example 9-11 shows such a method.

Example 9-11. Branching to download the header or file

```
- (void)downloadPlistWithHeader:(BOOL)headerOnly {
    NSURL *theUrl = [NSURL URLWithString:@"http://dannyg.com/dl/demo.plist"];

    self.theRequest = [NSMutableURLRequest requestWithURL:theUrl];
    if (headerOnly) {
        [theRequest setHTTPMethod:@"HEAD"];
    } else {
        [theRequest setHTTPMethod:@"GET"];
        self.incomingData = [[NSMutableData alloc] initWithCapacity:10000];
    }

    self.pListConnection = [NSURLConnection connectionWithRequest:theRequest
                                                        delegate:self];
}
```

You need the mutable form of NSURLRequest, because you begin by assigning the URL to it, but then you need to adjust the method part of the request to either HEAD (for the header) or GET (for the content). If you are performing only one retrieval per session, this is a suitable place to initialize the NSMutableData object, because the statement will be called only once when retrieving the file's content. Regardless of request method type, the request is passed to NSURLConnection to communicate with the server.

If the connection is made to retrieve only the header, the next stage of the remaining connection work is handled in the NSURLConnection object's connection:didReceive Response: delegate method. The key is to cast the NSURLResponse argument as its specialized NSHTTPURLResponse subclass. That argument lets you obtain header information in the form of an NSDictionary object. But because the connection:didReceiveRes ponse: method does double duty for both header and full content, you need to branch based on the HTTPMethod value of the NSMutableURLRequest property, as shown in Example 9-12.

Example 9-12. Reading a file's header before downloading the file

```
// If server file hasn't changed, cancel current connection
// so app will load cached version.
- (void)connection:(NSURLConnection *)connection
              didReceiveResponse:(NSHTTPURLResponse *)response {
    if ([[self.theRequest HTTPMethod] isEqualToString:@"HEAD"]) {
        NSDictionary *dictionary = [response allHeaderFields];

        // Verify actual header fields during development
        NSLog(@"Header dictionary: %@", dictionary);

        // Capture Last-Modified header field
        NSString *lastModifiedDate = [dictionary objectForKey:@"Last-Modified"];

        // Read previously-saved value (if any)
        NSUserDefaults *prefs = [NSUserDefaults standardUserDefaults];
        NSString *previousDateString = ([prefs objectForKey:@"lastUpdate"]) ?
            [prefs objectForKey:@"lastUpdate"] : @"none";

        // Compare the two
        if ([lastModifiedDate isEqualToString:previousDateString]) {
            // No change, so don't download
            NSLog(@"Connection Cancelled");
            [connection cancel];
        } else {
            // Save to user preferences on device
            [prefs setObject:lastModifiedDate forKey:@"lastUpdate"];
        }
    }
}
```

In this example, the date comparison is not particularly sophisticated. In fact, the comparison is strictly between the string values of the relevant header field. The makeup of the header will vary from server to server. The example outputs the header to the console so you can see exactly what your server is sending out. Here is the output from one of my servers as written to the console:

```
Header dictionary: {
    "Accept-Ranges" = bytes;
    Connection = "Keep-Alive";
```

```
    "Content-Length" = 1350;
    "Content-Type" = "text/plain";
    Date = "Thu, 27 May 2010 05:16:58 GMT";
    Etag = "\"6141533-546-4a28031e\"";
    "Keep-Alive" = "timeout=5, max=20";
    "Last-Modified" = "Thu, 04 Jun 2009 17:23:42 GMT";
    Server = "Apache/1.3.41 Ben-SSL/1.59 (Unix)";
}
```

These are key-value pairs, with the keys on the left. For this server, the key I'm interested in is labeled `Last-Modified`. That's the one whose value is examined in Example 9-12.

The connection is not canceled if the full download is needed. By not canceling the connection, the method tells `NSURLConnection` to continue normally with its header retrieval. All this means is that the `connectionDidFinishLoading:` delegate method is invoked. Here, again, you need to branch so that if the connection was only for the header, execution should run back to download the file, but without the header:

```
- (void)connectionDidFinishLoading:(NSURLConnection *)connection {
    if ([[self.theRequest HTTPMethod] isEqualToString:@"HEAD"]) {
        // Header says it's new, so go get file
        [self downloadPlistWithHeader:NO];
    } else {
        // Process the received data here
    }
}
```

With this foundation, you can build a sophisticated system of app data updates that operate in the background. The example demonstrates a property list, but you can use `NSURLConnection` to retrieve any type of data, including HTML and images. For example, I employ a system in my apps that retrieves news bulletins in HTML format that are displayed through a `UIWebView`. When the app launches, it checks to see whether a new version of the file has been put on the server. If so, the file is downloaded and saved to the device. A successful download sends an internal notification (through the `NS NotificationCenter`) to some view classes so one of the navigation bar icons changes to a different color. You can even turn the signal into a flashing image (using `NSTimer`).

Accounting for Fast App Switching

In iOS versions prior to iOS 4, when the user presses the Home button, the app quits (and `UIApplication` sends an `applicationWillTerminate:` message to the app delegate to let the app prepare for quitting). The next time the user accesses the app, it starts from scratch in a known, fresh state. In iOS 4, however, an app can go into a suspended state and later be awoken to resume where it left off. A major design decision you will consider for each app is what the user's expectation is when the app reawakens. For purposes of demonstration in the World Cup app, I chose to force the app to delete the downloaded *.plist* file when the app goes into the background. Then, no matter how long or short it may be that the app is suspended, when the user reactivates the app, the file will need to be downloaded again.

In addition to the `UIApplication` object sending messages to the app delegate about impended changes of state, it also triggers what are known in Cocoa Touch as notifications via the `NSNotificationCenter`. This system process allows any object to register with the center as an observer, waiting for a specific notification. When an iOS app is about to be suspended, a notification named `UIApplicationDidEnterBackground Notification` is sent through the center. Any object that has registered to be notified when that notification is sent is alerted and sends a message to an object, typically the current object (`self`).

The following code is a modified version of the `viewDidLoad:` method for the PList-Download project that includes the statement adding the notification observer:

```
- (void)viewDidAppear:(BOOL)animated {
    [super viewDidAppear:animated];
    // Alloc and initialize receptacle for retrieved plist data
    self.incomingPlistData = [[NSMutableData alloc] initWithCapacity:1000];

    // Set up notification observer for Fast App Switching suspend
    [[NSNotificationCenter defaultCenter] addObserver:self
                    selector:@selector(restoreApp)
                        name:@"UIApplicationDidEnterBackgroundNotification"
                    object:nil];

}
```

Whenever the named notification occurs, the `restoreApp` method (defined in the current class to delete the file and clear the results label) is invoked. You'll learn more about the `@selector` terminology later in this chapter. Every `addObserver:` method, however, should be balanced with a `removeObserver:` method. For this example, the `removeObserver:` method call is included in the `dealloc` method:

```
- (void)dealloc {
    NSNotificationCenter *notificationCenter =
        [NSNotificationCenter defaultCenter];
    [notificationCenter
        removeObserver:self
                  name:@"UIApplicationDidEnterBackgroundNotification"
                object:nil];

    [self.pListConnection release];
    [self.incomingPlistData release];
    [self.resultsLabel release];
    [super dealloc];
}
```

Each app has different needs for accommodating Fast App Switching. Consider the state of the app when it is brought back to life and what the user's expectations might be at that instant. Has so much time elapsed since the app went to sleep that it should look for possible updates from the server? Should an interrupted process be resumed or restarted? It's something you have to evaluate carefully during the design phase.

Reading and Writing Local Files

Until very recently, the idea of JavaScript in a browser having access to the client file-system in any fashion beyond cookies was blue-sky thinking. Security concerns are genuine issues on the Web, and handing hard disk access to any website you stumble upon (or are misled to visit) is a recipe for disaster and pwnage. But standalone applications have traditionally had access to the mass storage device(s) attached to the client. For example, there are plenty of disk utility software programs for Mac OS X, Windows (all flavors), Unix, and many other operating systems—utilities that have free rein over the most private of files. iOS meets you about halfway.

An important design consideration to bear in mind is that Apple's user interface design guidelines advise strongly against exposing iOS directory structures of any kind to users. Data storage is just supposed to happen, and that's all there is to it. For example, Apple's Notes app presents each document (note) as a page in the app. You can view a list of notes as a kind of table of contents, but they're not files in the user's eye. Any "file-ness" of content should be reserved for special interfaces, such as the File Sharing area of the iTunes display (in the Apps tab for the iPad OS 3.2 and iOS 4 or later).

If an iOS app developer follows the rules set down by Apple, access to files is somewhat limited. Each application is given room to read and write files, but only within the directory the OS creates for each application. That means no snooping around the rest of the filesystem. That doesn't mean you are totally blocked off from other data on the device. Apple provides numerous frameworks for accessing data in media libraries and the address book, but only through authorized APIs. Restrictions tend to loosen with subsequent OS versions, but it's unlikely you will ever be allowed to wander willy-nilly through low-level directories or other application data not designed to be shared.

The methods for reading and writing files on the device are pretty easy. Understanding the directory structure within an app's directory requires a bit of explanation, including rules about which areas are backed up during a sync with iTunes. Your knowledge of the directory (folder) structure is vital because to read or write a file, you must address the file by its pathname.

 Even though iOS devices do not have spinning hard-disk storage, you will frequently see references to saving a file "to disk." Because an iOS app creates a directory structure that resembles what you might encounter on a hard disk, reading and writing files are considered "disk" accesses.

iOS App Directories

When an app is installed on a device, the system creates a basic directory structure for the app. Conversely, when the app is deleted, so is the entire directory, which includes any files your app has created when it ran and user preferences the app saved through the prescribed preferences API (i.e., the `NSUserDefaults` class). If you had a Finder-like viewer into the structure of an app's directory, it would look like Figure 9-6.

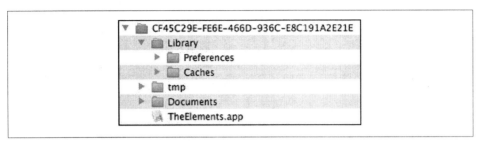

Figure 9-6. Default directory structure of an iOS app

The device assigns a unique ID to the directory that is your playground. The ID is unimportant to you because you have "legal" access only to the stuff *inside* that uniquely named directory. Cocoa Touch provides shortcuts (in a manner of speaking) to help you obtain the pathname to any of the app's subdirectories you see in Figure 9-6, automatically filling in the app's unique ID as part of the pathname.

The file with the *.app* extension is your *application bundle*, which contains all extra files you include in the project (e.g., *.plist* files containing initial data for the app). As part of the app submission process, you will authenticate the app through "codesigning" (putting a digital signature on the code), which means the bundle should not change once it is signed. Therefore, any data-oriented files you deliver to users with the bundle will be read-only (although your app can copy them to read-write files elsewhere in the app's directory system when the app runs the first time).

Not all subdirectories of the app directory are created equal when it comes to whether the contents are backed up during an iTunes sync. Only the *Documents* and *Preferences* directories are backed up. As you have probably experienced yourself, backups can take a long time. The smaller the amount of content you place in these directories, the shorter the backup time required for your app. Therefore, if you have lots of fixed data the user can download from sources (in the event the app needs to be restored from a backup), it's best to save that material in another directory (or a directory nested inside the *Documents* directory).

File Sharing

The Cocoa Touch frameworks have reserved the first level of the *Documents* directory as the designated storage place for files that can be transferred to another computer through the iTunes app. To enable this feature in your iPad 3.2 or later and iOS 4.0 or later app, add the `UIFileSharingEnabled` key to the *info.plist* file and enable the feature. Only when that key is enabled does the app appear in the File Sharing area of the App tab of a compatible device connected to iTunes.

Obtaining Directory Paths

The consistent way to obtain directory paths is to use a Foundation framework function, `NSSearchPathForDirectoriesInDomains()`, which relies on constant values to derive paths of two known directory places inside an app's directory. Syntax for the function is as follows:

```
NSArray * NSSearchPathForDirectoriesInDomains (
    NSSearchPathDirectory directory,
    NSSearchPathDomainMask domainMask,
    BOOL expandTilde
);
```

The only argument you need to worry about is the first, while the other two are always the same for use in iOS. The first argument consists of a constant value referring to a specific directory, either `NSDocumentDirectory` for the *Documents* directory (note the missing "s" in the constant name) or `NSCachesDirectory` for the *Library/Caches* directory. Because of its Mac OS X heritage, the method returns an array. For iOS, the array has only one member. The following code obtains the full pathname to the *Documents* directory of the current app:

```
NSArray *paths = NSSearchPathForDirectoriesInDomains(NSDocumentDirectory,
                                    NSUserDomainMask, YES);
NSString *theDocumentsDirectoryPath = [paths objectAtIndex:0];
```

To complete the path to a file, all you do is append the file's name to the path:

```
NSString *filenamePath = [theDocumentsDirectoryPath
                    stringByAppendingPathComponent:@"userData"];
```

You don't have to worry about the forward slash delimiter between the directory and filename, because the **stringByAppendingPathComponent:** method is smart enough to supply the slash if it's needed. The file's path is then applicable as an argument to methods that read from or write to disk (described in a moment).

You may have noticed that paths to the *Library/Preferences* and *tmp* directories don't have constant values for the `NSSearchPathForDirectoriesInDomains()` function. Preferences files should not be written directly by your code, but rather via the `NSUser Defaults` class, which uses key-value pairs to store preference values. To fill the gap for the *tmp* directory, Cocoa Touch offers a special function:

```
NSString *tmpDirectoryPath = NSTemporaryDirectory();
```

Write only disposable data to the *tmp* directory. The system may purge the directory if it needs disk space when your app is not running. But don't rely on the system to do all the work. You should manually manage the deletion of files from this directory when you no longer need them (such as when the app is about to quit, signaled by the `applicationWillTerminate:` delegate message sent to the app delegate class).

If you intend to create custom subdirectories for your app's data, do so inside known paths, such as the *Documents* or *Library/Caches* directories. You can also create a *Library/Application Support* directory and access it through the `NSSearchPathFor`

`DirectoriesInDomains()` function, using `NSApplicationSupportDirectory` as the constant. If you do this, you must create the directory yourself before you can use it as a path for reading and writing files (even though the function will return the correct path if the directory does not yet exist).

Obtaining Paths to Files Delivered with Your App

As mentioned earlier, your app and its resources are collected into a container (or package) known as a bundle. It's not uncommon to deliver a property list file with the bundle so the app reads the file each time it launches, creating data sources for tables or for other data-driven purposes (TheElements sample does this, as shown in Chapter 8). Except for some project-managed files, the files in a bundle are not nested in subdirectories of the bundle package (in fact, the directory structure of a bundle is of no concern to your app). You do, however, often need a way to obtain a valid path to a file inside the bundle.

To the rescue comes the `NSBundle` class. It features a class method, `mainBundle`, which creates an `NSBundle` object aimed at your app's bundle. Then the `pathForResource:ofType:` method lets you specify the filename and extension (separately). For example, if your bundle comes with a file named *USStates.plist*, your code can obtain a path to the file with the following:

```
NSString *path = [[NSBundle mainBundle] pathForResource:@"USStates"
                                                 ofType:@"plist"];
```

You can now use that path to load the file into an `NSArray` or `NSDictionary` object, depending on the class of root node in the property list.

Some other classes that rely on bundle files don't require the path. For example, the `UIImage` class offers a class method, `imageNamed:`, whose argument is a string of the entire image filename (including extension). The method does not require a directory name, because it searches for the file in the bundle.

 Do not write a file to the bundle. Changes to a bundle's signature will invalidate its provisioning and prevent the app from launching again.

Writing Files to Disk

Cocoa Touch provides file-writing methods for three classes whose instances accommodate a wide variety of data types: `NSArray`, `NSDictionary`, and `NSData` (and, by inheritance, their mutable subclasses). For example, all data you retrieve from a server via `NSURLConnection` is first stuffed into an `NSMutableData` object. If the data is an image, you can derive a viewable image from the data whenever you need it (using the `UIImage imageWithData:` method). But if you want to preserve the image data on disk, you can save the originally downloaded `NSData`. The `NSArray` and `NSDictionary` classes are handy if you want to save other types of Cocoa Touch objects to disk as collections. You get the added bonus of methods in those classes that stand ready to instantiate objects by directly reading information from files (you supply the path, as usual).

The following code assumes you have an NSDictionary collection in a variable called myRecipesDictionary. Save that dictionary to a file named *Recipes* in the *Documents* directory:

```
NSArray *paths = NSSearchPathForDirectoriesInDomains(NSDocumentDirectory,
                                      NSUserDomainMask, YES);
NSString *theDocumentsDirectoryPath = [paths objectAtIndex:0];
NSString *filenamePath = [theDocumentsDirectoryPath
                      stringByAppendingPathComponent:@"Recipes"];
BOOL writeSuccess = [myRecipesDictionary writeToFile:filenamePath
                                  atomically:YES];

if (!writeSuccess) {
    // Handle failure to write file
}
```

The second argument of the writeToFile:atomically: method is a Boolean value that controls how the file is written. When the argument is set to YES, the file is written to a temporary file until the writing is complete, at which point the temporary file is renamed to the name specified in the path. This sequence ensures that if a previous version of the file already exists, it is not overwritten until the new file has successfully been transferred to disk. An application crash, for example, can interrupt a write operation and leave the original file corrupted if you don't use the temporary file.

Writing an NSString object to a file requires additional information about how the string should be encoded. The file-writing method for NSString is defined as follows:

```
- (BOOL)writeToFile:(NSURL *)url
        atomically:(BOOL)flag
          encoding:(NSStringEncoding)encodingType
             error:(NSError **)error
```

Encoding types are defined as enumerated constants. The complete list of available encodings is long (as you'd expect from a framework that tries to work with as many worldwide systems as possible), but Table 9-8 shows the most common encodings you are likely to use.

Table 9-8. Selected NSStringEncoding values

Value	Constant
1	NSASCIIStringEncoding
4	NSUTF8StringEncoding
5	NSISOLatin1StringEncoding
10	NSUnicodeStringEncoding

Unless you know that the source of the string has a particular encoding type, you are usually safe specifying either the `NSUTF8StringEncoding` or `NSUnicodeStringEncoding` constants.

The file-writing method returns a Boolean signifying success or failure with the write action. Details of any errors are encapsulated and assigned to an `NSError` object, which you declare before the writing method and signify in the method with a pointer reference. For example, the following code attempts to write an `NSString` object to a *Documents* directory file and branches to handle any errors if the write fails:

```
NSArray *paths = NSSearchPathForDirectoriesInDomains(NSDocumentDirectory,
                        NSUserDomainMask, YES);
NSString *theDirectory = [paths objectAtIndex:0];
NSString *filenamePath = [theDirectory
                        stringByAppendingPathComponent:@"myString.txt"];

NSString *myString = @"Four score and seven years ago, our forefathers....";
NSError *stringWriteError; // Declare error object here
if (![myString writeToFile:filenamePath
                atomically:YES
                  encoding:NSUTF8StringEncoding
                     error:&stringWriteError]) {
    // Write failed, inspect error to find out what happened
    NSLog(@"String write error:%@", [stringWriteError localizedDescription]);
}
```

Notice how the main activity of writing the file is encased in an `if` condition expression because the method returns a Boolean value. This is a common construction.

Reading Files from Disk

Assuming you have saved data to a file via the `writeToFile:atomically:` methods of the `NSArray`, `NSDictionary`, or `NSData` objects, you can reverse the process by creating a new instance filled with the contents of that file. All of those classes have both instance and class methods that create objects from a file given a path to that file. The class methods are defined as follows:

```
+ (id)arrayWithContentsOfFile:(NSString *)path
+ (id)dictionaryWithContentsOfFile:(NSString *)path
+ (id)dataWithContentsOfFile:(NSString *)path
```

Compose pathnames for reading files the same way you do for writing files (described in the previous section). If you need the contents of the file to be mutable, send the messages to the mutable subclass, as in the following:

```
NSMutableDictionary *dictionaryFromFile =
        [NSMutableDictionary dictionaryWithContentsOfFile:dictionaryPath];
```

Other Cocoa Touch classes that rely on files have their own methods to obtain files. For example, the `UIImage` class has its own instance and class methods that load an image file (not in the bundle) into the object for potential display in its owning `UIImageView`:

```
- (id)initWithContentsOfFile:(NSString *)path
+ (UIImage *)imageWithContentsOfFile:(NSString *)path
```

As with writing NSString objects, reading a file into an NSString object poses character encoding issues for you to contend with. If you know the encoding that was used to generate the file, you should use the method that lets you specify encoding (class method version shown here):

```
+ (id)stringWithContentsOfFile:(NSString *)path
                      encoding:(NSStringEncoding)encodingType
                         error:(NSError **)error
```

But if you don't know the file's encoding type and want to learn what it is, another variation of the method returns the encoding type (provided the method successfully loads the data):

```
+ (id)stringWithContentsOfFile:(NSString *)path
                  usedEncoding:(NSStringEncoding *)encodingType
                         error:(NSError **)error
```

Notice the subtle difference in the second argument: the declaration includes a pointer star, meaning the argument can be written to. In fact, this version of the method not only returns the string contents to be assigned to an NSString variable like the first version (if the read is successful), but also assigns the encoding type (an enumerated value) to the previously declared NSStringEncoding type variable. The following example is the inverse of the earlier example that wrote a string to a file:

```
NSArray *paths = NSSearchPathForDirectoriesInDomains(NSDocumentDirectory,
                    NSUserDomainMask, YES);
NSString *theDirectory = [paths objectAtIndex:0];
NSString *filenamePath = [theDirectory
                    stringByAppendingPathComponent:@"myString.txt"];

NSError *stringReadError;
NSStringEncoding encodingType;
NSString *readString = [NSString stringWithContentsOfFile:filenamePath
                                usedEncoding:&encodingType
                                       error:&stringReadError];

NSLog(@"From file:\"%@\"", readString);
NSLog(@"String encodingType:%d", encodingType);
```

As an enumerated value, the encoding type can be read as an integer value. Table 9-8 lists common encoding type integer values and constant names.

Writing and Reading Property List Files

An earlier example project in this chapter (Example 9-5) downloads a property list file from a server, saves it to a local file, and later reads the file. Property lists can be saved in either XML or more compact binary formats. Data captured by NSURLConnection and accumulated in an NSMutableData object is binary, so you can use the writeToFile:atom ically: method directly on that object.

Most conveniently, if the property list's root entry is an array or dictionary data type, you can read the entire property list file directly into new instances of NSArray or NSDictionary. See the earlier discussion of the arrayWithContentsOfFile: and dictionaryWithContentsOfFile: methods.

Performing File Management Tasks

Use the NSFileManager class to assist you in file management duties, such as deleting files your app has written but no longer needs, or copying a file from your app's bundle to a working directory for possible modification. NSFileManager has a full complement of methods for nearly every type of filesystem activity (within your application's sandbox, that is), but I'll provide examples of two complementary operations.

To begin using NSFileManager, create an instance of the object using the following class method:

```
NSFileManager *fileManager = [NSFileManager defaultManager];
```

With that reference in hand, you can now invoke methods to act on files and directories.

In the *PlistDownload* project described earlier in this chapter, a property list file is downloaded from a server and saved to a *.plist* file in the *Documents* directory. Because this demonstration app should come to life each time with no saved file, the app deletes the saved file before quitting or (in iOS 4) suspending. The trigger for the action is a notification described earlier in this chapter. The notification observer sends the restoreApp message to the current view controller object. I have written that custom method to invoke two methods that delete the file and clear the results label. The sequence of methods is shown in Example 9-13.

Example 9-13. Methods that run when the PlistDownload app is suspended

```
// Delete file
- (void)deleteFile {
    NSString *plistFilenamePath = [self getDemoFilePath];
    NSFileManager *fileManager = [NSFileManager defaultManager];
    NSError *error;
    if ([fileManager fileExistsAtPath:plistFilenamePath]) {
        if (![fileManager removeItemAtPath:plistFilenamePath error:&error]) {
            // For demo, silently log removal failure
            NSLog(@"File removal failed:%@", error);
        }
    }
}

// Empty results label
- (void)emptyResultsLabel {
    [resultsLabel setText:@""];
}

// Restore file and label status as if freshly loaded
- (void)restoreApp {
```

```
    [self deleteFile];
    [self emptyResultsLabel];
}
```

Two file manager operations occur in the deleteFile method. One confirms that the file exists. If so, the file is deleted. Necessary ingredients include the path to the file (obtained from a supporting method defined elsewhere in the current class), a reference to an NSFileManager instance, and a declaration of an NSError object for use by one of the NSFileManager methods. The fileExistsAtPath: method returns a Boolean value, which makes it convenient as an if construction's conditional expression. The removeItemAtPath:error: method also returns a Boolean, allowing the code to branch for special handling in case of an unsuccessful operation. For purposes of the demonstration, the NSError object is output to the console, but for a real app, more robust error processing would certainly be in order.

Not all apps intensively manage files, create new subdirectories, and so on. But it's comforting to know the power is there if you need it.

Sorting Arrays

The NSArray class offers a few ways to sort the contents of an array, one of which will remind you instantly of JavaScript array sorting by way of a separate function. In all cases, pairs of array elements are compared against each other, just as they are in JavaScript. For any two-item comparison—whether the items are of type NSString, NSNumber, or NSDate—the sorting method reports whether the first item is lower, higher, or the same as the second item. Those states correspond to three simple values representing the result of the comparison of each pair of items. The sorting mechanism of NSArray compares pairs in quick succession and uses the results to arrange the elements. The sorted version is either returned as a new array in the sorted order (NSArray) or applied directly to the original array (NSMutableArray).

Your choice of sorting approach depends on the nature of the array. One approach is nicely suited to an array of simple objects (strings, numbers, and dates), while another lets you dig down deeper to sort on a key within an array of dictionaries. I'll start with the easy one.

Sorting with a Selector

In Objective-C, a *selector* is a reference to a method. Whenever a method argument calls for a selector, the syntax for the argument value is as follows:

```
@selector(methodName)
```

Yes, that's a compiler directive making an appearance somewhere within a message (not out at the left margin, as you've seen elsewhere). The expression is analogous to JavaScript referencing a function object by name (but Objective-C methods are not objects, so don't get carried away). Selectors are commonly used as arguments to methods that need to send a message during or after their execution. You saw a selector in action earlier in this chapter when specifying a method to be invoked when a system notification about the app being suspended was sent.

The NSString, NSNumber, and NSDate classes all have comparison methods that return a value of type NSComparisonResult. The NSNumber and NSDate classes have only one method, the compare: method. NSString offers several methods, the four most commonly used ones are:

```
compare:
caseInsensitiveCompare:
localizedCompare:
localizedCaseInsensitiveCompare:
```

Localized versions take into account the device's International language settings, which can impact the way characters are sorted.

Let's look more closely at the definition for the simplest of these methods:

```
- (NSComparisonResult)compare:(NSString *)aString
```

Remember that this is a method of NSString, so if you were to use this method in a standalone statement, it would look like the following:

```
NSComparisonResult result = [string1 compare:string2];
```

In other words, you are manually comparing two strings. Importantly, the receiver and argument of this message must be NSString values (or both NSNumber or both NSDate objects for their respective compare: methods).

If you have an array of NSString objects, you probably want to run pairs of array elements through this compare: method to establish the order of elements. You can do exactly that when you invoke the sortedArrayUsingSelector: method, passing @selector(compare:) as the argument, as follows:

```
NSArray *sortedNamesArray = [namesArray sortedArrayUsingSelector:@selector(compare:)];
```

The sortedArrayUsingSelector: method does all the work of passing pairs of array elements through the compare: method and creates a copy of the receiver sorted in ascending ASCII order. If you'd rather the sorting be done on a case-insensitive manner, use a different selector:

```
NSArray *sortedNamesArray =
    [namesArray sortedArrayUsingSelector:@selector(caseInsensitiveCompare:)];
```

Example 9-14 provides code you can run in Workbench. Replace the runMyCode: method with the code here.

Example 9-14. Simple string sorting

```
- (IBAction)runMyCode:(id)sender {

    NSArray *namesArray = [NSArray arrayWithObjects:@"Grover", @"Zoe", @"Oscar",
```

```
                    @"Bert", @"Ernie", @"Elmo",
                    @"Cookie", @"Rosita", nil];

    NSArray *sortedNamesArray =
    [namesArray sortedArrayUsingSelector:@selector(localizedCaseInsensitiveCompare:)];
    NSLog(@"sortedNames = %@", sortedNamesArray);
}
```

When you run the app and click the button, a sorted list of Muppet names appears in the console.

I should emphasize here that the selectors you can supply as the argument to the sorting method are limited to methods of the array element class that return an NSComparison Result data type. Therefore, for NSNumber and NSDate classes, you are limited to the simple @selector(compare:) selector.

The array returned from the sortedArrayUsingSelector: method is always in ascending order. Although there is no quick method to invert an array's order, you always have the option of iterating through the array in a for loop in reverse order.

Sorting with a Function

Using a function to direct the way each pair of array elements is compared should make you feel right at home from your JavaScript experience. The NSArray sortedArrayUsing Function:context: method operates the same way. In fact, you write a C function (rather than an Objective-C method) to assist with the sorting, so it's even more Java-Script-y. The sorting function's syntax outline is as follows:

```
NSInteger sortFunction(id value1, id value2, void *reverse) {

    // Operate on value1 and value2

    // Then return an NSComparisonResult value
    return comparisonValue;
}
```

Your array then invokes this function through its sorting method:

```
NSArray *sortedArray =
    [myArray sortedArrayUsingFunction:sortFunction context:nil];
```

 A sorting function (or any C function) is written in the same implementation file as the statement that invokes the function, but the function should come before the statement that invokes it. You can also code a C function in a different class file that you import into the current class, provided you have defined the function in the imported class's header file.

You are not limited to sorting simple values inside the sort function. The method sends pairs of top-level members of the array to the sort function in rapid succession. If those members happen to be `NSDictionary` objects, the sort function can dig into the objects and examine values of a specific key for comparison.

To demonstrate working with a dictionary, I created a property list file consisting of an array of dictionaries. Each dictionary has three objects—two `NSStrings` and one `NSNumber`—to hold information for a city name, state name, and annual average temperature for six west coast cities. Figure 9-7 shows a portion of the property list.

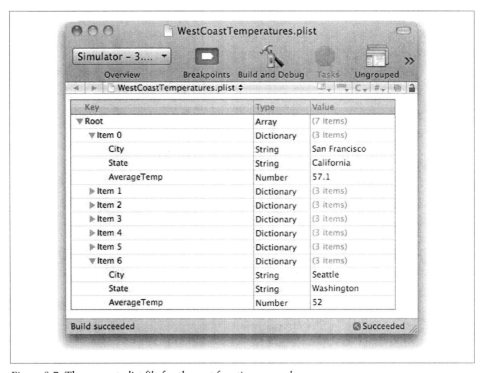

Figure 9-7. The property list file for the sort function example

After adding the *.plist* file to the Workbench project, I inserted a sorting function and `runMyCode:` method, as shown in Example 9-15.

Example 9-15. Workbench code to experiment with array sorting through a function

```
// Sorting function for AverageTemp dictionary key
NSInteger temperatureSort(id value1, id value2, void *reverse) {

    NSNumber *number1 = [value1 objectForKey:@"AverageTemp"];
    NSNumber *number2 = [value2 objectForKey:@"AverageTemp"];

    return [number1 compare:number2];
}

- (IBAction)runMyCode:(id)sender {
```

```
// Load property list file from bundle
NSString *path = [[NSBundle mainBundle]
            pathForResource:@"WestCoastTemperatures" ofType:@"plist"];
NSArray *tempsArray = [NSArray arrayWithContentsOfFile:path];

// Get copy of array sorted for temperature
NSArray *sortedTempsArray =
    [tempsArray sortedArrayUsingFunction:temperatureSort context:nil];

// Loop through sorted array and display one console line per city
for (int i = 0; i < [sortedTempsArray count]; i++) {
    NSLog(@"%@, %@ average temp: %@°F",
            [[sortedTempsArray objectAtIndex:i] objectForKey:@"City"],
            [[sortedTempsArray objectAtIndex:i] objectForKey:@"State"],
            [[sortedTempsArray objectAtIndex:i] objectForKey:@"AverageTemp"]);

}
// Extra line feeds in case I run it more than once
NSLog(@"\n\n");
}
```

In the sorting function, each incoming value is an NSDictionary, from which the function extracts the value for the AverageTemp key. Then the NSNumber compare: method is applied to each pair, returning one of the three integer values associated with an NSResultComparison value.

Sorting Arrays of Dictionaries with NSSortDescriptor

Using a sorting function for an array of dictionaries is fine for smaller arrays. But Cocoa Touch offers another array-sorting technique that is optimized for arrays of dictionaries: the sortedArrayUsingDescriptors: method. It can even sort on more than one key at a time in case you need secondary sorting. But I'll demonstrate it for just a single key, using the same average temperature data from the above example so you can get a better feel for how it works.

A descriptor is an NSSortDescriptor object that specifies the dictionary key on which you want to sort, plus sorting order and the comparison selector to use in the process. You pass an array of NSSortDescriptors to the sortedArrayUsingDescriptors: method, even if the array contains only one item. Example 9-16 shows the Workbench project runMyCode: method that sorts the property list data in descending order.

Example 9-16. Sorting an array of dictionaries with an NSSortDescriptor object

```
- (IBAction)runMyCode:(id)sender {

    // Load property list file from bundle
    NSString *path = [[NSBundle mainBundle]
                pathForResource:@"WestCoastTemperatures" ofType:@"plist"];
    NSArray *tempsArray = [NSArray arrayWithContentsOfFile:path];
```

```
// Create sort descriptor object for AverageTemp key
NSSortDescriptor *temperatureDescriptor = [[NSSortDescriptor alloc]
                               initWithKey:@"AverageTemp"
                                 ascending:NO
                                  selector:@selector(compare:)];
// Create array for our lone sort descriptor
NSArray *descriptorArray = [NSArray arrayWithObject:temperatureDescriptor];
[temperatureDescriptor release];
// Pass array to sorting method
NSArray *sortedTempsArray =
        [tempsArray sortedArrayUsingDescriptors:descriptorArray];

// Loop through sorted array and display one console line per city
for (int i = 0; i < [sortedTempsArray count]; i++) {
    NSLog(@"%@, %@ average temp: %@°F",
        [[sortedTempsArray objectAtIndex:i] objectForKey:@"City"],
        [[sortedTempsArray objectAtIndex:i] objectForKey:@"State"],
        [[sortedTempsArray objectAtIndex:i] objectForKey:@"AverageTemp"]);

}
// Extra line feeds in case I run it more than once
NSLog(@"\n\n");
}
```

Notice that you can directly specify sorting order as an attribute of a sort descriptor object. If you sort on multiple keys (i.e., one NSSortDescriptor per key), you can specify a different sort order for each key if that helps you achieve your sorting goal.

Capturing User-Entered Text

Like the two long-established text box elements in HTML (<text type="input"> and <textarea>), Cocoa Touch provides two types of text entry controls, UITextField and UITextView. The former is a one-line text box, while the latter allows for entry of multiple text lines in a scrollable area. In this section, you will add a UITextField to Workbench and learn how to obtain the text a user types into the text box.

Figure 9-8 shows how Workbench should look when you've finished this section. You will add both a UITextField and a UILabel so that when you finish entering text in the box, your code copies the text to the label and clears the text box in preparation for the next entry. To add just a little spice to the operation, the code converts the text to initial uppercase and applies one of three colors to the label's text, depending on the length of the typed text.

Figure 9-8. Workbench app equipped for UITextField demonstration

The Code Portion

Begin by adding the necessary code to the WorkbenchViewController class files. In the header file, insert the notation that this class implements the UITextFieldDelegate. This will allow the text field control to send messages to the class when various conditions arise (although for this demo, you're interested in acting only when editing ends with the press of the Return key on the keyboard). Next, add two instance variables and properties for the two user interface elements, plus a declaration of one IBAction method, as shown in Example 9-17. Notice that the two new properties are defined with IBOutlet designations. This will make it easy for the code to communicate with both controls when the action begins.

Example 9-17. WorkbenchViewController.h modified for the text field demonstration

```
#import <UIKit/UIKit.h>

@interface WorkbenchViewController : UIViewController <UITextFieldDelegate> {

    UITextField *myTextField;
    UILabel *myLabel;
```

```
}

@property (nonatomic, retain) IBOutlet UITextField *myTextField;
@property (nonatomic, retain) IBOutlet UILabel *myLabel;

- (IBAction)runMyCode:(id)sender;
- (IBAction)copyInput:(id)sender;

@end
```

Turn now to the companion class implementation file. Add the @synthesize directive for the two new properties you just declared in the header. Also, because those properties were set to be retained, add the corresponding release messages to the dealloc method. All action for this demo will occur in response to typing on the screen keyboard, so the runMyCode: method won't be used. Instead, add two methods, as shown in Example 9-18.

Example 9-18. WorkbenchViewController.m additions for the text field demonstration

```
@implementation WorkbenchViewController

@synthesize myTextField, myLabel;

// UITextField delegate message
- (BOOL)textFieldShouldReturn:(UITextField *)textField {
    // the user pressed the "return" button, so dismiss the keyboard
    [textField resignFirstResponder];
    return YES;
}

// Triggered by Editing Did End event
- (IBAction)copyInput:(id)sender {
    NSString *inputText = [sender text];
    int textLength = [inputText length];
    if (textLength < 10) {
        self.myLabel.textColor = [UIColor blackColor];
    } else if (textLength < 20) {
        self.myLabel.textColor = [UIColor blueColor];
    } else{
        self.myLabel.textColor = [UIColor redColor];
    }
    self.myLabel.text = [inputText capitalizedString];
    [sender setText:@""];
}

// No changes to intervening code
// ...

- (void)dealloc {
    [myLabel release];
    [myTextField release];
    [super dealloc];
}
```

@end

Most `UITextView` delegate messages signal intentions and seek approval to go ahead: the control is about to do something significant, so is it okay to proceed? That's why those methods return Boolean values. A tap of the keyboard Return or Done key (depending on the keyboard style) signals that the user has finished editing the text field. If you have multiple text fields and want a different behavior for each, you can use arbitrary integers to distinguish them. Assign a number as a tag to each control, inspect the `sender` argument to see which control is sending the delegate message, and act accordingly.

All user interface controls in iOS inherit from a class called `UIResponder`. All this means is that the control can react to events such as touches and keyboard events. For a `UITextField`, however, the responder action is automatic: when a user taps on the text box, that control becomes what is known as the *first responder*, meaning it receives the next event. For a text box, this triggers a lot of activity behind the scenes, but to the user, when a text box becomes the first responder, it means that a keyboard comes into view and the text box is the target of the next event. When the user has finished entering text into the field (signified by pressing the Return or Done key), the text field should hand control to whichever view gets it next (usually the `UIView` filling the screen). Therefore, Example 9-18 shows an implementation of the `textFieldShouldReturn:` delegate message, which means the user is ready to get out of the text field if approved. In this demo, the only handling needed is for the text field to resign from its temporary job as first responder and approve the action. When the text field resigns from being first responder, the keyboard gently slides out of view and the field no longer glows as being editable.

Because the `textFieldShouldReturn:` delegate method is invoked at a predictable point in the user interface sequence, you can also use it as the trigger for additional action on the content of the text field. But for this demonstration, the ensuing action is moved to a separate method that will be triggered by an event (and connected inside Interface Builder in a moment). In that separate `copyInput:` method, the text from the text box is copied into a variable whose character count is also extracted as an integer. One of three colors is assigned to the `UILabel`'s text, depending on the length of the string. Next, the text is transformed into initial uppercase (gratuitously for demo purposes) and assigned to replace the text of the label. Finally, the `UITextField`'s text is set to an empty string. This should all be pretty straightforward to you by now.

Specifying Cocoa Touch Colors

To apply a color to any object capable of changing colors, you go through the `UIColor` class (yes, there's a class for almost *everything*). For basic colors, the `UIColor` class offers 15 preset color class methods that return valid objects carrying values for the following colors: black, blue, brown, clear (transparent), cyan, dark gray, gray, green, light gray, magenta, orange, purple, red, white, and yellow. Example 9-18 shows how to apply those preset colors.

But the UIColor class has additional initializers (both instance and class methods) that let you produce color objects based on HSV (hue, saturation, and value) and RGB values (both plus alpha). Therefore, if you are accustomed to specifying CSS color values in RGB format, you should adapt fairly easily (although in UIColor, values range between 0 through 1.0 instead of decimal 0 through 255, so you'll have to get out your calculator to divide your old numbers by 255). For example, to generate a custom color and apply it to a label's text color, the code would look like the following:

```
UIColor *sortaOrangeColor = [UIColor colorWithRed:1.000
                                            green:0.412
                                             blue:0.208
                                            alpha:1.000];
self.myLabel.textColor = sortaOrangeColor ;
```

There is also a helpful developer tool that adds to the Interface Builder's color picker palette in the form of another icon in the palette's top toolbar. Once you select a color using any of the graphical sliders in the palette, you can switch to the Developer Picker tool to copy the UIColor message code with all the values plugged in to the clipboard, ready to paste into your code. You can find the add-in at *http://www.panic.com/~wade/picker/*.

The Interface Builder Portion

To add the text field and label to the Workbench app, double-click the *WorkbenchViewController.xib* file in Xcode to work with the nib file. Go to the Library palette and select Inputs & Values to make it easier to find the two items you need. First, drag a Label from the palette to the View window. Its precise location is not critical, but widen it until the edges activate the vertical guides near the left and right edges. In the Attributes inspector, select center alignment. For now, you can leave the default "Label" word there to help you spot the label area in the running app (or you can specify a background color).

Next, drag a Text Field from the Library palette to the View window and position it where you like. Widen it to the same dimensions as the label. In the Attributes palette, set alignment to center, add some placeholder text (which appears grayed out when the field is otherwise empty), and increase the font size to 14.0.

Now you have to make several connections between these elements and the code in the WorkbenchViewController class. Starting with the label, select it by clicking on it in the View window. Display the Connections inspector and drag from the empty circle to the right of "New Referencing Outlet" to the File's Owner item in the main document window. From the pop-up list that appears, select myLabel. That's the only connection for this item, because the code merely sends new text for it to display.

Select the text field and look at its Connections inspector. You will make three connections for this control. Although you can make the connections in any order, I'll lead you down the most logical path. First, in the bottom group ("Referencing Outlets"), drag from the empty circle to the right of "New Referencing Outlet" to the File's Owner item in the document window (just like you did for the label). Select `myTextField` from the pop-up list. That connects the `myTextField` property in the code with this visual text box. Because the view controller class needs to receive delegate messages from the text field, drag in the top group from the empty circle to the right of "delegate" to the File's Owner item in the document window. This tells the text box to direct all delegate messages to the `WorkbenchViewController` object (where the delegate method stands ready to go). Finally, drag from the empty circle to the right of "Editing Did End" to the File's Owner item in the document window. Select `copyInput:` from the pop-up list. This instructs the control to send the `copyInput:` message to `WorkbenchViewController` whenever the Editing Did End event occurs.

Save the Interface Builder file and return to your Xcode project. When I make a number of changes to a project, I usually type Cmd-B to perform only a project build (without installing). If that's a success, I build and install. When the app runs, click in the text box to make the keyboard appear. You can use your computer's keyboard to enter text and press Return if you like. Coming from web development, your first inclination might be to press the computer keyboard's Tab key to activate the text field again. But the touch-centric iOS user interface doesn't work that way. Keyboards are only for entering text after a touch event (including one simulated by code) has handed the first responder role to an editable text control. It's something you'll have to get used to.

Admittedly, the steps you had to go through to add a text field to a view, code its event, and obtain the field's text is a lot more work than adding a text input HTML element to a web page and inserting a few lines of JavaScript code to extract the field's value property. It's among the adjustments you make to develop native iOS apps.

Validating Text Entry with Regular Expressions

One of the earliest applications of JavaScript in web browsers was to perform prevalidation of form text fields prior to submitting the form to the server. The purpose of prevalidating in the browser is to provide instant feedback to obvious form entry errors, such as missing required fields or an incorrect data format. It is still necessary to perform validations again on the server for security and data integrity reasons, but by saving repeated roundtrips between browser and server to fix several entry errors, the user experience is improved with client-side validation. JavaScript has offered regular expression support for a long time now, making it easier to compare text entry against expected patterns, such as North American telephone numbers, US zip codes, and email addresses.

Surprisingly, general-purpose regular expressions have arrived late to the iOS platform, becoming first available in iOS 4. Therefore, this section applies only to apps that will be distributed with iOS 4 as the minimum platform. This section also assumes that you are familiar with regular expression syntax.

In JavaScript, regular expression patterns are allowed as arguments for a variety of String object methods, such as match(), replace(), and split(). This is in addition to a regular expression object instance, which contains a pattern you assign to it and offers methods—exec() and test()—to uncover matches in strings. Therefore, in JavaScript you can discover whether a string contains text matching a pattern from the point of view of either the string or the regular expression.

In contrast, Cocoa Touch lets you operate with regular expressions via the NSRegular Expression class. In this scenario, you create an instance of that class outfitted with a pattern and a list of options (e.g., specifying case sensitivity). Methods of that instance then apply the regular expression against an NSString or NSMutableString object that you pass as an argument.

Picking up from the previous example in this chapter that uses a UITextField for text entry, you'll produce a variant whose text field asks for an email address and then prevalidates the user's entry using a regular expression. Figure 9-9 shows the finished app after a user has entered an invalid email address and tapped the Return key on the keyboard. Unlike the previous example, the UITextField won't resign being first responder (and thus hide the keyboard) unless the entered email address matches the desired format.

Figure 9-9. Email address validation of a UITextField entry

Modifying the Code

Changes to the code occur only in the *Workbench.m* implementation file. No new instance variables are needed, and you do not need to declare the one new method as an instance method defined in the header file. Example 9-19 shows only the new and modified code from Example 9-18 (new and changed items in bold).

Example 9-19. Modifications to Example 9-18 to perform email validation via regular expression

```
- (BOOL)emailAddressIsValid:(NSString *)emailAddress {
    BOOL result = NO;

    NSString *emailAddressPattern = @"^[A-Z0-9+_.-]+@(?:[A-Z0-9-]+\\.)+[A-Z]{2,6}$";

    NSError *error = NULL;
    NSRegularExpression *regex =
        [NSRegularExpression regularExpressionWithPattern:emailAddressPattern
                                    options:NSRegularExpressionCaseInsensitive
                                      error:&error];
    if (regex == nil) {
        NSLog(@"RegExp Error: %@", [error localizedDescription]);
    } else {
        NSUInteger numberOfMatches =
            [regex numberOfMatchesInString:emailAddress
                            options:0
                              range:NSMakeRange(0, [emailAddress length])];
        result = (numberOfMatches == 1) ? YES : NO;
    }
    return result;
}


// UITextField delegate message
- (BOOL)textFieldShouldReturn:(UITextField *)textField {
    BOOL result = NO;
    // The user pressed the "Return" button
    if ([self emailAddressIsValid:textField.text]) {
        [textField resignFirstResponder];
        result = YES;
    } else {
        self.myLabel.textColor = [UIColor redColor];
        self.myLabel.text = @"Invalid Address. Try Again.";
        result = NO;
    }
    return result;
}


- (IBAction)copyInput:(id)sender {
    NSString *inputText = [sender text];
    int textLength = [inputText length];
    if (textLength < 10) {
        self.myLabel.textColor = [UIColor blackColor];
    } else if (textLength < 20) {
        self.myLabel.textColor = [UIColor blueColor];
    } else{
```

```
        self.myLabel.textColor = [UIColor redColor];
    }
    self.myLabel.text = [inputText lowercaseString];
    [sender setText:@""];
}
```

The basic execution flow is the same as before in that the UITextField sends the text FieldShouldReturn: delegate message to discover whether the Return key press should be processed. In this version, the code needs to validate the entry before allowing the Return key to proceed. If validation fails, a message is displayed in the label—perhaps not a world-class user experience, but sufficient for this demonstration. Only when the textFieldShouldReturn: delegate method returns YES does the UITextField send the copyInput: message to copy the typed text to the label. For this version, the entry is converted to all lowercase characters.

Validation occurs in the custom emailAddressIsValid: method. Because it simply needs to discover whether the typed text meets the pattern for an email address, I chose to use the numberOfMatchesInString:options:range: method of the NSRegularExpression class. This method returns an integer indicating how many times the regular expression found a match in a string passed as the first argument. If the pattern matches just one time, it means the string passed the test, and the method returns YES.

For the regular expression, I customized an email format regular expression from Recipe 4.1 of *Regular Expressions Cookbook* by Jan Goyvaerts and Steven Levithan (O'Reilly, *http://oreilly.com/catalog/9780596520694/*). It is a mix of moderately complex account and domain name patterns, with the assurance that the top-level domain name is between two and six characters long. Notice that the pattern is assigned as an NSString literal in the example. One of the characters is an explicit period acting as the delimiter between domain and top-level domain (approximately halfway in the group following "@"). Because a dot is a regular expression symbol meaning "any character," you must escape the character with a leading backslash (\) to indicate you mean the actual period character and not the "any character" regular expression symbol. But because the backslash character is, itself, an NSString symbol representing an escape, you have to escape the escape character so that the literal period character is represented by the \\. sequence. Regular expression recipes you find from outside sources won't have the double escape, so you'll have to understand the expression syntax well enough to know where to double-escape characters for the NSString version. This applies to common regular expression characters such as the word boundary (\b, which must be represented as \\b).

Cocoa Touch employs a more sophisticated regular expression syntax than that embodied in the ECMA standard. Documenting all of the differences and enhancements would exceed the scope of this book, but you will find that the basics have much in common.

To use a regular expression pattern once it is assigned to an NSString, the example code creates an autoreleased instance of the NSRegularExpression object through the

---

`regularExpressionWithPattern:options:error:` method. Like many Cocoa Touch methods, this one passes any errors encountered during its execution to an `NSError` object that is defined prior to execution of the method and passed as an indirect reference (via the `&` operator) as the `error` argument. If an error occurs, the method fails (the returned value would be `nil`) and you can then inspect properties of the `NSError` object to obtain details.

If the `NSRegularExpression` instance is created successfully, the code then sends it the `numberOfMatchesInString:options:range:` message. The first argument is the string to be tested. The second argument consists of a set of options different from the ones used in the creation of the `NSRegularExpression` object. These are known as matching options and don't apply to this method (at least in the current implementation). Therefore, the options are set to zero, meaning no options. Finally, the method requires a range of text to inspect. In this case, the complete string is being checked, so the `NSMakeRange()` function creates a range consisting of the entire string (starting at the first character for the length of the string). This method returns an integer count of matches. To be on the safe side, the method returns `YES` only if there is a single match.

If the validation fails, the `textFieldShouldReturn:` delegate method branches to display an error advisory and assign `NO` to the result. If the `UITextField` receives `NO` in response to this method, the keyboard remains in the view and the text field remains active as the first responder. In a production application, you would also provide a user interface control that allows the user to cancel out of this screen or operation so that failure to enter a valid email address doesn't trap the user in this mode.

Modifying the User Interface

For this demonstration, you don't really have to change the user interface to achieve the results, but it doesn't hurt to review how code changes might impact even minor UI elements. In this case, the placeholder text of the `UITextField` should prompt the user to enter an email address rather than just any old text. You can make the change to the *WorkbenchViewController.xib* file in the text field's Attributes inspector.

Using Regular Expressions for Text Search and Replace

As noted in Chapter 8, the Cocoa Touch `NSString` object does not offer a method to perform search and replace operations with regular expressions (as the JavaScript `String` object does). Instead, you can use the iOS 4 (or later) `NSRegularExpression` class to do the job. To demonstrate how this works, I'll once again use the `UITextField` example from earlier in this chapter as a basis. The goal of this version will be to strip out any extra spaces between words entered into the text field and display the results in the label below the field. Example 9-20 shows the one new method and two modified methods from Example 9-18.

Example 9-20. Modifications for regular expression search and replace

```
- (NSString *)stripExtraWhitespace:(NSString *)inputString {
    NSString *result = inputString;

    // One or more whitespace characters
    NSString *whiteSpacePattern = @"\\s+";
    NSString *replacementString = @" ";

    NSError *error = NULL;
    NSRegularExpression *regex =
        [NSRegularExpression regularExpressionWithPattern:whiteSpacePattern
                                                  options:0
                                                    error:&error];
    if (regex == nil) {
        NSLog(@"RegExp Error: %@", [error localizedDescription]);
    } else {
        result =
            [regex stringByReplacingMatchesInString:inputString
                                            options:0
                                              range:NSMakeRange(0, [inputString length])
                                       withTemplate:replacementString];
    }
    return result;
}

// UITextField delegate message
- (BOOL)textFieldShouldReturn:(UITextField *)textField {
    [textField resignFirstResponder];
    return YES;
}

- (IBAction)copyInput:(id)sender {
    NSString *inputText = [sender text];
    NSString *scrunchedText = [self stripExtraWhitespace:inputText];

    int scrunchedTextLength = [scrunchedText length];
    if (scrunchedTextLength < 10) {
        self.myLabel.textColor = [UIColor blackColor];
    } else if (scrunchedTextLength < 20) {
        self.myLabel.textColor = [UIColor blueColor];
    } else{
        self.myLabel.textColor = [UIColor redColor];
    }
    self.myLabel.text = scrunchedText;
    [sender setText:@""];
}
```

For the search-and-replace operation, I allow the UITextField to resign as first responder and let the copyInput: method be the controller. Text from the field is passed as an argument to the custom stripExtraWhitespace: method.

The original string is assigned to the result as a default: if the regular expression should fail, the original string is returned. One variable holds the whitespace pattern (note the double escape of the \s character), while another holds a single-space string as the replacement. An instance of NSRegularExpression is created just as in Example 9-19, along with error checking.

The difference comes in how the instance uses the replacement method, which returns a new string with the changes. You have the choice of limiting the range of the source string, but this example surveys the entire string. The replacement string is assigned to the withTemplate argument.

To try out the app in the iPhone simulator, you should temporarily disable the system-wide automatic period insertion in Settings→General→Keyboard. Type your expanded text into the text field, then click the Return button on the keyboard to see the scrunched text appear in the label. Figure 9-10 shows the screen before and after clicking the Return button.

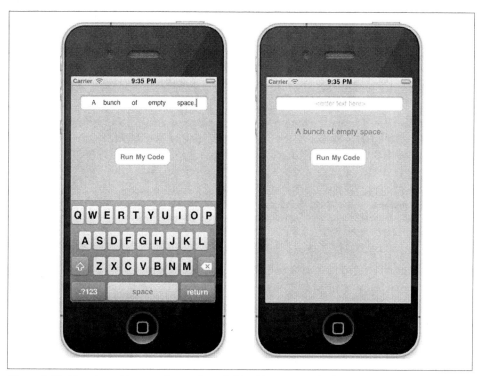

Figure 9-10. Entering wide-spaced text, then clicking Return to strip the extra spaces

Dragging a View Around the Screen

Recall that virtually every "thing" you see on an iOS device screen is descended from the UIView class. If you want your user to be able to drag something around the screen, you'll define the element as a UIView subclass. In HTML, CSS, DOM, and JavaScript terms, every view is the equivalent of an absolute-positioned element. It has a location within the coordinate system of the parent view and exists as its own layer that you can move independently of other views (and it takes its nested subviews along for the ride). In JavaScript on a browser running on a traditional computer, you use mouse events to detect when a user has engaged the element for movement, when the mouse moves the element, and when the user releases the mouse button. The equivalent events in iOS are called *touch events*.

Because UIView inherits from UIResponder, all views—when explicitly enabled—are capable of reacting to touch events. Touch events send messages to the view under the spot interpreted by the system as being the intended event coordinate. Despite the pudginess of fingers compared to the extremely small pixel points on the screen, the system calculates a point to report for each event. The ability to interpret and calculate this disparity well is a hallmark of a good touchscreen experience. We developers receive the benefits of that engineering for free.

A touch can be a quick tap or a lengthy drag around the screen. To accommodate those possibilities, the system sends four possible touch event messages to any view acting as a responder. If the view implements methods matching those messages, the view can act in response to the touch events. The four methods are as follows:

```
- (void)touchesBegan:(NSSet *)touches withEvent:(UIEvent *)event
- (void)touchesMoved:(NSSet *)touches withEvent:(UIEvent *)event
- (void)touchesEnded:(NSSet *)touches withEvent:(UIEvent *)event
- (void)touchesCancelled:(NSSet *)touches withEvent:(UIEvent *)event
```

A simple drag action encompasses at least the first three of the four methods above. The last method is called if, during a drag action, a notification of some kind (including an incoming telephone call) gets in the way between your fingers and your app's views.

All four methods share the same pair of arguments. The first is an NSSet type—an unordered collection of UITouch objects; the second is a UIEvent object. The reason the first argument can contain multiple UITouch objects is that a single event can have information about multiple touches—one touch per finger. For example, if you drag two fingers at the same time, each touchesMoved:withEvent: method call has information about each finger's touch location.

For the dragging demonstration in this section, you will be working with a single touch, even if multiple touches are in force during the event. You will add a UIImageView to Workbench and supplement the project's code to reposition the UIImageView during touch motions so that it tracks the position of your finger (or pseudofinger in the simulator).

The Code Portion

Example 9-21 shows the *WorkbenchViewController.h* header file stripped down to the bare minimums for this demonstration. Although the `runMyCode:` method isn't being used (nor its button in the interface), leave it in the declaration in case you wish to experiment with the `UIImageView` later.

Example 9-21. WorkbenchViewController.h for the drag demonstration

```
#import <UIKit/UIKit.h>

@interface WorkbenchViewController : UIViewController {

    UIImageView *movableImageView;

}

@property (nonatomic, retain) IBOutlet UIImageView *movableImageView;

- (IBAction)runMyCode:(id)sender;

@end
```

The only additions are the ivar and property declarations for the `UIImageView` that you will later add to the nib file. Notice the `IBOutlet` declaration, which will let us make the connection to the property in Interface Builder.

There is quite a bit new, however, in the implementation file, shown in Example 9-22. Some new Objective-C tidbits also creep in.

Example 9-22. WorkbenchViewController.m for the drag demonstration

```
#import "WorkbenchViewController.h"

@interface WorkbenchViewController()
// Private methods
- (void)animateTouchesBeganAtPoint:(CGPoint)touchPoint forView:(UIImageView *)theView;
- (void)animateTouchesEndedAtPoint:(CGPoint)releasePoint forView:(UIView *)theView;
@end

@implementation WorkbenchViewController

// Animation speed constant
#define kScaleAnimationDuration 0.15

@synthesize movableImageView;

#pragma mark -
#pragma mark Touch Event Methods

// First touch point
-(void)touchesBegan:(NSSet *)touches withEvent:(UIEvent *)event {
    UITouch *touch = [touches anyObject];
```

```
    // Activate only movableImageView
    if ([touch view] == movableImageView) {
        // Animate the first touch
        CGPoint touchPoint = [touch locationInView:self.view];
        [self animateTouchesBeganAtPoint:touchPoint forView:self.movableImageView];
    }
}

// "Drag" operation
-(void)touchesMoved:(NSSet *)touches withEvent:(UIEvent *)event {
    UITouch *touch = [touches anyObject];

    // Move only movableImageView view to its location
    if ([touch view] == movableImageView) {
        CGPoint location = [touch locationInView:self.view];
        movableImageView.center = location;
    }

}

// "Release" operation
-(void)touchesEnded:(NSSet *)touches withEvent:(UIEvent *)event {
    UITouch *touch = [touches anyObject];

    // Release movableImageView and return to normal size
    if ([touch view] == movableImageView) {
        CGPoint touchPoint = [touch locationInView:self.view];
        [self animateTouchesEndedAtPoint:touchPoint forView:self.movableImageView];
        return;
    }

}

#pragma mark -
#pragma mark Animation Methods

// Increase scale slightly for feedback
- (void)animateTouchesBeganAtPoint:(CGPoint)touchPoint forView:(UIImageView *)theView {
    [UIView beginAnimations:nil context:nil];
    [UIView setAnimationDuration:kScaleAnimationDuration];
    theView.transform = CGAffineTransformMakeScale(1.1, 1.1);
    [UIView commitAnimations];
}

// Return scale to original and drop image at touch position
- (void)animateTouchesEndedAtPoint:(CGPoint)releasePoint forView:(UIView *)theView {
    [UIView beginAnimations:nil context:NULL];
    [UIView setAnimationDuration:kScaleAnimationDuration];

    // Set the center to the ending touch position
    theView.center = releasePoint;

    theView.transform = CGAffineTransformIdentity;
    [UIView commitAnimations];
}
```

```
#pragma mark -
#pragma mark runMyCode

- (IBAction)runMyCode:(id)sender {

}

#pragma mark -
#pragma mark Memory Management Methods

- (void)didReceiveMemoryWarning {
    // Releases the view if it doesn't have a superview.
    [super didReceiveMemoryWarning];
}

- (void)dealloc {
    [movableImageView release];
    [super dealloc];
}

@end
```

Immediately following the #import directive for the header file comes what appears to be an additional @interface header section. The directive references the current class similar to the way a category header begins (Chapter 8), but the parentheses after the class name are empty. The net effect is to create an *extension* to the current class, offering a place to declare extra methods for the current class but methods that are not exposed to other classes. You must still implement the methods in the main @implementation section, but they are intended for "internal" use by other methods in the class. For this demo, you will declare two animation methods that will be invoked from within various touch methods in this fashion. User interface controls will not be calling these methods directly, so you can declare them as private for any instance of the class. A description of what these methods do is coming in a moment.

An additional preliminary task includes defining a constant value for how long upcoming animation is to take. The value will be applied in two locations later in the code. Next, synthesize the movableImageView property.

About #pragma mark Preprocessor Directives

You see several instances of #pragma mark in Example 9-20. To get a better view of what they do (and why you should use them), go to Xcode and select the implementation file containing these directives. Pull down the menu at the center-top of the editor window. You should see a list of elements contained in the file, as shown in Figure 9-11.

The #pragma mark directives instruct Xcode to display text, line spaces, and horizontal dividers (created with a single hyphen) to help you locate methods for editing. Although the implementation file in this demonstration is not particularly long, some files you generate can have many groups of methods. The more you can identify methods that work with each other, group them together, and label them accordingly, the easier it will be for you to find methods and navigate quickly to them. The system of labeling groups also helps you keep your source code organized and offers a bit of implied documentation. You'll thank yourself when you return to the code six months later and try to remember what you did.

The group of four methods acting in response to touch events comes next. At least the first three methods are invoked often as the user clicks/taps on the screen. Because the UIImageView will be set up (in Interface Builder) to allow only single touches, each touchesBegan:withEvent: message sent to the delegate will have only one touch object in the NSSet received as an argument. Therefore, the anyObject method of the NSSet returns the single UITouch event of interest to the code. Of course, there may be many single-touch events occurring for the WorkbenchViewController class, so the methods make sure they handle touches occurring only in the movableImageView.

Figure 9-11. #pragma mark directives help organize source code blocks

All three methods also need to read the coordinates of the event to assist with positioning of movableImageView for each event. Because movableImageView will be positioned within the coordinate system of the WorkbenchViewController's view, the touch object's locationInView: method takes the self.view reference as its argument. A coordinate point is preserved as a CGPoint type.

When a user clicks on the movableImageView, the code provides a bit of visual feedback that the view has been activated: the image scales upward slightly, with a smooth animation between the normal and larger size. This task is handed off to the `animate TouchesBeganAtPoint:forView:` custom method.

Animation is a much longer discussion than is appropriate for this book, but the two methods included here can help you get started with your investigations. The job of the `animateTouchesBeganAtPoint:forView:` method is to enlarge the `movableImageView` by a factor of 110% along both the horizontal and vertical axes. A change of this nature is called an *affine transform* (or transformation). Fortunately, all of the serious geometry required to understand affine transforms is built into the functions supplied to developers by Cocoa Touch (and specifically the Quartz 2-D drawing engine). A `UIView` subclass has a `transform` property, which can hold information about a specific type of transformation (or combinations of transformations). In other words, once the view knows its transform, it knows the nature of changes to its visual presentation (such as size scaling, inversion, rotation, and so on). If you encase the assignment of the transform inside an animation block, the previous rendering is held momentarily while other potential properties are set, such as how long the eventual animation should take. When all the properties are set, the animation can be committed, which causes the rendering to gradually change from the original display to the transformed display.

All of this takes place within the span of four lines of code in the `animateTouches BeganAtPoint:forView:` method. The point argument contains the coordinates of the touch event; the view argument is a reference to the `movableImageView`. An animation block begins so you can assign parameters about animation duration and nature of the intended transformation (scale the view by a factor of 1.1 along both axes). Then the animation is committed, causing the animation to appear on screen.

At the end of the drag operation, the `touchesEnded:withEvent:` method invokes another animation method, `animateTouchesEndedAtPoint:forView:`, which reverses the scaling. It does so by reverting the transform to its original state (`CGAffineTransformIdentity`). Additionally, the center of the `movableImageView` is placed at the location of the Touches Ended event.

It is the `touchesMoved:withEvent:` method that causes the `movableImageView` to track the position of the finger. At nearly every detected motion, the method is invoked so that the center of the control is positioned where the Touches Moved event occurred. This happens lots of times per second.

 For the moment, the `touchesCancelled:withEvent:` method is left undefined. The actions of this method commonly duplicate those of the `touchesEnded:withEvent:` method. In that case, you should refactor the current statements of the `touchesEnded:withEvent:` method into a separate method that is invoked by both touch event methods.

The Interface Builder Portion

Before switching over to Interface Builder, you need to add an image to the project if one does not yet exist. The image should be small enough to fit comfortably within the entire view. Something on the order of no more than 200 pixels in either dimension should work fine. In Xcode, choose Project→Add to Project and locate the desired image (preferably in PNG format). Copy the file to the project directory when prompted to do so.

Now double-click on the *WorkbenchViewController.xib* file to edit the file in Interface Builder. In the Library palette, choose Data Views and locate the Image View item. Drag that item to the View window and position it somewhere near the center of the view. Resize the image view as needed to provide the desired aspect ratio for your image. With the image view selected, activate the Image View Attributes inspector palette and select your image from the Image pop-up menu (all valid image files associated with the Xcode project are listed in the menu). Important: make sure the User Interaction Enabled checkbox is checked. In the Connections inspector, drag from the empty circle to the right of "New Referencing Outlet" to the File's Owner item in the document window. Select `movableImageView` from the pop-up list. This act connects the image view you just created to the `movableImageView` property in the `WorkbenchView Controller` class.

Save the nib file and switch back to Xcode. Build and run the project in the simulator. You should now be able to drag the image around the screen. Figure 9-12 shows the image while being dragged. When you use the app in the simulator, notice the scaling animation on both ends of the drag operation.

Figure 9-12. Dragging an image around the screen in the simulator

Recap

As this chapter aptly demonstrates, some of your JavaScript experience applies directly to developing native apps with the iOS SDK. In other instances, you have to forget what you know and learn techniques from scratch. The "classiness" of the SDK really stands out: intangible values, such as colors, are no longer just values, but classes unto themselves. The more you observe how the frameworks implement their worlds with classes, the more quickly you will start envisioning solutions to your app challenges in terms of subclasses of existing classes and your own custom classes.

The next stage in your mastery of iOS development is understanding in more detail how major view classes, navigation controllers, and table views operate. Beyond that, the specialties of your intended applications will guide you to areas for further study, whether it be more toward graphics and animation, intensive data handling with Core Data, communicating with other devices, media streaming, or dozens of other areas. Now that you are equipped with the basics of Objective-C and many Cocoa Touch facilities, you can take advantage of Apple's documentation, which offers a wealth of information and insight into the depths of the frameworks. Take advantage of those resources, as well as the Developer Forums at *http://developer.apple.com.*

You are now much closer to achieving your iOS app dreams.

Getting the Most from Xcode Documentation

The documentation that comes with the iOS SDK will become a frequent destination when you want to remind yourself about syntax details or discover frameworks features you may not have met yet. The amount of material is staggering, and Apple and its Developer Tools group must be congratulated for efforts to build a documentation system that is genuinely helpful to developers. Recent SDK versions have included more guides to using the documentation. Choosing Help→Developer Documentation in Xcode opens the documentation window with a Quick Start page. You can't go wrong taking advantage of the material presented there, including several tutorial videos that acquaint you with the overall system. What I hope to accomplish here, however, is to present tips on understanding some of the things you see once you start digging into the documentation and learn how to dig out the truly valuable pieces.

After you've watched the tutorial videos, I suggest visiting the "home page" of the iOS SDK documentation. In the documentation window, pull down the Home menu (near the top left corner) and choose the newest iOS SDK version listed. The window will fill with three panes that present an overview (perhaps overwhelming) of the documents relevant to iOS development, shown in Figure A-1.

Picking your way through the documentation the first time is a daunting experience. Apple has tried to make it more manageable by offering selected documents for getting started. It's all good reading, and worth the effort, even if it takes multiple times through some of the documents to drink it all in.

Until you get a better sense of the range of frameworks available to you, it's a good idea to scroll the table of contents pane on the left to scan through the list of framework groups. For example, you may not know whether a particular service is built into the Foundation framework or is more specialized, such as linking your app to the Address Book or adding mapping functionality. Selecting an item in the table of contents pane can reduce the list of relevant documents in the bottom right pane to a manageable

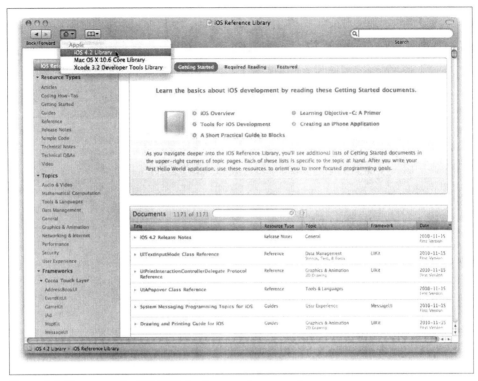

Figure A-1. Home page for iOS SDK development documentation

size, as you can sometimes cut down the entire list of over a thousand items to just dozens.

On a day-to-day basis, however, the search box in the upper right corner is where you will begin your discovery. If you know the exact name of a class, enter it into the search box. For example, if you want to see all of the features of the UITextView class, enter **uitextview** into the search box (search is not case-sensitive). The results pane (Figure A-2) appears at the far left.

Notice that the results for this search are divided into three groups: API, document title, and full-text search results. The documentation system is smart enough to recognize that if you are searching on a term that is found in API names, you are probably interested in API details. To uncover the range of methods and properties for classes, the specific class reference document is usually where you want to go. Results for both the UITextView API and the UITextView Class Reference point to the same document, as shown in Figure A-3. If you double-click an entry in the search results pane, the pane disappears, letting the remaining content fill the window.

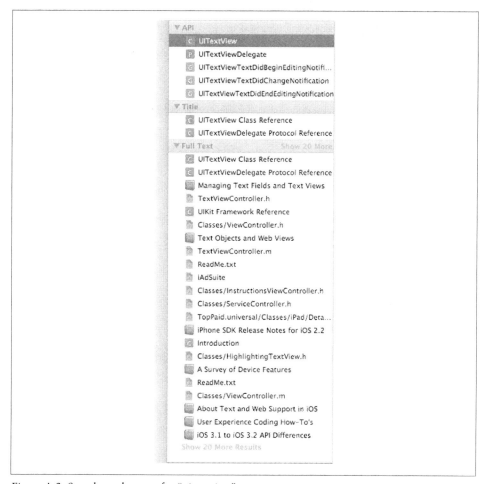

Figure A-2. Search results pane for "uitextview"

Even in this top-of-the-document view, you have a ton of vital information at your fingertips. First, if you know the method or constant name you're interested in, use the Jump To menu just above the document. The menu presents an alphabetical listing of entries within the document, grouped by methods and constants (or additional relevant groups as needed).

You can also perform a separate search within the document. Click anywhere in the document pane and type Cmd-F. A separate search field appears near the top of the window, and will look for matches to the text you enter there only within the current document. The total number of matches appears, and you can use Cmd-G to advance to each successive match (or Shift-Cmd-G to jump backward through the document).

Often, one of the most important pieces of information about a class is its inheritance chain, which is the first item in the class reference document. This information is

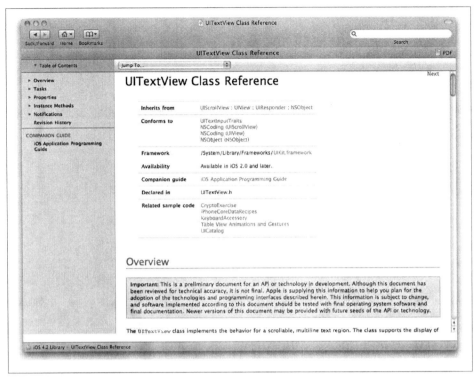

Figure A-3. A typical class reference document

especially useful for classes that have multiple generations of inheritance, such as UITextView, shown in Figure A-3. Methods and other features of superclasses are not repeated in the subclass reference documents. Therefore, you may need to follow the inheritance trail to discover whether a suspected method is implemented further up the chain. Fortunately, superclasses in the listing are active links to their respective class reference documents.

If the class is new to you, be sure to look at the framework for the class. Classes in your project that rely on the class whose document you're reading must import the framework. Most of the time, of course, you'll find one of the top three frameworks (Foundation, UIKit, or CoreGraphics), which are already added to projects generated from an Xcode template. But if you are interested in a class belonging to a more specialized framework, you will have to add that framework to the project and import the framework into the header files of your classes that reference the framework. It's too easy, when you're excited about unleashing a new power to your app, to forget to add and import the associated framework (leading to head-scratching compiler errors). At least with the help of the class reference document, you know which framework to work with.

Be alert to the recommended companion documentation noted for a class. Although the document mentioned in the UITextView reference in Figure A-3 is a fairly generic guide, you'll find other classes pointing to guides targeting very specific programming tasks. Such guides often provide practical contexts and code snippets that better explain usage of a class than the class reference document.

Most class reference documents contain links to sample code projects that demonstrate the current class. Numerous Apple engineers have created sample projects over the span of the SDK's public availability. You'll find a variety of programming styles and implementation decisions that are far from uniform (e.g., whether the project employs user interface features created through Interface Builder or code). Therefore, look to the samples not so much as paragons of iOS or Objective-C coding, but rather as suggested ways to implement very specific app or language features. The issue being targeted by the sample may be well done, but the supporting material may be less impressive. You can find instructions for installing sample apps in Chapter 2.

One point that I believe is missing from the top of a typical class reference document is a notice of whether the class has a companion delegate class (required or optional). For example, you can't tell from the UITextView class reference document header that a class you create that supports a UITextView object should implement the UITextView Delegate class to receive messages from a text view control. A sharp eye scanning the search results for UITextView might spot the companion delegate class (see Figure A-2), but not necessarily.

Every class reference document starts its body text with an Overview section. The depth of these sections across classes varies quite a bit. If a class is new to you, the overview usually provides a good sense of implementation requirements and occasional gotchas.

The heart of a class reference document, however, consists of the detailed listings of methods, properties, and constants. A summary list appears after the overview, usually organized into groups. Figure A-4 shows the beginning of the summary list for the NSArray class. The summaries always begin with methods for creating and initializing an instance of the class. Sometimes the instance and class methods are mixed together; other times they are separated into distinct groups, as shown for NSArray. If you do not see initialization methods at the top of the summary, you can tell the class relies on initialization methods of one or more of its superclasses. Each entry in the summary is a link to the detailed listing later in the document.

As you scroll through the rest of a class reference document, the grouping of items is usually different from the summary grouping. Sometimes properties are grouped together, as are tasks (methods). Your best route to finding what you're after, however, is through the summary listings at the top of their hyperlinks.

Figure A-5 shows the detail listing for the initWithFrame: method of the UIView class.

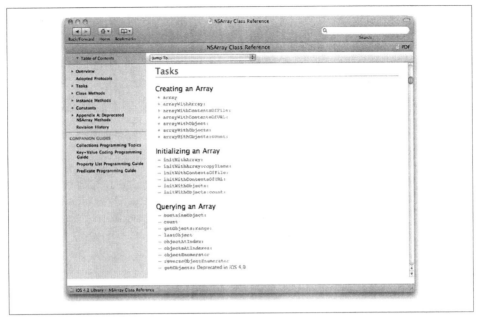

Figure A-4. NSArray class reference method summary

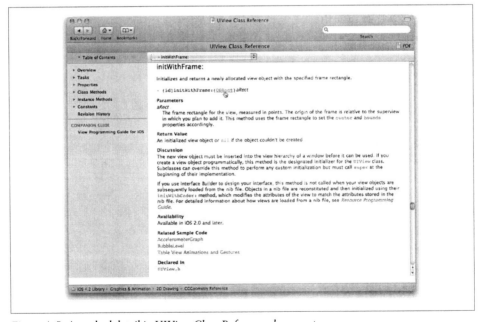

Figure A-5. A method detail in UIView Class Reference document

Method details always provide information about the arguments and return value (if any). Most of the time, an argument data type is shown as a hyperlink. In Figure A-5, the sole argument of the method is a CGRect type. If you are unsure what that data type represents, click the link and start following the trail through the documentation to uncover its components. This particular search is detailed in Chapter 7. If the data type is not represented as a hyperlink, you can always search the documentation for that value. Look in the search results list especially for API documents that name the type (preferably entries just consisting of the type name). For example, Figure A-6 shows a detail of an NSString method whose argument is shown to be an NSStringEncoding type.

---

stringByReplacingPercentEscapesUsingEncoding:

Returns a new string made by replacing in the receiver all percent escapes with the matching characters as determined by a given encoding.

- (NSString *)stringByReplacingPercentEscapesUsingEncoding:(NSStringEncoding)*encoding*

Figure A-6. An argument type without a link

The name is not a link, so you need to find the NSStringEncoding type. A documentation-wide search yields many results, but there are some listings in the API group for just this term. Clicking on the item shows that it is an enumerated list of constants (displayed in the very same NSString Class Reference document from which you started), as shown in Figure A-7.

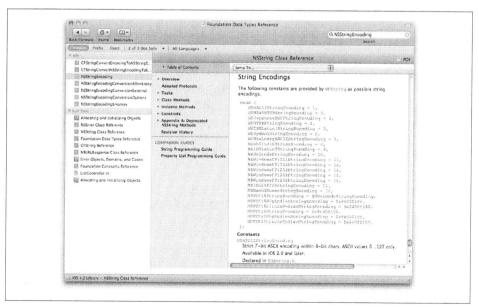

Figure A-7. Searching for the argument type

You will occasionally encounter entries in reference documents indicating that a method, property, or constant is deprecated, as shown in Figure A-8.

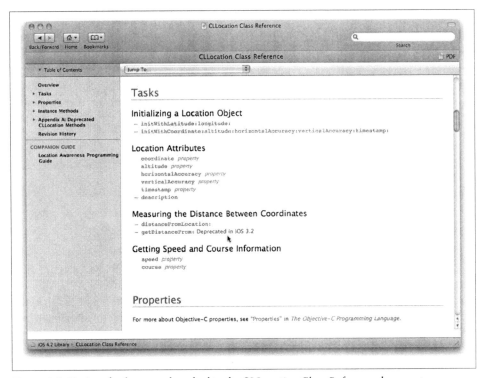

Figure A-8. Notice of a deprecated method in the CLLocation Class Reference document

Deprecation warnings appear in red to bring your attention to them. They also indicate in which version of iOS the deprecation warning begins. Should you use a deprecated item? Sometimes you have to. For example, the item shown in Figure A-8 states that it is deprecated in iPhone OS 3.2. If your app is designed to support older versions of iOS, you must continue using it in your code because the replacement probably isn't available in older OS versions (as is the case here). Deprecation notices signal impending removal, but without a specific deadline for removal. On the other hand, if you were developing a new app that targeted OS versions starting with 4.0 (which means iPads with iOS 4.2 or later), you should use the replacement instead of the deprecated method.

All is not perfect in the SDK documentation, however. You will occasionally encounter errors (which will be difficult for you to recognize), contradictions, or the sense that additional helpful information is lacking. For errors or inconsistencies, your next best friend is the Developer Forum, especially if an Apple engineer chimes in with some help. Google searches can also yield helpful discussions elsewhere, but answers may be less than definitive.

SDK documentation is still your first information resource. Embrace it.

Common Beginner Xcode Compiler Errors

When you've programmed in an environment for a while, you get to know the common errors and instinctively know what to look for in the code. Making the transition to a new environment means you may have to ignore all your previous experience and learn an entirely new vocabulary for error messages. And if you're moving from a loosely typed environment such as JavaScript to a language that is much more strongly typed, the error messages may not give you a sufficient clue about what's wrong. Even more potentially confusing is that a coding error in a header file may be exposed only when the compiler processes its companion implementation file. As the number of class files grows, you'll need Xcode's help more and more to find the file in which an error appears. Notice that an error displays a brief notice at the bottom right corner of any window you have open for the project. Click the icon to bring the Build Results window into view. There you'll find specific references to files and locations of errors. This appendix lists the compile-time error messages you are likely to encounter as you get acquainted with Objective-C, Xcode, and the Cocoa Touch frameworks.

You will soon learn that Xcode presents two types of messages: warnings and errors. Warnings do not prevent an app from compiling. That said, warnings are not necessarily harmless. They are advance signs that something is not right in your code. The app may compile and launch in the simulator or on a device, but don't be surprised if the app crashes unexpectedly. You should clear up all warnings before finalizing an app. If you want to make sure you don't skip over warnings, you can ask Xcode (on a project-by-project basis) to take warnings more seriously. Choose Project→Edit Project Settings, click the Build tab, and search for **treat**. Find the entry for "Treat Warnings as Errors" and activate the checkbox. Close the window when you're done.

Despite all of my advisories about how Xcode error messages differ from JavaScript errors, the two environments share one characteristic. If you attempt to build a project and the compiler reports several errors, start looking at the top of any file that contains an error. Some syntax errors can throw off the rest of the code in the file, causing a ripple effect of errors. It's a waste of time trying to fix something that really isn't broken, when the fault lies earlier in the file.

With that advice, let's begin the error message parade. Items in warning and error messages shown as *<someName>* indicate that the content in the message will refer to a class, method, or variable name from your source code.

Error Messages

Error Message: '<className>' undeclared
> Interpretation: You are most likely trying to reference a class whose header file has not been imported into the current class. This includes trying to reference a class in a framework you have forgotten to add to the project.

Error Message: '<methodName>' undeclared
> Interpretation: If this occurs in the line where a method definition occurs, there is likely a problem earlier in the code. Most likely the previous method definition has an imbalanced pair of curly braces.

Error Message: Expected ';' before '}' token
> Interpretation: A statement inside a code block is missing its semicolon delimiter.

Error Message: Expected ':', ',', ';', '}' or '__attribute__' before 'end'
> Interpretation: A property declaration above the error is missing its semicolon delimiter.

Error Message: Expected identifier before ';' token
> Interpretation: A method declaration in the header or definition in the implementation ends in a colon in anticipation of an argument, but the argument is missing.

Error Message: 'i' undeclared
> Interpretation: You tried to initialize a for loop index counter variable without declaring its int value type.

Error Message: Request for member '<propertyName>' in something not a structure or union
> Interpretation: You are trying to reference a dot-syntax property of a dynamically typed object (whose data type is id). Use accessor methods inside an Objective-C square-bracketed message instead. For instance, instead of object.property, say [object getProperty].

Error Message: Statically allocated instance of Objective-C class '<className>'
> Interpretation: A variable declaration for an Objective-C object (of the type explicitly named at the end of the error message) expected a pointer, but the pointer star is missing.

Error Message: Symbol(s) not found
> Interpretation: You have imported a framework into a class header, but you have not yet added the framework to the project.

Warning Messages

Warning Message: '<className>' may not respond to '<methodName>'
Interpretation: A message receiver is a class that does not have the named method defined for it. The method name in your message may be spelled or capitalized incorrectly. Alternatively, the receiver may belong to a different class than you think it is in.

Warning Message: Cannot find interface declaration for '<className>'
Interpretation: The implementation file does not include an `#import` directive for the header file.

Warning Message: Control reaches end of non-void function
Interpretation: Your method is declared to return a value, but the method does not contain a `return` statement. This commonly occurs when you insert an empty method as a placeholder in the implementation and the method is defined to return a non-void value.

*Warning Message: Incompatible Objective-C types initializing 'struct NSArray *', expected 'struct NSString *'*
Interpretation: A method declaration in the header states that the returned value is an `NSString`, but the implementation says the returned value is an `NSArray`. They need to be the same type.

*Warning Message: Incompatible Objective-C types returning 'struct NSString *', expected 'struct NSArray *'*
Interpretation: A method is defined to return an `NSArray`, but the returned value is defined as an `NSString` type.

Warning Message: Incomplete implementation of class '<className>'
Interpretation: The compiler can't match all declarations in the header with corresponding implementations. Look especially that methods are spelled, capitalized, and equipped with arguments identically between the two files. The warning is often accompanied by another warning with a reference to the problem method.

Warning Message: Initialization from incompatible pointer type
Interpretation: You are trying to assign an incorrect string value to an `NSString` pointer variable. Objective-C string literals must be defined with the @ directive in front of the quoted string.

Warning Message: Initialization makes pointer from integer without a cast
Interpretation: You are trying to assign an integer value to a pointer variable. If you need a string version of an integer, use the `stringWithFormat:` method of `NSString` to generate an `NSString` object with a value occupying the %d format specifier in the format.

Warning Message: Method definition for '-<methodName>:' not found
> Interpretation: You have declared a method in the header, but it is not defined in the corresponding implementation file.

Warning Message: Property '<ivarName>' requires method '-<ivarName>' to be defined - use @synthesize, @dynamic or provide a method implementation
> Interpretation: You defined a property in the header but forgot to synthesize the accessor methods in the implementation.

Warning Message: Return makes integer from pointer without a cast
> Interpretation: A method is defined to return a pointer value, but the value being returned is an integer.

Warning Message: Unused variable '<variableName>'
> Interpretation: You have defined a local variable inside a method, but no other statement in the method references the variable. This is harmless while you are still working on a method and wish to have the compiler check the validity of other statements. It serves as a reminder to use everything you declare.

Glossary

accessor methods

Two complementary methods of a class that allow instance variable values to be read and/or modified, usually known as getter and setter methods.

affine transform(ation)

A geometrically calculated change to a rendered object. Predefined transforms in the Quartz 2-D drawing system include operations such as rotation, inversion, and scaling of the displayed object.

application programming interface (API)

A description of the objects and methods programmers can use to control a particular system.

autorelease pool

A collection of references to memory allocations for objects. In iOS, autorelease pools automatically release memory for those objects at each cycle of the run loop. May also be manually created and drained on command.

autoreleased

An object that becomes a member of an autorelease pool.

base class

The class from which all other classes of a system are derived. For most (but not all) Cocoa Touch frameworks classes, `NSObject`.

bit mask

A system that uses the binary representation of numbers and the binary OR operator to arrive at unique values signifying each potential combination of values.

buffer

A memory space designed to accumulate data until its contents are retrieved and/or emptied.

bundle (application bundle)

A container of files consisting of the application binary and supporting files, such as images, nib files, and other resources.

cast

A conversion of one data type to another.

category

A definition of methods that are added to an existing class without subclassing.

class file

A definition of the methods, instance variables, and other characteristics of an object. Sometimes represented in a single file or divided into head (interface) and implementation files.

class method

In Objective-C, a method that is invoked by sending a message to the class rather than to an instance of the class. Initialization class methods for iPhone frameworks classes both allocate and initialize objects and return autoreleased objects.

compiler directive

A command (designated with the @ symbol) to be interpreted by the compiler.

data source

data source
> An array structure that a `UITableView` uses to populate cells of a table.

delegate
> An object that is handed a task to complete on behalf of another object.

design pattern
> In object-oriented programming, a set of guidelines that suggest the relationships among objects and how those objects should work together.

document window
> In Interface Builder, the primary nib file window that contains icons representing each object affiliated with the window or view being specified. It also has an icon for the view controller or application delegate class that "owns" the user interface being specified.

dynamic typing
> An important feature of Objective-C that allows a variable to be declared as an indeterminate data type (`id`) at compile time, but which can store an object of any data type at runtime. The runtime system recognizes the specific data type of the value currently stored in the variable and directs messages to the appropriate object class. Also known as late binding.

encapsulation
> In object-oriented programming, the ability to limit the scope of data and methods to classes or instances of classes. It allows for repetition of items such that a reference to an instance variable and method name in one instance does not conflict with an identically named reference belonging to another instance.

entry
> In a dictionary data structure, a value and its associated key.

extension
> In Objective-C, a technique of adding private methods to a class without subclassing.

external global variable
> In Objective-C, a global variable that is accessible by all classes and instances in the application.

format specifier
> In C and Objective-C, a placeholder within a string, such that values of different types may be represented in the string. A format specifier usually consists of the % symbol followed by a character denoting the type of data it can accept (e.g., %d for an integer, %f for a float).

frame
> In the iOS `UIKit` framework, a specification for a rectangle consisting of an origin point (top left corner), a width, and height. Represented as a `CGRect` value type.

framework
> In the iOS SDK, a collection of class (and other relevant) files that provide programmers an API to the device hardware and software systems. Some frameworks provide APIs for very specialized operations, such as location services and audio processing.

garbage collection
> A system of automatic release of allocated memory within an operating system. As of version 4.2, iOS does not provide garbage collection, which means programmers must be mindful of memory utilization.

getter
> See accessor methods.

header
> In Objective-C, the interface portion of a class definition. When stored as a separate file, denoted by the *.h* file extension.

implementation
> In Objective-C, the portion of a class definition that contains the program code for methods of a class. When stored as a separate file, denoted by the *.m* extension.

inheritance

In object-oriented programming, the ability of a parent class to expose all methods and instance variables to any of its child classes.

instance method

A method that is invoked when a message is sent to an instance of the class.

instance variable

A variable declared in a class header capable of storing a value separate from any other instance of the same class.

interface

In Objective-C, the portion of a class definition that contains instance variable declarations of a class.

See also **header**.

ivar

Shortcut terminology for instance variable. Pronounced EYE-var.

key

A label associated with a value.

key-value pair

A combination of a label and a value. In an `NSDictionary` class, a single entry.

late binding

See **dynamic typing**.

managed memory model

A design pattern in which the programmer is responsible for allocating and releasing memory while an application is running.

memory leak

A memory allocation that fails to be freed when it is no longer needed. That memory space becomes unavailable to any other process in the application.

message

A transmission directed to an object (a class or instance) conveying the name of a method to invoke (and any necessary arguments). In Objective-C, a message is surrounded by square brackets and consists of a reference to the intended recipient (the receiver) and the method call.

Model-View-Controller (MVC)

A design pattern consisting of three components such that the Model communicates with a View only by way of an intervening Controller.

mutable

A class whose instance values can be changed completely or in part without the developer having to create a new instance of the class for the modified value.

override

In object-oriented programming, to create a method in a subclass with the same name and arguments as in the superclass so that a message directed to the subclass causes the subclass method to run.

pointer

An address of the memory location where the first byte of a value is stored.

preprocessor directive

In Xcode, a command (designated with the # symbol) that signals the compiler to perform an action prior to compiling the code.

principal class

In iOS, the primary controller of the application. The `UIApplication` class.

property

In Objective-C, a representation of an instance variable that has accessor methods generated for the variable. Referenced as a member of an instance variable through dot syntax (`objectRef.property`).

receiver

In Objective-C, the object to which a message is sent.

reference count

See **retain count**.

retain count

In Objective-C, the number of times an object has been instructed to keep its memory allocation alive. The retain count of an object is increased by one by sending it a `retain` message; decreased by one by sending it a `release` message. When an object's retain count reaches zero, the memory allocation is returned for reuse.

scalar

In Objective-C, any of the numeric value types.

selector

In Objective-C, a reference to a method name. When used as a method argument (type SEL), the value is created via the @selector compiler directive (e.g., @selector(*methodName*)).

setter

See accessor methods.

static analyzer

A tool built into Xcode that performs an analysis of the source code to locate potential problems, such as memory leaks.

string constant

In Objective-C, a value that consists of the @ directive followed immediately by a quoted string of characters to create an NSString instance.

structure

From C, a data type that acts as a collection of multiple data types within a single entity. Each data member has a label associated with it. Also known as a struct.

subclass

A descendant of another class that inherits the instance variables and public methods of its ancestor. A subclass typically adds more specialized features.

superclass

An ancestor to a class. The base class is often the superclass of all objects in a system. In the case of multiple generations of inheritance, a subclass has one superclass, which, in turn, has its own superclass.

synthesize

In Objective-C, the process of writing accessor methods (behind the scenes) for an instance variable that has been declared as a property of the class. Invoked via the @synthesize compiler directive.

target-action pattern

A design pattern for processing events.

touch event

In iOS, an event caused by the contact, movement, or release of a finger on the screen.

Index

We'd like to hear your suggestions for improving our indexes. Send email to *index@oreilly.com*.

Math object functions and C equivalents, 155
   in Objective-C, 84
   sorting arrays with, 243–245

G

garbage collection, 126, 282
getters (see accessor methods)
global variables
   external, 282
   in JavaScript, 136
   in Objective-C, 141
Gregorian calendar, 212

H

hardware, native applications' access to, 3
header files, 61–64
   converting Xcode template class file to category header file, 166
   DGCar class (example), 59
   importing files that are not frameworks, 71
   importing frameworks, 62
   inheritance, 63
   specifying inheritance with @interface directive, 64
   specifying properties, 176
headers, 282
HTML, DOM module for, 64
HTML5, 1
   APIs, 52
Human Interface Guidelines, 175

I

IB (see Interface Builder)
IBActions, 45
   adding method in BlueViewController (example), 99
   assigning as return type for runMyCode: method, 76
   for date picker control, 209
   declaring for text field demonstration, 247
IBOutlet, 259
icons, 175
id data type, 76, 122
   using for keys in NSDictionary, 198
IDEs (integrated development environments), 9
image files, 175

images
   HTMLImage element, 64
   preserving data on disk, 237
implementation, 59, 282
@implementation compiler directive (see listing in Symbols section)
implementation files, 59
   converting Xcode template class file to category file, 167
   DGCar class (example), 60
   editing @implementation section in Xcode, 70
   synthesizing properties, 178, 248
#import directives
   importing class header files, 71
   importing framework header files, 62
indexes, array, 193
Info.plist files, 87
   contents of, 87
   TheElements project (example), 175
inheritance, 63
   defined, 283
   specifying with @interface compiler directive, 64
initialization methods, 69, 73
initWithCapacity: method, 226
instance methods
   accessor methods for, using class properties, 176
   defined, 283
   definitions in Objective-C, 72
instance variables, 68, 137
   automatic instantiation for UI elements, 96
   defined, 283
   getting and setting, 79–81
Instruments, 15
int data type, 116
   conversions, 123
integers, 116
integrated development environments (IDEs), 9
Interface Builder, 15, 35–49, 208
   (see also Attributes Inspector; Connections Inspector)
   adding button to View, 38
   adding text field and label to Workbench application (example), 250
   connecting button to a method, 43–45
   creating user interface for view, 100–105

MapKit framework, importing in class header file, 62
Maps application, 152
Math object (JavaScript), equivalents in C, 155–157
memory
    pointers and, 108
    representation of locations and blocks occupied by data, 108
memory leaks, 127, 283
memory management, 125
    autorelease pools, 129
    cleaning up unwanted objects, 126
    observing memory usage, 130
    retain count, 127
messages, 70, 84
    defined, 283
    sent from UIApplication to delegates, 86
    syntax, 72
methods, Objective-C
    argument labels, 74
    in class implementation files, 60, 72, 281
    colon following method name, 45
    connecting method to a button in Interface Builder, 43–45
    data types of return values and arguments, 113
    declarations, 69
    declaring
        data types, 118–122
    defining, 32, 71
    documentation, 271
    getters and setters, 79
    referencing, using selectors, 241
    return value as pointer, 112
    returning Boolean values, 155
    runMyCode: (example) method, 34, 76
    triggering execution of, 70
MKMapView class
    properties, 180
    setting map type, 152
Mobile Safari
    access to iOS location services, 52
    support for HTML5 offline application cache, 3
    web applications running in, access to hardware, 4
modal views, 100

Model-View-Controller pattern (see MVC design pattern)
models (MVC pattern), 93
    data model classes in TheElements (example), 174
month and day names, 218
mouse events, 258
mutable, 283
MVC (Model-View-Controller) design pattern, 92, 283

N

names in Objective-C, 70
naming projects, 29
native iPhone applications, 1–9
    Apple iOS Developer Program, 8
    authoring platform choices, 8
    disadvantages of, 6
    more access to hardware, 3
    more access to software, 4
    restrictions on content, 8
    updates to, 7
    using offline, 2
.nib files, 35
    main .nib file for application, 87
        NSMainNibFile value, 88
NO and YES Boolean values, 155
Node objects (DOM), 64
nonatomic attribute, 177
NSArray class, 151, 190–194
    arrayWithContentsOfFile: method, 238
    creating instances of, 192
    file-writing methods, 237
    methods, and JavaScript equivalents, 193
    reference method summary, 271
    retrieving array elements, 193
    searching Developer Documentation on, 16
    sortedArrayUsingSelector: method, 242
    sorting arrays with a function, 243–245
NSAutoreleasePool objects, 129
NSBundle class, 236
NSCalendar class, 211
    applying date components to instance, 212
    components:fromDate: method, 214
    components:fromDate:toDate:options: method, 220
    dateByAddingComponents:toDate:options: method, 219

UIWindow class, 96
undefined values, 138
Unicode
   date and time formatting, 215
   format specifiers for date and time, 215
universal applications, 28
URL strings, escaping and unescaping, 188
user interface
   building for Workbench application
      (example), 35–49
User Interface Guidelines, 175
user-entered text (see text)

V

values
   in NSDictionary objects, 195
   wrapping in NSValue objects, 191
variables
   data type in Objective-C, 115
   naming in C, 133
   Objective-C
      declarations, 118
   Objective-C, and pointers, 111
   scope, 136–141
      global variables, 141
      instance variables, 137
      local variables, 137
      local variables in control structure
         blocks, 138
      static local variables, 140
viewDidAppear: method, 225
views
   adding view to Workbench project
      (example), 97–106
      adding IBAction method, 100
      code to display blue view, 105
      creating user interface, 100–105
   application window, UIWindow, 96
   dragging around the screen, 258–265
   importance of, 95
   in MVC pattern, 93
   types of, 95

W

warning messages, Xcode, 279
weakly-typed languages, 115
web applications
   Ajax in, 222

restricted access to hardware, 3
web browsers, security and privacy
      considerations, 3
web page for this book, xv
WebKit, 1
windows
   application window, UIWindow class, 96
   document window in Interface Builder, 37,
      282
writeToFile:atomically: method, 237

X

Xcode, 9, 11, 14
   accessing developer documentation, 15
   creating a project, 26
      default view-based project window, 29
      editing files, 31–33
      naming and saving project, 29
      runMyCode (example) method, 34
      selecting project type, 26
   creating DGCar class files (example), 65–
      75
   directing to build application for simulator,
      22
   documentation, 267–275
   hardware and OS requirements for, 11
   loading code samples, 18
   setting base SDK for project, 21
.xcodeproj files, 19
.xib files, 35
XMLHttpRequest objects, in web applications,
   222

Y

YES and NO Boolean values, 155

About the Author

Danny Goodman has been writing about personal computers and consumer electronics since the late 1970s. A freelance writer and programmer, he's published hundreds of magazine articles, several commercial software products, and three dozen computer books. His most popular book titles—on HyperCard, AppleScript, and JavaScript—have covered programming environments that are both accessible to non-professionals yet powerful enough to engage experts. He is currently an independent iOS app developer, with three products available on the App Store and more in the pipeline.

Colophon

The dog on the cover of *Learning the iOS 4 SDK for JavaScript Programmers* is a King Charles Spaniel. Today's Cavalier King Charles Spaniel is descended from a small, "toy" type of spaniel that was popular in 16th-century England. King Charles II, from whom the breed gets its name, was so fond of these dogs that he decreed that they were to be allowed in any public place, and it was said that "His Majesty was seldom seen without his little dogs." These spaniels were often referred to as "Comforters"; in the winter, a noble lady riding in a carriage was likely to keep a spaniel in her lap for warmth. While used by some for hunting small game, the King Charles Spaniel was typically valued for its companionship and considered more of a luxury item than a utilitarian pet.

Today's King Charles Spaniel emerged in part from interbreeding with the pug—which was in fashion in England during the reign of King William III and Queen Mary II—and the longer-nosed spaniels Charles II was so fond of. Their pointed noses, flat heads, and almond-shaped eyes were replaced with the shorter muzzles, domed skulls, and large, round eyes that characterize them today. The turn of the 20th century saw a final attempt to revive the breed as it existed during King Charles's time, but the modern King Charles Spaniel—named "Cavalier King Charles Spaniel" by the Cavalier Club in 1928—persisted. During World War II, the breed declined significantly (with one registered kennel dropping from 60 to 3 Caveliers), but regained popularity after the war and throughout the 1940s.

Today, the Cavalier King Charles Spaniel is gaining popularity worldwide. There are national Cavalier breed clubs in about a dozen countries, including Finland, Italy, New Zealand, and South Africa. The Kennel Club reports that the Cavalier was the sixth most popular dog in the UK in 2007, and according to statistics from the American Kennel Club, they were the 25th most popular in the US in 2008, particularly in San Francisco, New York City, Boston, and Washington, D.C..

The cover image is from Wood's *Animate Creation, Vol. I*. The cover font is Adobe ITC Garamond. The text font is Linotype Birka; the heading font is Adobe Myriad Condensed; and the code font is LucasFont's TheSansMonoCondensed.

Get even more for your money.

Join the O'Reilly Community, and register the O'Reilly books you own. It's free, and you'll get:

- $4.99 ebook upgrade offer
- 40% upgrade offer on O'Reilly print books
- Membership discounts on books and events
- Free lifetime updates to ebooks and videos
- Multiple ebook formats, DRM FREE
- Participation in the O'Reilly community
- Newsletters
- Account management
- 100% Satisfaction Guarantee

Signing up is easy:

1. **Go to: oreilly.com/go/register**
2. **Create an O'Reilly login.**
3. **Provide your address.**
4. **Register your books.**

Note: English-language books only

To order books online:
oreilly.com/store

For questions about products or an order:
orders@oreilly.com

To sign up to get topic-specific email announcements and/or news about upcoming books, conferences, special offers, and new technologies:
elists@oreilly.com

For technical questions about book content:
booktech@oreilly.com

To submit new book proposals to our editors:
proposals@oreilly.com

O'Reilly books are available in multiple DRM-free ebook formats. For more information:
oreilly.com/ebooks

Spreading the knowledge of innovators   oreilly.com

©2010 O'Reilly Media, Inc. O'Reilly logo is a registered trademark of O'Reilly Media, Inc. 00000

Buy this book and get access to the online edition for 45 days—for free!

Learning the iOS 4 SDK for JavaScript Programmers
By Danny Goodman
December 2010, $34.99
ISBN 9781449388454

With Safari Books Online, you can:

Access the contents of thousands of technology and business books

- Quickly search over 7000 books and certification guides
- Download whole books or chapters in PDF format, at no extra cost, to print or read on the go
- Copy and paste code
- Save up to 35% on O'Reilly print books
- **New!** Access mobile-friendly books directly from cell phones and mobile devices

Stay up-to-date on emerging topics before the books are published

- Get on-demand access to evolving manuscripts.
- Interact directly with authors of upcoming books

Explore thousands of hours of video on technology and design topics

- Learn from expert video tutorials
- Watch and replay recorded conference sessions

To try out Safari and the online edition of this book FREE for 45 days, go to *www.oreilly.com/go/safarienabled* and enter the coupon code NKKHTZG. To see the complete Safari Library, visit safari.oreilly.com.

Spreading the knowledge of innovators

safari.oreilly.com

©2009 O'Reilly Media, Inc. O'Reilly logo is a registered trademark of O'Reilly Media, Inc. 0000

LaVergne, TN USA
18 January 2011

212971LV00003B/19-94/P

9 781449 388454